GRAMMAR AND BEYOND

Laurie Blass
Susan Iannuzzi
Alice Savage
Deborah Gordon
with Randi Reppen

3A

CAMBRIDGE
UNIVERSITY PRESS

CAMBRIDGE
UNIVERSITY PRESS

32 Avenue of the Americas, New York NY 10013-2473, USA

Cambridge University Press is part of the University of Cambridge.

It furthers the University's mission by disseminating knowledge in the pursuit of education, learning and research at the highest international levels of excellence.

www.cambridge.org
Information on this title: www.cambridge.org/9780521143158

First published 2012
7th printing 2015

Printed in Mexico by Editorial Impresora Apolo, S.A. de C.V.

A catalog record for this publication is available from the British Library.

ISBN 978-0-521-14298-4 Student's Book 3
ISBN 978-0-521-14315-8 Student's Book 3A
ISBN 978-0-521-14319-6 Student's Book 3B
ISBN 978-1-107-60197-0 Workbook 3
ISBN 978-1-107-60198-7 Workbook 3A
ISBN 978-1-107-60199-4 Workbook 3B
ISBN 978-1-107-68502-4 Teacher Support Resource Book with CD-ROM 3
ISBN 978-0-521-14339-4 Class Audio CD 3
ISBN 978-1-139-06187-2 Writing Skills Interactive 3

Art direction, book design, layout services, and photo research: Integra
Audio production: John Marshall Media

Contents

PART 3 The Future

PART 4 Modals and Modal-like Expressions

PART 5 Nouns and Pronouns

PART 6 Gerunds and Infinitives

Appendices

Introduction to *Grammar and Beyond*

Grammar and Beyond is a research-based and content-rich grammar series for beginning- to advanced-level students of North American English. The series focuses on the grammar structures most commonly used in North American English, with an emphasis on the application of these grammar structures to academic writing. The series practices all four skills in a variety of authentic and communicative contexts. It is designed for use both in the classroom and as a self-study learning tool.

Grammar and Beyond Is Research-Based

The grammar presented in this series is informed by years of research on the grammar of written and spoken North American English as it is used in college lectures, textbooks, academic essays, high school classrooms, and conversations between instructors and students. This research, and the analysis of over one billion words of authentic written and spoken language data known as the *Cambridge International Corpus*, has enabled the authors to:

- Present grammar rules that accurately represent how North American English is actually spoken and written

- Identify and teach differences between the grammar of written and spoken English

- Focus more attention on the structures that are commonly used, and less attention on those that are rarely used, in written and spoken North American English

- Help students avoid the most common mistakes that English language learners make

- Choose reading and writing topics that will naturally elicit examples of the target grammar structure

- Introduce important vocabulary from the Academic Word List

Grammar and Beyond Teaches Academic Writing Skills

Grammar and Beyond helps students make the transition from understanding grammar structures to applying them in their academic writing.

In the Student's Books

At Levels 1 through 3 of the series, every Student's Book unit ends with a section devoted to the hands-on application of grammar to writing. This section, called Grammar for Writing, explores how and where the target grammar structures function in writing and offers controlled practice, exposure to writing models, and a guided but open-ended writing task.

At Level 4, the most advanced level, the syllabus is organized around the academic essay types that college students write (e.g., persuasive, cause and effect) and is aimed at teaching students the grammar, vocabulary, and writing skills that they need in order to be successful at writing those kinds of essays.

Online

Grammar and Beyond also offers *Writing Skills Interactive*, an interactive online course in academic writing skills and vocabulary that correlates with the Student's Books. Each unit of the writing skills course focuses on a specific writing skill, such as avoiding sentence fragments or developing strong topic sentences.

Special Features of *Grammar and Beyond*

Realistic Grammar Presentations

Grammar is presented in clear and simple charts. The grammar points presented in these charts have been tested against real-world data from the *Cambridge International Corpus* to ensure that they are authentic representations of actual use of North American English.

Data from the Real World

Many of the grammar presentations and application sections in the Student's Book include a feature called Data from the Real World, in which concrete and useful points discovered through analysis of corpus data are presented. These points are practiced in the exercises that follow.

Avoid Common Mistakes

Each Student's Book unit features an Avoid Common Mistakes section that develops students' awareness of the most common mistakes made by English language learners and gives them an opportunity to practice detecting and correcting these errors in running text. This section helps students avoid these mistakes in their own work. The mistakes highlighted in this section are drawn from a body of authentic data on learner English known as the *Cambridge Learner Corpus*, a database of over 35 million words from student essays written by nonnative speakers of English and information from experienced classroom teachers.

Academic Vocabulary

Every unit in *Grammar and Beyond* includes words from the Academic Word List (AWL), a research-based list of words and word families that appear with high frequency in English-language academic texts. These words are introduced in the opening text of the unit, recycled in the charts and exercises, and used to support the theme throughout the unit. The same vocabulary items are reviewed and practiced in *Writing Skills Interactive*, the online writing skills course. By the time students finish each level, they will have been exposed several times to a carefully selected set of level-appropriate AWL words, as well as content words from a variety of academic disciplines.

Series Levels

The following table provides a general idea of the difficulty of the material at each level of *Grammar and Beyond*. These are not meant to be interpreted as precise correlations.

	Description	TOEFL IBT	CEFR Levels
Level 1	beginning	20 – 34	A1 – A2
Level 2	low intermediate to intermediate	35 – 54	A2 – B1
Level 3	high intermediate	55 – 74	B1 – B2
Level 4	advanced	75 – 95	B2 – C1

Components for Students

Student's Book

The Student's Books for Levels 1 through 3 teach all of the grammar points appropriate at each level in short, manageable cycles of presentation and practice organized around a high-interest unit theme. The Level 4 Student's Book focuses on the structure of the academic essay in addition to the grammar rules, conventions, and structures that students need to master in order to be successful college writers. Please see the Tour of a Unit on pages xiv–xvii for a more detailed view of the contents and structure of the Student's Book units.

Workbook

The Workbook provides additional practice of the grammar presented in each unit of the Student's Book. The exercises offer both discrete and consolidated practice of grammar points and can be used for homework or in class. Each unit also offers practice correcting the errors highlighted in the Avoid Common Mistakes section in the Student's Book to help students master these troublesome errors. Self-Assessment sections at the end of each unit allow students to test their mastery of what they have learned.

Writing Skills Interactive

This online course provides graduated instruction and practice in writing skills, while reinforcing vocabulary presented in the Student's Books. Each unit includes a vocabulary review activity, followed by a short text that builds on the theme presented in the Student's Book and provides an additional context for the vocabulary. The text is followed by an animated interactive presentation of the target writing skill of the unit, after which students have the opportunity to practice the target skill in three different activities. Each unit closes with a quiz, which allows students to assess their progress.

Teacher Resources

Teacher Support Resource Book with CD-ROM

This comprehensive book provides a range of support materials for instructors, including:

- Suggestions for applying the target grammar to all four major skill areas, helping instructors facilitate dynamic and comprehensive grammar classes

- An answer key and audio script for the Student's Book

- A CD-ROM containing:

  - Ready-made, easily scored Unit Tests

  - PowerPoint presentations to streamline lesson preparation and encourage lively heads-up interaction

Class Audio CD

The class audio CD for each level provide the Student's Book listening material for in-class use.

Teacher Support Website

www.cambridge.org/grammarandbeyond

The website for *Grammar and Beyond* contains even more resources for instructors, including:

- Unit-by-unit teaching tips, helping instructors plan their lessons

- Downloadable communicative activities to add more in-class speaking practice

- A monthly newsletter on grammar teaching, providing ongoing professional development

We hope you enjoy using this series, and we welcome your feedback! Please send any comments to the authors and editorial staff at Cambridge University Press, at grammarandbeyond@cambridge.org.

About the Authors

Laurie Blass has more than 25 years' experience teaching and creating materials for ESL students in the United States and abroad. She is currently a full-time materials developer with a special interest in ESL for academic success and educational technology. Laurie is co-author of *Writers at Work: From Sentence to Paragraph*, published by Cambridge University Press, among many other titles.

Susan Iannuzzi has been teaching ESL for more than 20 years. She has trained English teachers on five continents and consulted on the national English curricula for countries in Africa, Asia, and the Middle East. She has authored or co-authored more than 10 English courses in use today. *Grammar and Beyond* is her first publication with Cambridge University Press.

Alice Savage is an English Language Teacher and Materials Writer. She attended the School for International Training in Vermont and is an author on the *Read This!* series, published by Cambridge University Press. She lives in Houston, Texas with her husband and two children.

Deborah Gordon, creator of the Grammar for Writing sections, has more than 25 years' experience teaching ESL students and training ESL teachers in the United States and abroad. She is currently an ESL instructor at Santa Barbara City College and a TESOL Certificate instructor at the University of California, Santa Barbara Extension. Deborah is coauthor of *Writers at Work: From Sentence to Paragraph*, published by Cambridge University Press, among many other titles.

 Randi Reppen is Professor of Applied Linguistics and TESL at Northern Arizona University (NAU) in Flagstaff, Arizona. She has over 20 years' experience teaching ESL students and training ESL teachers, including 11 years as the Director of NAU's Program in Intensive English. Randi's research interests focus on the use of corpora for language teaching and materials development. In addition to numerous academic articles and books, she is the author of *Using Corpora in the Language Classroom* and a co-author of *Basic Vocabulary in Use*, 2nd edition, both published by Cambridge University Press.

Advisory Panel

The ESL advisory panel has helped to guide the development of this series and provided invaluable information about the needs of ESL students and teachers in high schools, colleges, universities, and private language schools throughout North America.

Neta Simpkins Cahill, Skagit Valley College, Mount Vernon, WA

Shelly Hedstrom, Palm Beach State College, Lake Worth, FL

Richard Morasci, Foothill College, Los Altos Hills, CA

Stacey Russo, East Hampton High School, East Hampton, NY

Alice Savage, North Harris College, Houston, TX

Acknowledgments

The publisher and authors would like to thank these reviewers and consultants for their insights and participation:

Marty Attiyeh, The College of DuPage, Glen Ellyn, IL

Shannon Bailey, Austin Community College, Austin, TX

Jamila Barton, North Seattle Community College, Seattle, WA

Kim Bayer, Hunter College IELI, New York, NY

Linda Berendsen, Oakton Community College, Skokie, IL

Anita Biber, Tarrant County College Northwest, Fort Worth, TX

Jane Breaux, Community College of Aurora, Aurora, CO

Anna Budzinski, San Antonio College, San Antonio, TX

Britta Burton, Mission College, Santa Clara, CA

Jean Carroll, Fresno City College, Fresno, CA

Chris Cashman, Oak Park High School and Elmwood Park High School, Chicago, IL

Annette M. Charron, Bakersfield College, Bakersfield, CA

Patrick Colabucci, ALI at San Diego State University, San Diego, CA

Lin Cui, Harper College, Palatine, IL

Jennifer Duclos, Boston University CELOP, Boston, MA

Joy Durighello, San Francisco City College, San Francisco, CA

Kathleen Flynn, Glendale Community College, Glendale, CA

Raquel Fundora, Miami Dade College, Miami, FL

Patricia Gillie, New Trier Township High School District, Winnetka, IL

Laurie Gluck, LaGuardia Community College, Long Island City, NY

Kathleen Golata, Galileo Academy of Science & Technology, San Francisco, CA

Ellen Goldman, Mission College, Santa Clara, CA

Ekaterina Goussakova, Seminole Community College, Sanford, FL

Marianne Grayston, Prince George's Community College, Largo, MD

Mary Greiss Shipley, Georgia Gwinnett College, Lawrenceville, GA

Sudeepa Gulati, Long Beach City College, Long Beach, CA

Nicole Hammond Carrasquel, University of Central Florida, Orlando, FL

Vicki Hendricks, Broward College, Fort Lauderdale, FL

Kelly Hernandez, Miami Dade College, Miami, FL

Ann Johnston, Tidewater Community College, Virginia Beach, VA

Julia Karet, Chaffey College, Claremont, CA

Jeanne Lachowski, English Language Institute, University of Utah, Salt Lake City, UT

Noga Laor, Rennert, New York, NY

Min Lu, Central Florida Community College, Ocala, FL

Michael Luchuk, Kaplan International Centers, New York, NY

Craig Machado, Norwalk Community College, Norwalk, CT

Denise Maduli-Williams, City College of San Francisco, San Francisco, CA

Diane Mahin, University of Miami, Coral Gables, FL

Melanie Majeski, Naugatuck Valley Community College, Waterbury, CT

Jeanne Malcolm, University of North Carolina at Charlotte, Charlotte, NC

Lourdes Marx, Palm Beach State College, Boca Raton, FL

Susan G. McFalls, Maryville College, Maryville, TN

Nancy McKay, Cuyahoga Community College, Cleveland, OH

Dominika McPartland, Long Island Business Institute, Flushing, NY

Amy Metcalf, UNR/Intensive English Language Center, University of Nevada, Reno, NV

Robert Miller, EF International Language School San Francisco – Mills, San Francisco, CA

Marcie Pachino, Jordan High School, Durham, NC

Myshie Pagel, El Paso Community College, El Paso, TX

Bernadette Pedagno, University of San Francisco, San Francisco, CA

Tam Q Pham, Dallas Theological Seminary, Fort Smith, AR

Mary Beth Pickett, Global-LT, Rochester, MI
Maria Reamore, Baltimore City Public Schools, Baltimore, MD
Alison M. Rice, Hunter College IELI, New York, NY
Sydney Rice, Imperial Valley College, Imperial, CA
Kathleen Romstedt, Ohio State University, Columbus, OH
Alexandra Rowe, University of South Carolina, Columbia, SC
Irma Sanders, Baldwin Park Adult and Community Education, Baldwin Park, CA
Caren Shoup, Lone Star College – CyFair, Cypress, TX
Karen Sid, Mission College, Foothill College, De Anza College, Santa Clara, CA
Michelle Thomas, Miami Dade College, Miami, FL
Sharon Van Houte, Lorain County Community College, Elyria, OH

Margi Wald, UC Berkeley, Berkeley, CA
Walli Weitz, Riverside County Office of Ed., Indio, CA
Bart Weyand, University of Southern Maine, Portland, ME
Donna Weyrich, Columbus State Community College, Columbus, OH
Marilyn Whitehorse, Santa Barbara City College, Ojai, CA
Jessica Wilson, Rutgers University – Newark, Newark, NJ
Sue Wilson, San Jose City College, San Jose, CA
Margaret Wilster, Mid-Florida Tech, Orlando, FL
Anne York-Herjeczki, Santa Monica College, Santa Monica, CA
Hoda Zaki, Camden County College, Camden, NJ

We would also like to thank these teachers and programs for allowing us to visit:

Richard Appelbaum, Broward College, Fort Lauderdale, FL
Carmela Arnoldt, Glendale Community College, Glendale, AZ
JaNae Barrow, Desert Vista High School, Phoenix, AZ
Ted Christensen, Mesa Community College, Mesa, AZ
Richard Ciriello, Lower East Side Preparatory High School, New York, NY
Virginia Edwards, Chandler-Gilbert Community College, Chandler, AZ
Nusia Frankel, Miami Dade College, Miami, FL
Raquel Fundora, Miami Dade College, Miami, FL
Vicki Hendricks, Broward College, Fort Lauderdale, FL
Kelly Hernandez, Miami Dade College, Miami, FL
Stephen Johnson, Miami Dade College, Miami, FL
Barbara Jordan, Mesa Community College, Mesa, AZ
Nancy Kersten, GateWay Community College, Phoenix, AZ
Lewis Levine, Hostos Community College, Bronx, NY
John Liffiton, Scottsdale Community College, Scottsdale, AZ
Cheryl Lira-Layne, Gilbert Public School District, Gilbert, AZ

Mary Livingston, Arizona State University, Tempe, AZ
Elizabeth Macdonald, Thunderbird School of Global Management, Glendale, AZ
Terri Martinez, Mesa Community College, Mesa, AZ
Lourdes Marx, Palm Beach State College, Boca Raton, FL
Paul Kei Matsuda, Arizona State University, Tempe, AZ
David Miller, Glendale Community College, Glendale, AZ
Martha Polin, Lower East Side Preparatory High School, New York, NY
Patricia Pullenza, Mesa Community College, Mesa, AZ
Victoria Rasinskaya, Lower East Side Preparatory High School, New York, NY
Vanda Salls, Tempe Union High School District, Tempe, AZ
Kim Sanabria, Hostos Community College, Bronx, NY
Cynthia Schuemann, Miami Dade College, Miami, FL
Michelle Thomas, Miami Dade College, Miami, FL
Dongmei Zeng, Borough of Manhattan Community College, New York, NY

Tour of a Unit

Grammar in the Real World presents the unit's grammar in a **realistic** context using **contemporary** texts.

Notice activities draw students' attention to the **structure**, guiding their own **analysis** of form, meaning, and use.

UNIT

4

Past Perfect and Past Perfect Progressive

Nature vs. Nurture

1 Grammar in the Real World

A Have you ever reconnected with someone from your past? Read the web article about twins who lived apart for many years. What surprised the twins when they reconnected?

The Science of Twins

Twins, especially identical[1] twins, have always fascinated scientists. Identical twins develop from one egg, have identical DNA,[2] and are usually very similar in appearance
5 and behavior. There have been many studies of identical twins raised in the same family. There have also been a number of studies of identical twins separated at birth and raised in separate families. These studies have provided
10 interesting information about the impact of *nature* (genetics) and *nurture* (the environment) on the development of the individual. However, some of the studies have been controversial.[3]

Take the case of Elyse Schein and Paula Bernstein. Elyse and Paula were identical twins separated at birth. Both girls knew that their parents **had adopted** them as infants, but
15 neither girl knew about her twin. When Elyse grew up, she longed to meet her biological mother, so she contacted the agency that **had arranged** the adoption. She **had been doing** research on her birth mother when she made a surprising discovery. She had an identical twin. Even more surprising, she learned that she **had been** part of a secret scientific study. At the time of the adoption, the agency **had allowed** different families to
20 adopt each twin. The agency **had told** the families that their child was part of a scientific study. However, it **had** never **told** the families the goal of the study: for scientists to investigate nature versus nurture.

[1]**identical:** exactly the same | [2]**DNA:** the abbreviation for deoxyribonucleic acid, a chemical that controls the structure and purpose of every cell | [3]**controversial:** causing or likely to cause disagreement

---

Past Perfect and Past Perfect Progressive

When Elyse and Paula finally met as adults, they were amazed. They had many similarities. They looked almost identical. They **had** both **studied** film. They both loved
25 to write. Together, the twins discovered that the researchers **had stopped** the study before the end because the public strongly disapproved of this type of research.

Although that study ended early, many scientists today make a strong case for the dominant[4] role of nature. Schein and Bernstein agree that genetics explains many of their similarities. However, recent research suggests that nurture is equally important. It
30 is clear that the nature versus nurture debate will occupy scientists for years to come.

[4]**dominant:** more important, strong, or noticeable

B *Comprehension Check* Answer the questions.

1. What was surprising about the twins' adoption?
2. What characteristics and interests did Elyse and Paula have in common?
3. What is the nature versus nurture debate?

C *Notice* Underline the verbs in each sentence.

1. Both girls knew that their parents had adopted them as infants.
2. She had been doing research on her birth mother when she made a surprising discovery.
3. Even more surprising, she learned that she had been part of a secret scientific study.

Which event happened first in each sentence? What event followed? Write the verbs. What do you notice about the form of the verbs?

1. First: _____   Then: _____
2. First: _____   Then: _____
3. First: _____   Then: _____

2 Past Perfect

▶ Grammar Presentation

The past perfect is used to describe a completed event that happened before another event in the past.	*Elyse finally met her sister, Paula. Paula **had been** married for several years.* (First, Paula got married; Elyse met Paula at a later time.)

46

Nature vs. Nurture 4

The ***Grammar Presentation*** begins with an **overview** that describes the grammar in an **easy-to-understand** summary.

Charts provide clear guidance on the form, meaning, and use of the target grammar, for **ease of instruction and reference**.

Data from the Real World, a feature **unique** to this series, takes students **beyond traditional information** and teaches them how the unit's grammar is used in authentic situations, including differences between spoken and written use.

2.1 Forming Past Perfect

Form the past perfect with *had* + the past participle of the main verb. Form the negative by adding *not* after *had*. The form is the same for all subjects.

*Elyse and Paula did not grow up together. They **had lived** with different families.*
*They were available for adoption because their birthmother **had given** them up.*
*"**Had** she **talked** about the study to anyone at the time?"*
*"No, she **hadn't**."*
*"What **had** you **heard** about this study before that time?"*
*"**I'd heard** very little about it."*

▶ Irregular Verbs: See page A1.

2.2 Using Past Perfect with Simple Past

a. Use the past perfect to describe an event in a time period that leads up to another past event or time period. Use the simple past to describe the later event or time period.

LATER TIME   EARLIER TIME
*She **learned** that she **had been** part of a secret study.*
LATER TIME   EARLIER TIME
*The twins **discovered** that they **had** both **studied** psychology.*

b. The prepositions *before, by,* or *until* can introduce the later time period.

EARLIER TIME   LATER TIME
*Their mother **had known** about the study before her death.*
EARLIER TIME   LATER TIME
*Sue **hadn't met** her sister until last year.*
EARLIER TIME   LATER TIME
*Studies on twins **had become** common by the 1960s.*

c. The past perfect is often used to give reasons or background information for later past events.

REASON
*She was late. She **had forgotten** to set her alarm clock.*
BACKGROUND INFORMATION   LATER PAST EVENT
*He **had** never **taken** a subway before he moved to New York.*

Data from the Real World

In writing, these verbs are commonly used in the past perfect: *come, have, leave, make,* and *take. Had been* is the most common past perfect form in speaking and writing.

*The twins **had not gone** to the same school as children.*
*The family thought that they **had made** the right decision.*
*Psychologists praised the study because the researchers **had been** very careful in their work.*
*The researchers **had not been** aware of each other's work on twins until they met.*

▶ ## Grammar Application

Exercise 2.1 Past Perfect

Complete the sentences about twins who met as adults. Use the past perfect form of the verbs in parentheses.

1. Two separate Illinois families ___had adopted___ (adopt) Anne Green and Annie Smith before the twins were three days old.
2. When the girls met, they were fascinated by their similarities. For example, they _____ (live) near each other before the Greens moved away.
3. As children, both Anne and Annie _____ (go) to the same summer camp.
4. Anne _____ (not / go) to college, and Annie _____ (not / attend) college, either.
5. Both _____ (marry) for the first time by the age of 22.
6. Anne _____ (get) divorced and _____ (remarry). Annie _____ (not / get) divorced and was still married.
7. Both Anne and Annie were allergic to cats and dogs and _____ never _____ (own) pets.
8. Both _____ (give) the same name – Heather – to their daughters.
9. Both _____ previously _____ (work) in the hospitality industry.
10. Anne _____ (work) as a hotel manager. However, Annie _____ (not / work) in hotels; she _____ (be) a restaurant manager.

Theme-related exercises allow students to **apply the grammar** in a variety of natural contexts.

Exercise 4.2 Past Perfect Progressive, Past Perfect, or Simple Past?

A Complete the interview with a woman who found her three siblings after many years. Use the past perfect progressive, the past perfect, or the simple past form of the verbs in parentheses. Use contractions when possible. Sometimes more than one answer is possible.

Vijay Tell us how you found your family.

Paula I *'d been looking* (look) for my sister all my life. I _____
(1)   (2)
(not / have) much luck, though. Then one day, I turned on the TV. A talk show was on. The host of the show was interviewing three siblings – two brothers and a half sister.[1] Different families _____ (adopt) the siblings many
(3)
years before.

Vijay And?

Paula They _____ (talk) about me before I turned on the program.
(4)
The siblings had recently reunited, and they _____ (search)
(5)
for a fourth sibling for the past several months. I called the TV station, and we all
finally _____ (meet).
(6)

Vijay So, you _____ (look) for a sister all your life, and you found
(7)
three siblings!

Paula Yes, it was wonderful! We all met at one of the network offices the following week.
After we _____ (speak) for a while, it was obvious to me that
(8)
they _____ (look) for me all their lives, too.
(9)

¹**half sister:** a sister who is biologically related by one parent only

B *Pair Work* Discuss these questions with a partner.

• Choose a sentence in A in which you can use either the past perfect or the past perfect progressive. Why are both possible here?
• In which sentence in A is only the past perfect correct?

C *Over to You* Do an online search for twins, siblings, or other family members who reunited after many years. Write five sentences about their experiences. Use the past perfect and the past perfect progressive.

5 Avoid Common Mistakes ⚠

1. **Use the past perfect or past perfect progressive to give background information for a past tense event.**
   had
   I ~~have~~ never seen my sister in real life, so I was nervous the first time we met.
   had been dreaming
   I ~~have dreamed~~ about meeting her, and I finally did.

2. **Use the past perfect or past perfect progressive to give a reason for a past event.**
   had been crying
   Her eyes were red and puffy because she ~~cried~~.

3. **Use the past perfect (not the past perfect progressive) for a completed earlier event.**
   arranged
   They ~~had been arranging~~ a time to meet, but both of them forgot about it.

4. **Use the past perfect (not present perfect) to describe a completed event that happened before a past event.**
   had
   I ~~have~~ visited her in Maine twice before she came to visit me.

Editing Task

Find and correct seven more mistakes in the paragraphs about sibling differences.

    had
    I ~~have~~ never really thought about sibling differences until my own children were
    born. When we had our first child, my husband and I have lived in Chicago for just a few
    months. We have not made many friends yet, so we spent all our time with our child. Baby
    Gilbert was happy to be the center of attention. He depended on us for everything.
5   By the time our second son, Chase, was born, we have developed a community of
    friends and a busier social life. We frequently visited friends and left the children at home
    with a babysitter. As a result of our busy schedules, Chase was more independent. One
    day I had just been hanging up the phone when Chase came into the room. Chase picked
    up the phone and started talking into it. I thought he was pretending, but I was wrong. He
10 had been figuring out how to use the phone!
        When my husband came home, he was tired because he worked all day. When I
    told him about Chase's phone conversation, though, he became very excited. Gilbert has
    never used the phone as a child. At first, we were surprised that Chase was so different
    from Gilbert. Then we realized that because of our busy lifestyles, Chase had learned to be
15 independent.

> *Grammar for Writing* connects the unit's grammar to specific **applications** in writing.

> The final writing exercise **brings everything together** as students apply their knowledge of the unit's grammar in a level-appropriate **writing task.**

Grammar for Writing ✏

Using Past Perfect to Provide Background Information and Reasons

Writers use the past perfect to provide background information and reasons for past situations and actions. Read these examples:

I had always thought that I was an only child, but I recently discovered that I have a sister. My parents had given me up for adoption. When I was 15, I decided to find my biological parents.

Pre-writing Task

1 Read the paragraph. What does the writer believe about the influence of the environment on relationships? What example does the writer use to explain this?

The Effects of Friends on Sibling Relationships

I believe that the experiences that a person has outside the home can be as influential as experiences inside the home. Examples of this are siblings who start out very similar but become very different from one another as they grow older. For example, Andy and Frank are two brothers who are only two years apart. They did everything together and were best friends until they started junior high. After Andy had been in seventh grade for a little while, he started to change. He had made new friends at school, so he and Frank did not see each other much during the day. Frank had made new friends, too. In fact, Andy's new friends did not like Frank very much, so Andy did not feel comfortable asking Frank to spend time with them. By the time Andy and Frank were in high school, they had grown very far apart. They had made different friends and they had developed different interests. They had been similar when they were young, but Andy and Frank had very little in common as young adults.

2 Read the paragraph again. Underline the sentences that contain both simple past and past perfect verbs. Double underline the sentences with verbs only in the past perfect. Circle the time clauses. Notice how the time clauses help clarify the earlier time period.

Writing Task

1 *Write* Use the paragraph in the Pre-writing Task to help you write about different conditions that influence people's behavior. Give examples from events and situations you have observed to support your opinion.

2 *Self-Edit* Use the editing tips to improve your paragraph. Make any necessary changes.

1. Did you use the past perfect to give background information and provide reasons?
2. Did you use time words and time clauses to clarify the time periods in your sentences or emphasize that some events happened earlier than others?
3. Did you avoid the mistakes in the Avoid Common Mistakes chart on page 59?

> A **Pre-writing Task** uses a model to guide students' **analysis** of grammar in **writing.**

1

Simple Present and Present Progressive

First Impressions

1 | Grammar in the Real World

A When you meet someone for the first time, what do you notice about the person? Read the article about first impressions. What influences your first impressions?

First Impressions

Here is an interesting fact: The average person **forms** a first impression of someone in less than 30 seconds. *First impressions* **are** the opinions someone **has** about you when
5 you **meet** for the first time. What **is** your smile **telling** the other person? What **is** the way you dress **saying** about you? These factors can make a difference in the way the person **thinks** about you.
10   Handshakes, facial expressions, and general appearance **help** to create first impressions. People are constantly **forming** these impressions of others. We do not make these impressions consciously.[1] They **are** largely subconscious.[2] However, they **tend**[3] to be extremely difficult to change.
     Some psychologists today **are researching** the factors that influence how
15 people react to others. For example, psychologist Brian Nosek **is** currently **using** a collection of tests known as the IAT, or Implicit Association Test, for his research. These tests **are helping** to reveal our thinking processes, both conscious and subconscious, as we form our impressions of others. Specifically, Nosek is **investigating** our use of stereotypes and attitudes about others in
20 forming first impressions.
     Each test **measures** what happens while people **are making** judgments. The results **demonstrate** that people have stereotypes, and that these stereotypes **influence** their first impressions. For example, both young and old people **tend** to associate the word *good* with pictures of young people.
25   Since first impressions **influence** what a person **thinks** about you to a great degree, it **is** important to always do your best to make a good first impression.

[1]**consciously:** aware of what is happening | [2]**subconscious:** existing in the mind but not in one's awareness | [3]**tend:** be likely

B *Comprehension Check* Answer the questions.

1. How long does it take to form a first impression?

2. What is the collection of tests known as the IAT helping to reveal?

3. What is one stereotype that young and old people share?

C *Notice* Find the sentences in the article and complete them. Circle the correct verbs. Then check (✔) the box that best describes the function of each verb.

1. The average person **forms / is forming** a first impression of someone in less than 30 seconds.

   ☐ general fact or habit   ☐ temporary action

2. Handshakes, facial expressions, and general appearance **help / are helping** to create first impressions.

   ☐ general fact or habit   ☐ temporary action

3. Some psychologists today **research / are researching** the factors that influence how people react to others.

   ☐ general fact or habit   ☐ temporary action

4. Specifically, Nosek **investigates / is investigating** our use of stereotypes and attitudes about others in forming first impressions.

   ☐ general fact or habit   ☐ temporary action

What do the verbs in the simple present describe? What do the verbs in the present progressive describe?

2 Simple Present vs. Present Progressive

▶ Grammar Presentation

The simple present and the present progressive both describe present time. The simple present describes things that are more permanent, such as general facts or habits. The present progressive describes things that are temporary, such as things in progress now or around now.

*The average person **forms** a first impression in less than 30 seconds.*

*Psychologists **are researching** the factors that influence how people react.*

2.1 Simple Present

a. Use the simple present for general facts and permanent situations.

*People **form** a first impression within 30 seconds.*
*First impressions **influence** what a person thinks about you.*
*I **dress** conservatively at work.*

b. Use the simple present to describe routines and habits.

*The manager **asks** a lot of questions.*
*We **work** for eight hours every day.*

You can use time expressions such as *always, usually, often, sometimes, never, on Mondays, once a week, two days a week,* and *twice a month.*

*The hiring manager <u>always</u> **writes** a report after an interview.*
*We <u>usually</u> **follow** her recommendations.*
*She **doesn't** interview candidates <u>on Mondays</u>.*
*We **discuss** the manager's reports <u>once a week</u>.*

c. Use the simple present for routines, scheduled events, and timetables.

*The office **opens** at 9:00 a.m.*
*The train to Boston **departs** from platform 11 at 2:00 p.m.*
*"**Does** the meeting always **begin** at noon?"*
*"Yes, it **does**."*

▶▶ Irregular Verbs : See page A1.

Data from the Real World

Research shows that we use some adverbs with the simple present more often in academic writing than in speaking.

More common in writing: *typically, frequently, traditionally*	*The interview **typically** takes 3 hours.*
Common in both speaking and writing: *generally, usually, normally*	*The team **generally** meets on Tuesdays.* *How do you **normally** handle complaints?*

2.2 Present Progressive

a. Use the present progressive to describe what is in progress now or around the present time.

*Mr. Rask **is interviewing** a candidate at the moment.* (The interview is happening now.)
*We **are interviewing** candidates all month.* (Interviews may not be in progress now, but they are in progress during this month.)

b. Use the present progressive to describe temporary events or changing situations.

*I **am studying** stereotypes in the workplace.* (My studies will end in the future.)

Data from the Real World

Research shows that we often use the present progressive for habits that are noteworthy or unusual. This is sometimes, but not always, because these habits are not desirable. You can use *always* or *constantly* for emphasis. *Constantly* is more formal than *always*.

She **is always disturbing** me when I am trying to study.
My boss **is constantly asking** me to stay late at work.

The present progressive form is also common with verbs that describe changing or temporary situations.

The workers at that store **are constantly changing.** Every week there is someone new.
We **are always looking** for new ideas and people with special talents.

▶ Grammar Application

Exercise 2.1 Simple Present

Complete the sentences with the simple present of the verbs in the box.

give   have   have   help   ~~make~~   meet   show   start   teach   videotape

1. According to many studies, most people _make_ judgments about others in only a few seconds.
2. Communication trainer Mary Hernandez _____ job seekers make a good first impression.
3. Ms. Hernandez _____ a course called Making a Good First Impression at the community college.
4. The class _____ on Mondays and Wednesdays.
5. At the first class meeting, Ms. Hernandez typically _____ students a self-assessment test.
6. The self-assessment test _____ how the students judge themselves.
7. Students almost always _____ a positive impression of themselves.
8. After the self-assessment, Ms. Hernandez usually _____ the students in mock interviews.
9. On the last day of class, students _____ real interviews with a representative from a local company.
10. Ms. Hernandez's class _____ at 6:30 p.m. and ends at 9:00 p.m.

Exercise 2.2 Simple Present or Present Progressive?

Complete the questions about Josh and Rachel with the simple present or present progressive form of the words in parentheses. Then write answers using the information in the picture.

1. Where _are Josh and Rachel working_ (Josh and Rachel / work) this summer?
   Josh and Rachel are working at the Bursar's Office this summer.

2. How often _____ (Josh and Rachel / work)?
   _____

3. When _____ (Josh / start his job) in the mornings?
   _____

4. _____ (Rachel / talk) to a student right now?
   _____

5. How many _____ (students / wait) in Josh's line?
   _____

6. _____ (who / make) a better first impression on the
   students who need help?
   _____

7. When _____ (Rachel / finish) work in the afternoons?
   _____

8. _____ (who / not help) students at the moment?
   _____

Exercise 2.3 More Simple Present or Present Progressive?

A Complete the sentences from a brochure that participants received at a job fair. Use the simple present or present progressive form of the verbs in parentheses.

Welcome to the State Employment Agency Job Fair!

careers services support contact

Representatives from over 30 big regional corporations _are participating_ (1) (participate) in today's state job fair. The job fair _____ (2) (take) place every year. Every year, interviews _____ (3) (begin) at 9:00 a.m. and _____ (4) (continue) throughout the day until 6:00 p.m. The long list of participating companies is on the back of this brochure. This year, companies A–G _____ (5) (interview) candidates in room 245 on the second floor. Companies H–Z _____ (6) (meet) candidates in room 252.

Tips for Job Seekers

Interviews generally _____ (7) (take) about 30 minutes. An interviewer usually _____ (8) (spend) a few minutes reading your résumé. He or she sometimes _____ (9) (ask) you to fill out an application. An interview typically _____ (10) (end) with a question-and-answer period. The average employer _____ (11) (expect) you to know a lot about the company – this is an opportunity to demonstrate your knowledge. Also, employers _____ (12) always _____ (12) (look) for new ideas, and these ideas may come from you!

B *Pair Work* Compare your answers with a partner. Discuss the reason for each of your answers.

A *I used the present progressive in number 1 because the phrase* today's job fair *tells me that the sentence is about something that is happening now.*

B *I agree with you. For number 2, I used . . .*

3 | Stative Verbs

▶ Grammar Presentation

Stative verbs describe states and conditions. Generally, they do not describe actions.	That **sounds** like a great project. We **don't have** two chances to make a first impression.

3.1 Non-action or Stative Verbs

Use the simple present with stative verbs. Here are some common stative verb categories:

Description: *appear, be, exist, look, seem, sound*

Measurement: *cost, weigh*

Knowledge: *believe, forget, know, remember, think*

Emotions: *feel, hate, like, love, prefer*

Possession / Relationship: *belong, contain, have, need, own, want*

Senses: *hear, see, smell, taste*

Perception: *notice, see, understand*

She **seems** like a hard worker.

It **doesn't cost** anything to send your application.

He **doesn't believe** that first impressions are true.

I **know** stereotypes aren't true.

Employers **prefer** motivated workers.

I **don't have** a good impression of him.

I **need** a challenging career.

Can you **see** the water from your office?

When you explain the problem in that way, I **see** your point. I **understand** your viewpoint.

▶▶ Stative (Non-Action) Verbs: See page A2.

3.2 Verbs with Stative and Action Meanings

Some verbs have both stative and action meanings. You can use the present progressive with the action meanings of these verbs. Examples of verbs with stative and action meanings include *be, have, see, taste, think,* and *weigh.*

SIMPLE PRESENT (STATIVE MEANING)	PRESENT PROGRESSIVE (ACTION MEANING)
I **think** first impressions are important. (*think* = believe)	I **am thinking** about how to make a good first impression. (*think* = use the mind)
Do you **have** an interesting career? (*have* = own)	**Are** you **having** trouble at work? (*have* = experience)
She **is** the new manager. (*be* = description)	She **is being** difficult. (*be* = act)
He noticed that he doesn't **see** very well anymore. (*see* = view with the eyes)	He **is seeing** the eye doctor for an exam next week. (*see* = meet with)

▶ Grammar Application

Exercise 3.1 Verbs with Stative and Action Meanings

A Complete the article from a college newspaper. Circle the correct form of the verbs.

A Study on Stereotypes

Lisa James is majoring in psychology here at Carlson College. This semester, she **thinks/(is thinking)** about participating in a study on stereotypes in Professor Green's
(1)
Psychology 101 class. According to Dr. Green, many people **have/are having** fixed
(2)
ideas about members of their own and other cultures. This is true even when they
know/are knowing that the stereotypes they **have/are having** are false.
(3)   (4)
Dr. Green **believes/is believing** that when most people make generalizations
(5)
about other cultures, they **don't seem/are not seeming** to make these judgments
(6)
on observation. Instead, they **appear/are appearing** to base their judgments on
(7)
ideas that they grew up with in their own cultures.

This semester, Dr. Green **has/is having** an interesting time giving his students
(8)
two tests: a self-assessment test and a personality test. In the self-assessment test,
students describe the traits they **think/are thinking** members of their own culture
(9)
have. The personality test gives basic information about what a person is really like.
Dr. Green **believes/is believing** the results of the personality test will conflict with
(10)
the results of the cultural self-assessment test. Here's an example: People from one
culture in the study **believe/are believing** that they are hostile and argumentative.
(11)
However, when these people take the personality test, they usually **get/are getting**
(12)
very high scores for kindness and helpfulness.

The results of studies such as Dr. Green's **appear/are appearing** to show
(13)
that cultural stereotypes are almost always mistaken. Lisa is looking forward to
discovering what the tests say about her. Although she believes that she does not
have stereotypes about people, she knows that Dr. Green **believes/is believing** that
(14)
almost everyone has stereotypes of some people.

B *Pair Work* Compare your answers with a partner. Discuss the reason for each of your answers.

I used the present progressive with the verb think in number 1 because the action is happening now.

Exercise 3.2 Stative or Action Meaning?

Complete the conversation about stereotypes at work. Use the simple present or present progressive form of the verbs in parentheses. Use contractions when possible.

Alan Claudia, how are your interview follow-up reports going? Are you still

working on them?

Claudia I ___think___ (think) they're going well. I'm almost finished.
         (1)

Alan That's wonderful news. How many reports _____ you
                                                      (2)

_____ (have)?
        (2)

Claudia Eight. I have three more to do.

Alan Oh, I see. So you're just a little more than half finished. Our meeting

_____ (be) always at 4:30 on Wednesdays. Why are you still
        (3)

working on them?

Claudia I don't usually take this long, but this time I'm spending a lot of time on the

reports because I _____ (be) very careful. I interviewed a lot
                            (4)

of people from many different cultures, both young and old, and from cities as

well as from the countryside.

Alan So?

Claudia Some of the reports _____ (be) finished, but I don't want to base
                                      (5)

my judgments on only partial information. I _____ (not think)
                                                        (6)

that the information would be useful if it's not complete.

Alan I _____ (know) what you mean.
              (7)

Claudia This time, I _____ (have) a hard time separating things like
                              (8)

culture and appearance from people's actual abilities.

Alan Well, it's good that you _____ (be) aware of this. Let's discuss
                                          (9)

it later.

Exercise 3.3 More Stative or Action Meaning?

A 🔊 Listen to the interview about first impressions. Write the missing words.

Reporter When you __*meet*__ someone for the first time, how does
(1)
the person's appearance affect your judgment? Today, we
_____ people to describe how they make
(2)
judgments about others.

Marta I know I _____ unfair stereotypes when I meet someone
(3)
new. To me, older people always _____ like they need
(4)
help. When I meet an older person, I _____
(5)
about my grandparents. I speak slowly and clearly, in case the person
can't hear. I _____ it's wrong to think all older people are
(6)
like that, but I can't help it.

Marc I feel that I _____ always very fair when I meet a
(7)
new person. I _____ people's appearances don't
(8)
always say who they really are. For example, if I meet a person who
_____ sloppy,[1] I _____ that he
(9)   (10)
or she is a lazy person.

Bin For me, it depends on the situation. When I am interviewing
people at work, I take their appearance very seriously. For example,
I always notice how a person dresses for an interview. If a person's
appearance _____ sloppy or careless in an interview,
(11)
I _____ he or she will be a sloppy and careless worker.
(12)

[1]**sloppy:** messy, not tidy

B *Pair Work* Discuss these questions with a partner: Which person in A are you most
like? How much do stereotypes affect the judgments you make about people when you
first meet them? Give an example.

*I think I'm like Marc. I don't like to judge someone right away. For example, my landlord
seems somewhat reserved when you meet him, but he's actually a really nice guy.*

4 | Special Meanings and Uses of Simple Present

▶ Grammar Presentation

The simple present is frequently used for summarizing and reviewing as well as for explaining procedures or giving instructions.	Malcolm Gladwell's book Blink **persuades** the reader to believe in first impressions. Participants **follow** strict procedures for the Implicit Association Test.

4.1 Special Meanings and Uses of Simple Present

a. Use the simple present to summarize scientific writing or review artistic works such as books, plays, and movies.	The Implicit Association Test **measures** people's responses. Malcolm Gladwell's book Blink **discusses** the importance of first impressions. He **argues** that first impressions **are** often accurate, even if the mind **doesn't realize** it.
b. Use the simple present to explain procedures or instructions.	To administer the test, we always **follow** the same procedures. First, we **seat** participants in every other chair. We **don't** usually **put** them next to each other.
Commonly used expressions that show sequencing include *first, then, next, after that,* and *finally*.	When you arrive at the job fair, first you **go** to the desk and **sign** in. Then you **take** a look at the list of companies and **plan** which companies you **want** to see.

▶ Grammar Application

Exercise 4.1 Uses of Simple Present

Read the sentences. Then label each sentence *R* (book reviews), *P* (procedures and instructions), or *O* (other uses – facts, routines, schedules) according to where the text comes from.

1. First, students write their names at the top of the paper.   *P*

2. The authors end with a set of tips for always creating good first impressions.   _____

3. The class meets on Tuesdays and Thursdays from 11:30 a.m. to 1:00 p.m.   _____

4. This book helps readers understand the difference between how they see themselves and how other people see them.   _____

5. The required reading for this course is *Making a Good Impression* by Dr. Al Stone.   _____

6. *Making a Good Impression* includes summaries of many of the latest studies on how people make first impressions.   _____

7. To complete the online test, students select their answers and click "Submit."   _____

Exercise 4.2 Summarizing an Article

Use the words to write sentences that describe the main points from an article on the problems with personality tests.

1. personality tests / always / not be / accurate

   Personality tests are not always accurate.

2. job candidates / sometimes / not tell / the truth

3. a job candidate's score / always / not reflect / the candidate's personality

4. candidates who take some personality tests twice / sometimes / get / different scores

5. these tests / not match / people to jobs well

Exercise 4.3 Giving Instructions

Pair Work Choose a situation with a partner in which it is important to make a good first impression, such as a job interview or a first meeting with an important person. Describe the scene and how the person makes a good first impression. Remember to use sequencing words such as *First, . . .*; *Then . . .*; *After that, . . .*; and *Finally, ...*

On the first day of work: First, the new employee shakes hands and makes eye contact with the people he or she meets.

5 Avoid Common Mistakes ⚠️

1. **Use the simple present with stative verbs.**

   First impressions are mattering when you want to establish a relationship. (matter)

2. **Use the simple present to express facts, routines, or habits unlikely to change.**

   Sessions are requiring 10 to 15 minutes to complete. (require)

3. **Use the present progressive to show that something is in progress or temporary.**

   He doesn't interview for jobs this year because he still studies. (isn't interviewing / is still studying)

4. **Use the -ing form, not the base form of the verb, when using the present progressive.**

   He is work as a store clerk. (working)

Editing Task

Find and correct eight more mistakes in the paragraphs about first impressions.

Without a doubt, first impressions are important. Current research ~~is showing~~ *shows* that a first impression can last a long time. These days it seems that everyone talks about the significance of the first 30 seconds of a job interview or a meeting with a client. However, I am believing there is another side to this story.

5   Some people are having the ability to make a good first impression, but the impression may be false. I believe that time and experience are telling the truth about a person's character. Whenever I talk with someone who smiles at me and seems completely charming, I am getting suspicious. I think that the person is not sincere, and that he or she wants something from me. On the other hand, I often find that quieter,

10 more reserved people are more willing to help me when I ask. My colleague Jim is a good example. This fall he is work on a special project, so he is very busy, and sometimes he appears unfriendly. However, he usually stops and helps me when I ask. My friendlier colleagues usually smile, but when I ask them for help, they are making excuses.

In short, I am not believing that everyone who makes a good first impression

15 deserves my trust. Maybe I am too suspicious with friendly people, but I will always give awkward or shy people a second chance. After all, I think that I may be one of them.

6 | Grammar for Writing

Using Simple Present and Present Progressive to Write About Present Time Situations

Writers use the simple present to discuss facts and give general information. They use the present progressive to describe scenes or temporary situations. Read these examples:

People <u>are</u> often nervous at job interviews.
Most people <u>worry</u> about job interviews.
These days, many people <u>are looking</u> for jobs.

Pre-writing Task

1 Read the paragraph. Which days are best for a job interview?

Best Interview Times

Most people worry about making a good impression at a job interview. They generally think about what to wear and what questions to prepare. One thing that people usually do not think about is the day of the appointment. However, some job experts believe that the actual day makes a difference. For example, some say that normally
5 the worst days are Monday and Friday, whereas Tuesday and Wednesday are the best. Monday is not ideal because on that day the interviewer is probably still thinking about the weekend, and on Friday, the interviewer is usually watching the clock and waiting for the weekend to start. On the other hand, Tuesday and Wednesday are typically much better because the interviewer does not feel as much stress as later in the week. There
10 are others who believe that any day is good, but morning appointments are better than afternoon ones because interviewers still feel relaxed in the morning. People who want to have a successful job interview might want to choose the right interview day in addition to the perfect outfit.

2 Read the paragraph again. Circle the simple present verbs. Underline the present progressive verbs. Why did the writer choose to use the present progressive for these verbs and not the simple present? <u>Double underline</u> the stative verbs.

Writing Task

1 *Write* Use the paragraph in the Pre-writing Task to help you write a good job interview tip or a tip for making a good first impression.

2 *Self-Edit* Use the editing tips to improve your paragraph. Make any necessary changes.

1. Did you use the simple present to express factual situations, routines, and habits?
2. Did you use the present progressive to express situations that are in progress or temporary?
3. Did you avoid the mistakes in the Avoid Common Mistakes chart on page 13?

UNIT
2

Simple Past and Past Progressive; *Used To, Would*

Global Marketing

---

1 | Grammar in the Real World

A What is a *global market*? Read the web article about global marketing. What makes global marketing campaigns successful?

🌐 Global Marketing

In 2009, an American toy company **opened** a huge store on the main shopping street in a major city in China. The store **featured** the company's famous doll. At that time, the sales of the doll **were falling** slightly in the United States, so the
5 company **was working** on developing new markets in other countries. At the store, there **were not** many sales. Customers **would come** in and look, but few **were buying** the dolls. The company **did** some research and **found out** why. The doll's image **did not appeal**[1] to young Chinese women. They **had** a preference for dolls
10 that looked cute and **adorable**.[2] They also **wanted** more affordable prices. The toy company eventually **closed** the store.

Shanghai

Around the same time, another American company **was showing** a series of advertisements in the United States for a shampoo product. In one ad, "real women" **showed** their
15 hair and **talked** about how much they liked the shampoo. These women **looked** like your friends and neighbors, not like models. The advertisements **were** a great success. The company **decided** to create similar advertisements in Malaysia. While it **was working on** these advertisements,
20 it **was** also **doing** research on the Malaysian culture. The company **discovered** that some Malaysian women **thought** that it was inappropriate[3] to show their hair in public, so it **realized** that its approach[4] **would not be** successful. As a result, the company **adapted** its advertising to fit the local culture. In the new Malaysian advertisements, the women **did not show** their hair. They only **talked** about it.
25 The ads **were** a tremendous success.

Kuala Lumpur

[1]**appeal:** interest or attract someone │ [2]**adorable:** attractive and easy to love │ [3]**inappropriate:** unsuitable, especially for the particular time, place, or situation │ [4]**approach:** a method or way of doing something

In the past, companies **would create** one advertisement and one product for all markets. Today's markets include places all over the world, and the success of global marketing campaigns depends on two simple rules: understand the local culture and adapt the marketing and product to that culture.

B *Comprehension Check* Answer the questions.

1. What are some reasons customers in China did not buy the dolls at first?
2. Why was the campaign in Malaysia successful?
3. How are advertising campaigns different today from in the past?

C *Notice* Read the sentences from the article. Check (✓) the sentence that describes an action that continued for a period of time in the past. Does the verb end in *-ing* or *-ed*?

_____ 1. Around the same time, another American company **was showing** a series of advertisements in the United States for a shampoo product.

_____ 2. As a result, the company **adapted** its advertising to fit the local culture.

2 Simple Past vs. Past Progressive

▶ Grammar Presentation

The simple past and the past progressive describe actions in the past.	*American consumers **wanted** affordable prices.* *While the company **was working** on these advertisements, it **was** also **doing** research on the Malaysian culture.*

2.1 Simple Past

Use the simple past to describe actions, situations, or events that are completed. Use the simple past for actions that happened once or repeatedly in the past.	*Company executives **decided** to market the dolls in China in 2009.* *The dolls **weren't** popular in China a few years ago.* *What **did** the company **market** in Malaysia?* *The company executives **visited** Malaysia a few times.*
Past time markers, such as *yesterday, last week, two months ago,* and *in 2011* can be used with the simple past.	*A company **studied** Malaysian culture <u>last year</u>.* ***Did** it **get** good local advice <u>last time</u>?* *Who **gave** the company advice <u>last week</u>?*

▶▶ Irregular Verbs: See page A1.

2.2 Past Progressive

Use the past progressive to describe an activity or event in progress over a period of time in the past.	*The company **wasn't selling** dolls in China at that time.* *Why **weren't** many people **buying** them?* *What **was happening** during that period?*

2.3 Simple Past and Past Progressive Contrasted

a. Use the past progressive to describe background activities. These activities were in progress at the same time as the main event in the sentence. Use the simple past for the main event.	BACKGROUND ACTIVITY *They **were planning** a new advertising campaign* MAIN EVENT *in the country, so they **did** some research on the culture.*
b. Use the simple past, not the past progressive, with stative verbs.	*The company **understood** the culture.* NOT *The company ~~was understanding~~ the culture.*

▶ Grammar Application

Exercise 2.1 Simple Past and Past Progressive

A Underline the past forms of the verbs in this paragraph about early American advertising.

Benjamin Franklin is one of the fathers of American advertising. He <u>was</u> an early American politician and inventor. In the early 1700s, Franklin was working in Philadelphia, Pennsylvania, as a publisher and inventor. He published a variety of books, and he was also the publisher of the newspaper *The Pennsylvania Gazette*. He used *The Pennsylvania Gazette* to advertise his inventions. Franklin filled the newspaper with ads. He also advertised books, both his own and other people's. Because of the ads in his newspaper, Franklin was making a lot of money and was selling a lot of books. These were among the first advertisements in America.

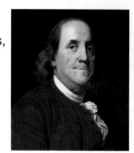

B *Pair Work* Compare your answers with a partner. Discuss which verbs are simple past and which are past progressive.

Exercise 2.2 Simple Past or Past Progressive?

A Read the paragraphs about a successful advertising campaign.[1] Circle the simple past or past progressive form of the verbs. Sometimes more than one answer is possible.

In the years after World War II, the U.S. government **promoted /(was promoting)**
(1)
milk as a health product. In the 1960s, however, soft-drink[2] companies began to market
their products very aggressively. As a result, people **soon drank / were soon drinking**
(2)
more soft drinks and less milk. The California Milk Advisory Board (CMAB) realized that
the old health-focused advertising **didn't work / wasn't working**.
(3)

Beginning in the mid-1970s, milk sales **went / were going** down in the United
(4)
States, and the CMAB **decided / was deciding** to do something to increase sales. The
(5)
CMAB members **learned / were learning** that the majority of people believed that
(6)
milk was good for them, but they weren't drinking it.

In 1993, a new board was formed, the California Milk Processor Board (MilkPEP).
This new board **hired / were hiring** an advertising agency to design a new
(7)
advertisement for milk. The agency **designed / were designing** a very original ad. The
(8)
ad showed a person eating something sweet or sticky (like cake or peanut butter). The
ad was funny because the person really needed milk to drink, but he or she didn't have
it. This **became / was becoming** the very successful "Got milk?"[3] campaign. In 1994,
(9)
milk sales **increased / were increasing** by over 10 million gallons a year. This was a
(10)
clear indication that the new campaign was a success.

[1]**campaign:** series of advertisements │ [2]**soft-drink:** a carbonated, nonalcoholic drink, also known as "pop," "soda," or "cola" │
[3]**Got milk?:** an informal way of saying "Do you have milk?"

B *Pair Work* Compare your answers with a partner. Then ask and answer questions about the information in A. Use the simple past and the past progressive.

  A *What was happening in the United States beginning in the mid-1970s?*
  B *Milk sales were going down.*

3 | Time Clauses with Simple Past and Past Progressive

▶ Grammar Presentation

The simple past and past progressive are used with time clauses to show the order of two past events.

We **changed** our minds about the product **after we saw the ads for it**.
While he was presenting the product, the audience **listened** attentively.

3.1 Using Time Clauses with Simple Past

a. Use time clauses beginning with the time words and phrases *after*, *as soon as*, *before*, *once*, *until*, and *when* to show the order in which two events happened.

When the time clause comes first in the sentence, use a comma.

We found out that the ad wasn't appropriate for consumers **when we were doing research on the market**.
When we were doing research on the market, we found out that the ad wasn't appropriate for consumers.

b. Use *after* to introduce the first event.

FIRST EVENT   SECOND EVENT
After the store opened, people didn't buy the dolls.

c. Use *before* to introduce the *second* event.

FIRST EVENT
The company worked with an advertising team
SECOND EVENT
before it marketed the shampoo.

d. Use *as soon as* or *once* to introduce the first event when the second event happens immediately after.

FIRST EVENT
As soon as the company made prices
SECOND EVENT
affordable, sales improved.

SECOND EVENT   FIRST EVENT
Women bought the shampoo **once the ad fit the local culture**.

e. *Until* means "up to that time." Use *until* to indicate the second event.

FIRST EVENT   SECOND EVENT
There were not many sales **until the company changed its advertising**.

f. Use *when* to introduce the first event. *When* means "at almost the same time."

FIRST EVENT   SECOND EVENT
When we thought about the low sales, we got a little worried.

3.2 Using Time Clauses with Simple Past and Past Progressive

a. Use the past progressive to describe an ongoing action. Use *while* or *when* to introduce the ongoing action.

ONGOING EVENT
While we were developing an advertising campaign,

INTERRUPTION
I got sick.

Use the simple past to describe an action that interrupts the ongoing action. Use *when* to introduce the interruption.

ONGOING EVENT
We were discussing the new ad campaign

INTERRUPTION
when we heard about the low sales.

b. Use the past progressive in both clauses to talk about two actions in progress at the same time.

While they were studying Malaysian culture,* they *were developing *an advertising campaign.*

Data from the Real World

In formal writing, *when* is more common than *while*.

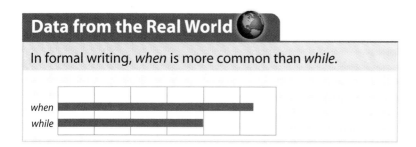

when

while

► # Grammar Application

Exercise 3.1 Time Clauses with *After, Before, Once,* and *When*

Read the sentences about marketing milk. Circle the time words. Underline the time clauses. Label the earlier event with *1* and the later event with *2*.

1. (After) World War II ended, the milk companies in the United States wanted people to drink milk. They marketed milk as a health drink.

2. People drank more milk than soft drinks before soft-drink companies started marketing their drinks as "fun."

3. When soft-drink companies began marketing their drinks as "fun," the California Milk Advisory Board (CMAB) realized it needed to market milk differently.

4. The CMAB learned that people thought milk was boring after the board completed its market research.

5. When the CMAB discovered that 70 percent of Californians already drank milk, it decided to create a campaign to persuade them to drink more milk.

6. Before it started a new ad campaign, the new California Milk Processor Board, MilkPEP, learned that most people drink milk at home with foods like cookies and cake.

7. When the new milk ads appeared, they immediately became famous.

8. MilkPEP created a successful Spanish-language milk ad once it had success with the "Got milk?" campaign.

Exercise 3.2 Time Clauses with *As Soon As, Before, Until,* and *While*

Read the facts about the history of advertising. Combine the sentences with the time words in parentheses. Sometimes more than one answer is possible.

1. First event: Advertising already existed in Europe.

   Second event: Europeans came to the Americas in the 1400s.

   (before) *Before Europeans came to the Americas in the 1400s, advertising already existed in Europe./Advertising already existed in Europe before Europeans came to the Americas in the 1400s.*

2. First event: Europeans were exploring the world from the fifteenth to the seventeenth centuries.

   Second event: They found new and interesting kinds of food and spices.

   (while) _____

   _____

3. First event: European explorers came home.

   Second event: They introduced the items to the people from their countries.

   (as soon as) _____

   _____

4. First event: Europeans didn't know anything about coffee.

   Second event: They read the ads that explained what it was.

   (before) _____

   _____

5. First event: Early advertisements had no words because most people couldn't read.

   Second event: Literacy became widespread in the eighteenth century.

   (until) _____

   _____

6. First event: Newspapers were the most common form of advertising.

   Second event: Radio was invented in the 1920s.

   (before) _____

   _____

Exercise 3.3 Using Time Clauses with *When* and *While*

Complete the sentences from a report on a global marketing lecture. Use the simple past and past progressive forms of the verbs in parentheses.

1. The head of marketing of a restaurant chain _was speaking_ (speak) when I _arrived_ (arrive).

2. When his company _____ (consider) opening new restaurants, they _____ (realize) that they needed some vegetarian food items.

3. The market researchers _____ (do) research on the vegetarian consumer when the managers _____ (decide) they needed a new, healthy menu.

4. The managers _____ (learn) that they had to eliminate many ingredients with eggs and dairy products when the market researchers _____ (interview) vegan[1] customers.

5. While they _____ (listen) to customers explain how busy they were, the market researchers _____ (get) the idea that the company should offer delivery service.

6. The head of marketing _____ (think) about opening up restaurants in Chicago when he _____ (learn) that more people ordered take-out food in New York City than in Chicago.

7. While the managers _____ (contemplate) the idea of opening up a place in New York City, a restaurant in a busy location _____ (become) available, and the company bought the place immediately.

[1] **vegan:** a vegetarian who eats no animal or dairy products

Exercise 3.4 More Using Time Clauses with *When* and *While*

A *Over to You* Think about important decisions you have made in your life. Write an answer to one of these questions. Use *when* and *while*.

- What were you doing when you decided to study here?
- What were you doing when you made an important decision about your life?

  I was working in two different jobs when I decided to take classes here.

B *Pair Work* Discuss your sentences with a partner.

 Used To and Would

▶ Grammar Presentation

Used to and *would* describe past routines or repeated actions. *Used to* expresses states or habits that existed in the past, but do not exist now. *Would* can only express repeated actions.	*Our company **used to sell** shampoo around the world. We **would study** the local customs. Then we **would create** local marketing campaigns.*

4.1 *Used To*

a. *Used to* is followed by the base form of the verb. It can be used for actions or states.	*Some companies **used to ignore** local customs.* (But they don't do that now.) *This building **used to be** a TV studio.* *I **used to know** the manager's name, but I've forgotten it.*
Use *use to* not *used to* in questions with *did*.	*Where **did** you **use to go** to school when you were young?*
The negative is *didn't use to* + the base form.	*Our company **didn't use to ask** for advice from the local markets.* (But our company does now.)
b. Use the simple past, not *used to*, to talk about completed actions in the past.	*The company **made** its sales goals last year.* NOT *The company ~~used to make~~ its sales goals last year.* *The company made its sales goals for a decade.* NOT *The company ~~used to make~~ its sales goals for a decade.* *The company made its sales goals three times.* NOT *The company ~~used to make~~ its sales goals three times.*

4.2 *Would*

a. *Would* is followed by the base form of the verb.	*In the past, companies **would create** one advertisement for all markets.*
A time expression, such as *in the past*, shows the context for the action.	*In the past, we **would meet** for an hour every Friday to talk about marketing techniques. (But we don't do that now.)*
b. *Would* is only used for actions, not states.	*Twenty years ago, many smaller companies **wouldn't do** a lot of marketing in other countries.* *Usually, the president of our company **would not attend** our weekly meetings.* *In the past, companies **were not** sensitive to local customs.* NOT *In the past, companies ~~wouldn't be~~ sensitive to local customs.*
c. Use the simple past, not *would*, to talk about completed actions in the past.	*The sales team **attended** a conference last week.* NOT *The sales team ~~would attend~~ a conference last week.*

▶ # Grammar Application

Exercise 4.1 *Would*

Complete part of a lecture on the history of radio and TV advertising. Use *would* and the correct verbs in the boxes.

    appear   not use   ~~produce~~   read

TV commercials developed from radio commercials. In the early days of radio, radio stations sold advertising time to support themselves. Many companies

___would produce___ entire radio programs in order to advertise their products.
(1)

Famous Hollywood stars of the day _____ on these
(2)

programs. In the early days of radio, radio stations _____
(3)

ads that were on tape.[1] Instead, people performed the ads live. That is, an announcer

_____ an advertisement on the air.[2] Today, some radio ads are
(4)

still live, but many ads are also prerecorded.

[1]**on tape:** prerecorded │ [2]**on the air:** while broadcasting

advertise   buy   create   match

When television appeared, advertisers _____ time (5) during a TV program for their commercials. They _____ (6) short, 10-second advertisements to show during these programs. They

_____ a program with viewers who were likely to buy their (7) product. For example, they _____ laundry soap to housewives (8) who stayed home and watched serial dramas ("soap operas") during the day.

Exercise 4.2 *Used To, Would,* or *Simple Past?*

A ◀») Listen to an interview about how TV advertising has changed. Write the correct form of the verbs that you hear.

Zach How has TV advertising changed over the years?

Dave In the past, we ___*used to create*___ commercials with very direct messages. (1) Commercials _____ the consumer exactly what to do. We never (2)

_____ vague¹ about the message at all. In addition, (3) commercials _____ to entertain the viewer. (4)

Zach So, how _____ you _____ an advertising message in the old (5) (5) days?

Dave A commercial for our product _____: "Drink Fruity Juice." (6) We _____ the product several times in a commercial. We (7)

_____ the product. (8)

Zach What changed?

Dave We _____ some research a few years ago. It _____ (9) (10) that people no longer pay attention to commercials like those. As a result,

we _____ to change our style. Now we are producing (11) "mystery ads." Mystery ads don't show the product until the very end of the

commercial. They entertain the viewer because the viewer has to figure out

what the product is.

¹**vague:** unclear

B ◀») Listen again and check your answers.

Exercise 4.3 Using *Used To*, *Would*, and Simple Past

Group Work Describe your TV viewing habits in the past and in the present. In groups, discuss your answers to the following questions. Use affirmative and negative forms of *used to* and *would*.

- When you were younger, what types of TV shows did you use to watch?
- How much TV did you use to watch as a child?
- Would your family watch TV together, or did people in your family watch different programs?
- Did you use to believe everything you saw on TV? Do you believe what you see now? Why or why not?
- Did you use to pay attention to TV commercials in the past? Do you pay attention now? Why or why not?

A *When I was younger, I used to watch a few sitcoms[1] and sports games. What about you?*

B *I didn't use to watch TV much at all. But I would always watch cartoons on Saturday mornings.*

[1]**sitcom:** a situation-comedy show

5 Avoid Common Mistakes ⚠

1. Use the base form of the verb after *would* and *used to*.

 live
He used to ~~living~~ in Bangladesh, where he studied economics.

2. Use *was* or *were* with the verb + -*ing* to describe actions in progress in the past, including in sentences with two clauses.

 was
The new dolls were selling well, and the company making a lot of money.

3. Use the simple past when describing specific events in the past.

 had
She knew that she ~~has~~ a problem in one of her markets.

4. Use the past progressive to provide background information for an event.

was studying
I ~~studied~~ business administration in Malaysia when I got my first job.

Editing Task

Find and correct eight more mistakes in the transcript from a meeting.

Hello, everyone! Welcome to the meeting.

As many of you know, this past year $\overset{was}{\wedge}$ disappointing for many companies.
However, we ended up doing quite well here at ABC Cell Phones. At the beginning
of the year, things looking bad. In fact, our sales fell when I started here. However,
5 our excellent marketing team did their research, and they create new and
extremely successful advertisements after they discover two shifts in consumer
spending.

The first shift they saw was a shift to green marketing. Last year we noticed
that consumers would paid more for environmentally friendly products. Therefore,
10 our first advertisement of last year showed how good our cell phone batteries are
for the environment.

The second shift was in who advertised our products. While we wrote our most
recent advertisement, research arrived that showed that celebrities sell products
better. In October we began showing famous actors and actresses using our
15 phones, and last month alone, our sales rise by 25 percent.

In short, while some businesses were struggling, we increasing our profits.

6 | Grammar for Writing

Using Past and Present Forms to Write About Changes

Writers use both past forms and present forms of verbs to describe changes. They use
past forms to express background information about what something was like in the
past. They use present forms to describe what the subject is like now. Read this example
paragraph:

> Years ago, most companies used to hold focus groups to find out what
> consumers wanted. They asked consumers questions and gave them products to
> review. These days, companies still employ techniques like focus groups. However,
> many companies use the Internet to find out what people want. Advertisers collect
> information about consumers based on the websites they look at.

Pre-writing Task

1 Read the paragraph. What kind of music did advertisers use to use? What kind of music are advertisers using these days?

Music in Advertising

Music in advertising has gone through different stages throughout the years. In the 1950s and 1960s, every product used to have a jingle, a short piece of music that is appealing and singable. A product would have several different advertisements, but the jingle was always the same. Jingles used to be effective because consumers would

5 sing them at different times to themselves, and the songs would remind them about the product. In the 1980s, advertisers stopped using jingles and started using hit songs. Nike was the first to do this. It successfully used the Beatles's song "Revolution" in its advertisements. Other companies followed Nike. Today, an interesting thing is happening. Companies are creating jingles for their products again. However, the jingles of today are

10 different because they have to compete with the short, snappy songs on MP3 players and the songs used as ringtones. They simply don't stand out as being different from regular songs anymore.

2 Read the paragraph again. Underline *used to* + verb and circle *would* + verb. Double underline the simple past verbs. Why did the writer sometimes choose to use present forms instead of a past form?

Writing Task

1 *Write* Use the paragraph in the Pre-writing Task to help you write about a change in advertising. How did it use to be? How is it now? Why did it change? You can write about one of these topics or use your own ideas.

- advertising on the Internet
- advertising on the sides of cars and buses
- billboard advertising
- changes in advertising because of DVRs or watching TV on the Internet

2 *Self-Edit* Use the editing tips to improve your paragraph. Make any necessary changes.

1. Did you use the simple past to focus on completed actions?
2. Did you use *used to* + the base form of verb and *would* + the base form of verb to write about the way things were in the past?
3. Did you use the present to write about the current situation and to highlight the differences between now and how it used to be?
4. Did you avoid the mistakes in the Avoid Common Mistakes chart on page 27?

UNIT
3

Present Perfect and Present Perfect Progressive

Success

---

1 Grammar in the Real World

A What are the characteristics of a successful person? Read the article about Mahatma Gandhi and Bill Gates. What qualities do they have in common?

The Making of Success

Some people **have said** that a successful person is like a sore thumb: The person sticks out[1] wherever he or she goes. People always seem to notice something special about the person. **Have** you ever **wondered** why? What makes someone successful?

5 For some time, researchers **have been trying** to answer this question. They **have been looking** closely at people who **have achieved** success in their lives, and they **have discovered** some very interesting traits.[2]

Mahatma Gandhi is one person the researchers **have studied**. Gandhi was born in India in 1869. Although he **died** in 1948, his life and principles **have**
10 **been inspiring**[3] people all over the world since then.

Gandhi **believed** in nonviolence, and he **used** this principle to help India gain independence from the British. His example **has been guiding** movements for civil rights[4] and freedom around the world ever
15 since. In spite of great personal risk, he never **gave up** on his goals to help the poor and the underprivileged, such as ethnic minorities. Additionally, he always **aimed** to live a simple life. At the time of Gandhi's death, the prime minister of India **announced** on the radio: "The
20 light **has gone out**[5] of our lives, and there is darkness everywhere."

[1]**stick out:** be easily noticed │ [2]**trait:** a characteristic, especially of a personality │ [3]**inspire:** fill someone with confidence and the desire to do something │ [4]**civil rights:** the rights of every person in a society, including equality under law │ [5]**light goes out:** an idiom meaning joy and hope disappear

Many people consider Bill Gates one of the most successful people in the world, and certainly one of the richest. Gates **founded** the Microsoft Corporation
25 in 1975. In 1994, he **formed** the Bill and Melinda Gates Foundation. Through this foundation, he **has contributed** billions of dollars to organizations and programs working in global health, including public-health organizations, and he continues to work for
30 world health and education.

The secret of the success of Gandhi, Gates, and other successful people is strikingly similar. They **have found** a purpose in life and are not afraid to take action, to take risks, or to work hard. Sometimes they **have**
35 **failed**, but they **have** always **gone on** to reach their goal.

B *Comprehension Check* Answer the questions.

1. What principle did Mahatma Gandhi support?
2. What does the Bill and Melinda Gates Foundation do?
3. What is the secret of successful people?

C *Notice* Find the sentences in the article and complete them. Circle the correct verb forms.

1. Although he died in 1948, his life and principles _____ people all over the world since then.
   a. inspired   b. have inspired   c. have been inspiring

2. His example _____ movements for civil rights and freedom around the world ever since.
   a. guided   b. has guided   c. has been guiding

3. Gates _____ the Microsoft Corporation in 1975.
   a. founded   b. has founded   c. has been founding

Which verbs describe actions that are still happening now?

2 | Present Perfect

▶ Grammar Presentation

The present perfect is used to describe an event that happened at an unspecified time in the past. This event may be completed, or it may not be completed and may continue into the future.	Winners of the Gandhi Peace Prize **have contributed** to world peace. Sociologists **have studied** the definition of success for a long time.

2.1 Using Present Perfect

a. Use the present perfect to describe an action or event that happened at an unspecified time in the past.	Researchers **have discovered** similar traits in successful people.
The adverbs *already, ever, never,* and *(not) yet* can be used with the present perfect. *Ever* means "at any time in the past."	*"Has* she **received** an award *yet?"* *"Yes, she* **has** *already* **received** *two awards."* *"No, she* **has**n't **received** *one* *yet."* *"Have* you *ever* **thought** *about the meaning of success?"* *"I've never* **thought** *about it."*
b. Use the present perfect for actions or events that started in the past and continue into the present.	How long **has** she **been** a successful businessperson?
For, since, so far, and *still* help link between the past and the present. Other common expressions are *all day, all my life,* and *all year.*	She**'s owned** a successful business *for 15 years*. They**'ve worked** here *since May*. *So far*, he **hasn't changed** jobs. I *still* **haven't learned** to relax on weekends. They**'ve been** in the lab *all day*. He **has lived** here *all his life*.
c. Use the present perfect to describe a recent action.	Breaking news: The judges **have awarded** the Nobel Peace Prize.
The adverbs *just* and *recently* emphasize the recent past time.	I **have** *just* **discovered** the answer. He **has** *recently* **given** money to the foundation.

2.2 Present Perfect with *For* and *Since*

a. Use *for* to show the duration of time of an event that continues into the present moment.	She **hasn't worked** here <u>for</u> several years.
b. In negative sentences, the preposition *in* may replace *for*.	She **hasn't seen** her <u>in</u> several years.
c. Use *since* with specific dates or times to show the start of an event that continues into the present moment.	He **has lived** here <u>since</u> last year. She **hasn't worked** here <u>since</u> 2008.

▶ Grammar Application

Exercise 2.1 Uses of Present Perfect

Read about Blake Mycoskie, a businessperson and a humanitarian. Label the bold and underlined verbs *U* (unspecified time in the past), *C* (time that continues to the present), or *R* (recent action) according to the use of the present perfect.

Blake Mycoskie is an American businessperson. He started

a shoe company called TOMS in 2006. He sells a special type

of shoe, the *alpargata*. He discovered the shoe in Argentina.

C
Argentinean farmers **have worn** alpargatas for over 100 years.

5   Recently, experts **have discovered** a link between children going barefoot and

getting certain diseases. Mycoskie **has** always **wanted** to help children stay healthy.

Therefore, every time someone buys a pair of TOMS shoes, his company gives a free

pair of new shoes to a child who needs shoes. Since he started TOMS, Mycoskie

has given over a million pairs of alpargatas to children in South Africa, Ethiopia,

10 Rwanda, Argentina, Guatemala, Haiti, and the United States.

Not long ago, Mycoskie **started** a shoe factory in Ethiopia. He **has** also **created** a

special shoe that helps prevent a serious foot disease. Mycoskie's favorite quote comes

from Gandhi: "Be the change you wish to see in the world."

Exercise 2.2 Using Present Perfect

A Complete the interview about success. Use the present perfect form of the verbs in parentheses. Use contractions when possible.

Reporter	Today, we are asking a few people about success. Are you successful? Do you know anyone who is successful? What makes someone successful?
Carlos	My friend Marta is successful. She _'s wanted_ (want) to own a restaurant for years, and now she _____ (achieve) her goal. Three years ago, she bought a restaurant. She _____ (have) a successful business ever since.
Reporter	How long _____ you _____ (know) Marta?
Carlos	I _____ (know) her for 10 years.
Reporter	_____ she always _____ (be) interested in food?
Carlos	So far, that _____ (be) her only interest!
Annie	Well, I think my parents are very successful people. They _____ (not/have) any problems in years. They _____ (raise) five happy, successful children. In fact, my youngest brother _____ just _____ (graduate) from college, and my older sister _____ recently _____ (get) married.
Ian	You know, I _____ never _____ (think) about it. I guess I _____ (not/achieve) anything yet. I'm very happy, though! That's my idea of success!

(1) (2) (3) (4) (4) (5) (6) (6) (7) (8) (9) (10) (10) (11) (11) (12) (12) (13)

B *Group Work* Read the definitions of success. Choose one definition and give examples of it using your experiences or those of someone you know. Use the present perfect and *already*, *never*, *yet*, *for*, *since*, *so far*, *still*, *just*, and *recently*.

Definitions
Success is having a goal and then achieving it.
Success is doing work that you love.
Success is having a lot of money.
Success is having good relationships with family and friends.

I think that success is having a goal and achieving it. My brother has always wanted to climb Mount Everest. He hasn't done it yet, but he has climbed several other mountains.

Exercise 2.3 *For* or *Since*?

Complete the sentences about successful people. Circle *for* or *since*.

1. Blake Mycoskie has started five businesses (since) / **for** he graduated from college.

2. Bill Gates has worked part-time for Microsoft and part-time for the Bill and Melinda Gates Foundation **since** / **for** the past several years.

3. Bill Gates has given over $28 billion to charity **since** / **for** 2007.

4. Oprah Winfrey has helped poor people **since** / **for** many years.

5. **Since** / **For** the last several years, the actor George Clooney has spent a great deal of time trying to help end the conflict in Darfur, Sudan.

Exercise 2.4 More *For* or *Since*?

Use the words to write sentences about successful people. Use the present perfect and *for* or *since*.

1. Joe and Ling have a successful marriage. They / be married / more than 30 years.
   They have been married for more than 30 years.

2. They / have / only / one fight / they first met

3. They / not spend / a night apart / 1980

4. Mark and Amy have a successful friendship. They / be friends / high school

5. They / speak / on the phone every day / the past 10 years

6. Verónica / be / a successful single parent / many years

7. She / raise / her three children by herself / her divorce

3 | Present Perfect vs. Simple Past

▶ Grammar Presentation

The present perfect can refer to events that began in the past, continue until now, and may continue in the future. The simple past expresses completed events.

*"**Have** you **read** any books about successful people?"*
*"Yes. I **read** one about Raul Julia last week."*

3.1 Present Perfect and Simple Past Contrasted

a. Use the present perfect to refer to events or repeated actions that continue into the present moment.	*Gandhi **has inspired** people all over the world. (Gandhi inspired people for many years, and his ideas still inspire people now.)*
Use the simple past to refer to completed actions.	*Gandhi **promoted** nonviolence against British rule. (Gandhi did this while he was alive.)*
b. Use the present perfect to refer to an action completed at an unspecified time in the past that has an effect in the present.	*The Gates Foundation **has supported** health care in poor countries. (Poor countries are benefiting from this care now.)*
Use the simple past to refer to a completed action in the past that doesn't have an effect in the present.	*Bill Gates **founded** the Microsoft Corporation in 1975. (This is a fact about Bill Gates's past.)*

Data from the Real World

In informal speaking, people sometimes use the simple past with *already* and *yet* instead of the present perfect.	*We **haven't finished** <u>yet</u>.* *We **didn't finish** <u>yet</u>. (informal speaking)*
In academic writing, always use the present perfect with *already* and *yet*.	*The foundation **has** <u>already</u> **given** millions of dollars to charities this year.*

already   ■ with present perfect
yet   ■ with simple past

▶ Grammar Application

Exercise 3.1 Present Perfect or Simple Past?

A Complete the online interview about the actress Marlee Matlin. Circle the correct form of the verbs.

Marlee Matlin is a successful actress, writer, and producer. She is also hearing impaired. She cannot hear, but she is able to communicate in spoken English. She won an Oscar for Best Actress and has received other acting awards as well.

Kate I really admire Marlee Matlin. She didn't let her disability stop her from achieving her dreams.

Alex I don't know that much about her.

Kate Well, she began acting at a very young age. She **played**/'s played (1) Dorothy in *The Wizard of Oz* when she was seven years old.

Alex Wow. **Did she use/Has she used** sign language in that role? (2)

Kate Yes, she **did/has**. That play was produced by a hearing-impaired (3) children's organization. In 1986, she **played/'s played** a hearing-impaired (4) woman in *Children of a Lesser God*, and she won an Oscar.

Alex Has she ever played a hearing person?

Kate So far, she **performed/'s performed** mostly hearing-impaired roles, (5) but in 1994, she **played/'ve played** a hearing woman in the television (6) movie *Against Her Will*.

Alex What else **did she do/has she done** besides acting? (7)

Kate In 1999, she **produced/'s produced** a television movie. In addition, (8) she **was/'s been** very busy raising four children! Her oldest child (9) **was/has been** born in 1996. She **had/has had** her last child in 2003. (10) (11)

B *Pair Work* Compare your answers with a partner. Discuss the reason for each of your answers.

I chose the past for number 1 because the action happened at a specific time in the past – when she was seven years old.

Exercise 3.2 More Present Perfect or Simple Past?

A Read the time line about Diane, a successful clothing designer. Complete the sentences with the present perfect or simple past.

1999	Come to the United States; not speak English
2000	Move to Florida; study English at a school for fashion design
2002	Finish college; work as a seamstress in Miami
2003	Move to New York; get a job at Smith Designs
2005	Become a designer at Smith Designs
2006	Leave Smith Designs; start a company, Sorel Designs
2006 to present	Work at Sorel Designs
2009 to present	Make movie costumes

1. In 1999, *Diane came to the United States. She did not speak English* .
2. In 2000, _____ .
3. In 2002, _____ .
4. In 2003, _____ .
5. In 2005, _____ .
6. In 2006, _____ .
7. Since 2006, _____ .
8. Since 2009, _____ .

B *Over to You* Think about a successful person you know: a friend, a relative, or a famous person. On a separate piece of paper, write five facts about that person's life and accomplishments. Use the simple past and present perfect. Then share your sentences with a partner.

4 Present Perfect vs. Present Perfect Progressive

▶ Grammar Presentation

The present perfect and present perfect progressive can sometimes have similar meanings. However, the present perfect progressive focuses on the ongoing nature of the activity. The present perfect often suggests that the action is finished.	*I've worn / I've been wearing glasses all my life.* *I've been writing an article about the meaning of success.* (I haven't finished it yet.) *I've written an article about the meaning of success.* (I've already finished it.)

4.1 Similar Meaning: Habitual and Ongoing Actions

a. Use either the present perfect or present perfect progressive for habitual actions that began in the past and continue up to the present. Some verbs that show habitual action are *live*, *study*, *teach*, *wear*, and *work*.	*Bill Gates has worked hard all his life.* *Bill Gates has been working hard all his life.*
b. Use *how long* to ask about the duration of habitual actions.	*"How long have you lived / have you been living here?"* *"I've lived / I've been living here for 4 years."*

4.2 Different Meanings: Completed vs. Ongoing Actions

a. Use the present perfect for an event that was completed at an unspecified time in the past.	*She has read a biography of Gandhi.* (She finished it. She is no longer reading it.)
Use the present perfect progressive for an event that began in the past and is still ongoing. It emphasizes the duration of the activity.	*She has been reading a biography of Gandhi.* (She is still reading it.)
Stative verbs are usually in the present perfect (not the present perfect progressive). Stative verbs include *be*, *have*, *like*, and *see*.	*They've been good friends for ages.* *He's had a lot of experience in this business.* *I've always liked learning about successful people.*
b. Use the present perfect to express *how much / how many*.	*A friend of mine has painted at least 100 paintings.* (*at least 100 paintings* = how many)
Use the present perfect progressive to express *how long*.	*She has been painting for more than 10 years.* (*more than 10 years* = how long)

▶ Grammar Application

Exercise 4.1 Completed or Ongoing Actions?

Read the sentences. Check (✓) whether the action is completed or ongoing.

	Completed	Ongoing
1. Lara has learned Spanish very well.	☑	☐
2. Michelle has also been studying French and Japanese this semester.	☐	☐
3. Enrico has been learning a lot of languages.	☐	☐
4. Tony has been working as a chef for the past 8 years.	☐	☐
5. Alex has been running his own business since he was 19.	☐	☐
6. Joe has lived in Madrid.	☐	☐
7. Ron has been living in California since 2010.	☐	☐
8. We've already eaten dinner.	☐	☐
9. Sasha and Janet have been working there since 2008.	☐	☐
10. Raymond has won three prizes for his poetry.	☐	☐
11. I've been traveling for four weeks.	☐	☐
12. Bryn has been dancing since she was a child.	☐	☐
13. My mother has been cooking since she was 12.	☐	☐
14. Luisa has written four letters to her senator.	☐	☐

Exercise 4.2 Simple Past, Present Perfect, and Present Perfect Progressive

A Complete the following podcast transcript with the correct forms of the verbs in parentheses. Sometimes more than one answer is possible.

Zaha Hadid is an architect. She _has designed_ (design) (1) many famous buildings around the world, including the Rosenthal Center for Contemporary Art in Cincinnati. Hadid was born in Iraq, and she _____ (study) (2) architecture in London in the late 1970s. Since the 1980s, she _____ (work) at a design company, (3) and she _____ (teach) architecture at (4) several universities.

Richard Branson is one of the world's most successful businesspeople. He was born in England. He _____ (have) a hard time in school because (5) he had a learning disability.[1] Reading was difficult for him. As a result, he _____ (leave) school at age 16. (6) After that, he _____ (start) his first business. (7) Later, he _____ (open) a record shop called (8) Virgin Records. Since then, he _____ (start) (9) new businesses in many different industries, including transportation, entertainment, and communications.

[1] **learning disability:** a condition that affects a person's ability to learn

B *Pair Work* Compare your answers with a partner. Discuss the reason for each of your answers.

In number 1, I wrote has designed *because the action continues into the present, but the action seems complete. So, I didn't choose* has been designing.

C ◀)) Listen to the podcast and check your answers.

D *Over to You* Think about your life story. Write answers to these questions on a separate piece of paper. Use the simple past, the present perfect, and the present perfect progressive. Share your answers with a partner.

- Have you accomplished something important (for example, learned a language, graduated from high school, saved money for an important purchase)? How did you do it?
- What are some things that you have done recently that make you feel happy? How long have you been doing them?
- What have you been doing recently that makes you feel successful?

5 | Avoid Common Mistakes ⚠

1. Use correct subject-verb agreement when forming the present perfect.
> have
> Young people ~~has~~ always gone to college with high expectations.

2. Use the present perfect (not the present perfect progressive) for a time period that starts in the past and is completed.
> finished
> He has ~~been finishing~~ two books since last week.

3. Remember to include *been* for the present perfect progressive.
> been
> The definition of success has ʌchanging over the years.

4. Use the present perfect progressive (not the present progressive) for actions that began in the past and are still continuing.
> has been
> He ~~is~~ studying for six hours, and he refuses to stop.

Editing Task

Find and correct eight more mistakes in the paragraphs about a student's success in his job.

I am a college student by day and a sous-chef[1] by night. My studies are important,

has
but my restaurant job ~~have~~ taught me what I really need to know about success. I am

working in the kitchen of Da Lat, a French-Vietnamese bistro, for three years, and the job

has been a wonderful experience for me because I have learned many new skills.

[1]**sous-chef:** the head chef's assistant

5   First, I have been becoming a much better planner since I started working at Da Lat. Planning and preparation are very important in a kitchen. If the chef have not prepared the ingredients well beforehand, it will take too long to make each dish, and customers will complain. We start our preparation early each day, and by the time the first customer comes, we have working for 6 hours.

10   Second, I have developing better interpersonal skills. For example, I have been receiving two promotions in the last two years. Last year, I became a line cook because I had learned to pay attention to what others might need before they ask. I think that for the past few months, I am paying better attention in other areas of my life as well.

My college education is important, but I will always be grateful for my job at Da Lat.

15 This job have given me mental and social skills for my future.

6 | Grammar for Writing

Using Present Perfect, Present Perfect Progressive, and Simple Past to Describe a Series of Events

When writing about a living person, writers use the simple present, the simple past, the present perfect, and the present perfect progressive to talk about different points in the person's life:

- Use the simple present or present progressive to describe the person's current situation.
- Use the simple past to describe actions that were completed at a specific time in the past.
- Use the present perfect to describe situations or actions that occurred at unspecified times in the past or that continue into the present.
- Use the present perfect progressive to focus on the ongoing nature of something that began in the past.

Read this example paragraph:

Shakira Isabel Mebarak Ripoll is a Colombian musician. She recorded her first album at the age of 13, and since then she has sold more albums than any other Colombian recording artist in history. For the past few years, she has been working with several charities, including an organization that she helped create.

Pre-writing Task

1 Read the paragraph. What was the first important achievement of the person in the paragraph? Why was it so special? What has she done since that accomplishment?

An Artist or an Architect?

Maya Lin is an incredible American architect and artist. Her career began when she won a national competition to design the Vietnam Veterans Memorial in 1981. Lin was just 21 years old and was still an undergraduate in college at that time. This memorial became famous almost immediately. Millions of people have traveled to Washington,

5 D.C., to see it over the years. Since then, Lin has accomplished many more things. She completed her master's in architecture in 1986, and she has been designing monuments, parks, and other important structures ever since. She has designed many of her structures to draw people's attention to nature, to the environment, and to social issues. Recently she has been creating a lot of landscape art. Because Lin is both an artist and an architect, she

10 combines both of her interests in her designs. People have been questioning whether her work is art or architecture for many years. Lin likes to think of her work as a combination of both. Lin has won awards and honorary degrees throughout her career. Not all of Lin's designs have been popular, but Maya Lin has been a very successful architect and artist since she was a very young woman.

2 Read the paragraph again. Underline the present perfect verbs that are used to show a time period that extends up to now. <u>Double underline</u> the present perfect progressive verbs that are used to show duration up to now. Circle the simple past verbs.

Writing Task

1 *Write* Use the paragraph in the Pre-writing Task to help you write about the achievements of a person you admire. Describe specific events in the person's life, and include current activities the person is involved in.

2 *Self-Edit* Use the editing tips to improve your paragraph. Make any necessary changes.

1. Did you use the present perfect to write about events that happened at an unspecified time in the past?
2. Did you use the present perfect and present perfect progressive to describe situations that started in the past but are still ongoing in the present?
3. Did you use the simple past to write about actions that happened at specified times in the past?
4. Did you use the simple present or present progressive to write about the person's current activities?
5. Did you avoid the mistakes in the Avoid Common Mistakes chart on page 42?

Past Perfect and Past Perfect Progressive

Nature vs. Nurture

1 Grammar in the Real World

A Have you ever reconnected with someone from your past? Read the web article about twins who lived apart for many years. What surprised the twins when they reconnected?

The Science of Twins

Twins, especially identical[1] twins, have always fascinated scientists. Identical twins develop from one egg, have identical DNA,[2] and are usually very similar in appearance
5 and behavior. There have been many studies of identical twins raised in the same family. There have also been a number of studies of identical twins separated at birth and raised in separate families. These studies have provided
10 interesting information about the impact of
nature (genetics) and nurture (the environment) on the development of the individual. However, some of the studies have been controversial.[3]

Take the case of Elyse Schein and Paula Bernstein. Elyse and Paula were identical twins separated at birth. Both girls knew that their parents **had adopted** them as infants, but
15 neither girl knew about her twin. When Elyse grew up, she longed to meet her biological mother, so she contacted the agency that **had arranged** the adoption. She **had been doing** research on her birth mother when she made a surprising discovery. She had an identical twin. Even more surprising, she learned that she **had been** part of a secret scientific study. At the time of the adoption, the agency **had allowed** different families to
20 adopt each twin. The agency **had told** the families that their child was part of a scientific study. However, it **had** never **told** the families the goal of the study: for scientists to investigate nature versus nurture.

[1]**identical:** exactly the same | [2]**DNA:** the abbreviation for deoxyribonucleic acid, a chemical that controls the structure and purpose of every cell | [3]**controversial:** causing or likely to cause disagreement

When Elyse and Paula finally met as adults, they were amazed. They had many similarities. They looked almost identical. They **had** both **studied** film. They both loved to write. Together, the twins discovered that the researchers **had stopped** the study before the end because the public strongly disapproved of this type of research.

Although that study ended early, many scientists today make a strong case for the dominant[4] role of nature. Schein and Bernstein agree that genetics explains many of their similarities. However, recent research suggests that nurture is equally important. It is clear that the nature versus nurture debate will occupy scientists for years to come.

[4]**dominant:** more important, strong, or noticeable

B *Comprehension Check* Answer the questions.

1. What was surprising about the twins' adoption?
2. What characteristics and interests did Elyse and Paula have in common?
3. What is the nature versus nurture debate?

C *Notice* Underline the verbs in each sentence.

1. Both girls knew that their parents had adopted them as infants.
2. She had been doing research on her birth mother when she made a surprising discovery.
3. Even more surprising, she learned that she had been part of a secret scientific study.

Which event happened first in each sentence? What event followed? Write the verbs. What do you notice about the form of the verbs?

1. First: _____   Then: _____
2. First: _____   Then: _____
3. First: _____   Then: _____

2 | Past Perfect

▶ Grammar Presentation

The past perfect is used to describe a completed event that happened before another event in the past.	*Elyse finally met her sister, Paula. Paula **had been** married for several years.* (First, Paula got married; Elyse met Paula at a later time.)

2.1 Forming Past Perfect

Form the past perfect with *had* + the past participle of the main verb. Form the negative by adding *not* after *had*. The form is the same for all subjects.

*Elyse and Paula did not grow up together. They **had lived** with different families.*
*They were available for adoption because their birthmother **had given** them up.*
*"**Had** she **talked** about the study to anyone at the time?"*
*"No, she **hadn't**."*
*"What **had** you **heard** about this study before that time?"*
*"**I'd heard** very little about it."*

▸◂ Irregular Verbs: See page A1.

2.2 Using Past Perfect with Simple Past

a. Use the past perfect to describe an event in a time period that leads up to another past event or time period. Use the simple past to describe the later event or time period.

LATER TIME   EARLIER TIME
*She **learned** that she **had been** part of a secret study.*
          LATER TIME   EARLIER TIME
*The twins **discovered** that they **had** both **studied** psychology.*

b. The prepositions *before*, *by*, or *until* can introduce the later time period.

          EARLIER TIME   LATER TIME
*Their mother **had known** about the study before her death.*
          EARLIER TIME   LATER TIME
*Sue **hadn't met** her sister until last year.*
                    EARLIER TIME   LATER TIME
*Studies on twins **had become** common by the 1960s.*

c. The past perfect is often used to give reasons or background information for later past events.

                              REASON
*She was late. She **had forgotten** to set her alarm clock.*
BACKGROUND INFORMATION   LATER PAST EVENT
*He **had** never **taken** a subway before he moved to New York.*

Data from the Real World

In writing, these verbs are commonly used in the past perfect: *come, have, leave, make,* and *take.* *Had been* is the most common past perfect form in speaking and writing.	The twins **had not gone** to the same school as children. The family thought that they **had made** the right decision. Psychologists praised the study because the researchers **had been** very careful in their work. The researchers **had not been** aware of each other's work on twins until they met.

▶ Grammar Application

Exercise 2.1 Past Perfect

Complete the sentences about twins who met as adults. Use the past perfect form of the verbs in parentheses.

1. Two separate Illinois families ___*had adopted*___ (adopt) Anne Green and Annie Smith before the twins were three days old.

2. When the girls met, they were fascinated by their similarities. For example, they _____ (live) near each other before the Greens moved away.

3. As children, both Anne and Annie _____ (go) to the same summer camp.

4. Anne _____ (not / go) to college, and Annie _____ (not / attend) college, either.

5. Both _____ (marry) for the first time by the age of 22.

6. Anne _____ (get) divorced and _____ (remarry). Annie _____ (not / get) divorced and was still married.

7. Both Anne and Annie were allergic to cats and dogs and _____ never _____ (own) pets.

8. Both _____ (give) the same name – Heather – to their daughters.

9. Both _____ previously _____ (work) in the hospitality industry.

10. Anne _____ (work) as a hotel manager. However, Annie _____ (not / work) in hotels; she _____ (be) a restaurant manager.

Exercise 2.2 Past Perfect and Simple Past

A Read the article about a famous twin study. Underline the simple past forms. Double underline the past perfect forms.

The University of Minnesota is the birthplace of one of the most important twin studies in the world. It started in 1979. Thomas J. Bouchard had already been on the faculty¹ of the university for some time when he began his study of identical twins. Bouchard read an article about a set of twins who had been separated at birth. The twins had recently met and had found many similarities. They found out that they had lived near each other for years. Bouchard was amazed by the twins' story and decided to start the Minnesota Twins Reared Apart Study. Bouchard began to study sets of twins that had been separated at birth. Over the years, the Minnesota Twins Reared Apart Study has studied more than 8,000 sets of twins. The study continues today.

¹**faculty:** the people who teach in a department in a school

B *Pair Work* Compare your answers with a partner. Discuss the reason for each of your answers.

In line 2, had been *refers to the first event. Dr. Bouchard joined the faculty before the twin study. The twin study began later. The study is the second event, so* started *is in the simple past.*

Exercise 2.3 More Past Perfect and Simple Past

A 🔊 Listen to an interview with twins who are actors. Complete the sentences with the verbs you hear.

Claudia Today, I'm interviewing Alex and Andrew Underhill. They appear in the *Spy Twins* movie series based on the books of the same name. How did you get the part in the first *Spy Twins* movie?

Alex A friend _had seen_ the advertisement
            (1)
in the newspaper and later

_____ us about it. We
            (2)

_____ any acting before
            (3)

then, but we _____ to
                         (4)

try out anyway.

Claudia How many twins were at the audition?

Andrew When we got there, we _____ (5) that about five other sets of twins _____ (6) for the audition.

Alex We also noticed that all the twins were wearing matching outfits. Until that audition, we _____ (7) never _____ (7) the same clothes in our whole lives. We decided to run out to the nearest shopping mall to buy some matching clothes. The audition _____ (8) just _____ (8) when we _____ (9) .

Claudia _____ (10) you _____ (10) the *Spy Twins* novels before your audition?

Andrew Yes. The third book _____ (11) when we _____ (12) to the first audition.

Claudia What's it like being twins? Are you two close? Do you do the same things?

Alex Yes, in lots of ways.

Andrew We definitely think the same way.

Alex Right! Once, we took the same test in school. Of course, we were in the same grade, but we had different teachers. We had exactly the same answers correct, even though we _____ (13) in the same classroom!

Claudia Wow! I guess you're a lot alike in many ways! Well, thanks, Alex and Andrew. It's been great talking with you.

B 🔊 Listen again and check your answers.

C Use the time line to complete the sentences about Alex and Andrew. Use the past perfect form of the verbs in the box.

build   decide   graduate   ~~make~~   record   start

1986	The twins are born.
1993	The twins audition for the first *Spy Twins* movie.
1995	They record their first pop song and make a TV movie.
1996	The twins start a fashion company for young men's clothing.
1997 to 2003	The twins make three more *Spy Twins* movies.
2004	They graduate from high school; they start college.
2005	The twins decide to stop acting.
2008	They graduate from college.
2008 to present	They work as fashion designers for their clothing company.

1. By 2004, Alex and Andrew _*had made*_ four *Spy Twins* movies.

2. Before 1995, the twins _____ (not) a pop song.

3. By 2006, the twins _____ to stop acting.

4. The twins _____ (not) a fashion company yet in 1995.

5. The twins _____ from high school by 2005.

6. They _____ a successful career before the age of 30.

D *Over to You* Make a time line about yourself from your birth to the present. Write five sentences about your life. Use the past perfect with *before*, *by*, and *until*.

3 | Past Perfect with Time Clauses

▶ Grammar Presentation

The past perfect is often used with time clauses for events that occurred in an earlier time period leading up to a later event or time period.	*By the time Elyse discovered her sister, people **had forgotten** about the twin study.*

3.1 Order of Events

a. Use time clauses to show two separate past time periods. Use the past perfect to signal an event that occurred in an earlier time period.	Elyse **had moved** <u>by the time</u> the researchers called her.
The time words *after, as soon as, before, by the time, until,* and *when* can introduce the time clauses.	<u>After</u> they **had met**, they noticed their many similarities. <u>Until</u> Elyse started her research, she **hadn't known** about the twin study.
b. With *before* and *after*, the past perfect is not always necessary because the order is clear. In this case, the past perfect emphasizes the earlier time period.	Elyse **moved** <u>before</u> she met her twin. OR Elyse **had moved** <u>before</u> she met her twin.
c. In time clauses with *when*, the use of the past perfect in the main clause usually shows a good amount of time between events.	<u>When</u> Paula met Elyse, she **had** already **learned** about the research. (She learned about the research. She met Elyse some time later.)
d. The use of *as soon as* with the past perfect shows that one event happened very soon after the other.	*As soon as* the researchers **had learned** about the public's reaction to the study, they **stopped** it. (The scientists learned about the public's reaction to the study. They stopped the study very soon after that.)
The use of the simple past in both clauses shows that one event happened very soon after the other.	<u>When</u> Paula met Elyse, she **learned** about the research. (She learned about the research very soon after she met Elyse.)

▶ Grammar Application

Exercise 3.1 Order of Events

A Read the blog entry about twin studies. Underline the past perfect form of the verbs.

Twin World by Cory Daniels

Before her twins were born, Kim Lee <u>had read</u> a lot about twin studies. After she had done a little research, Kim found an early reading study for twins. She contacted the researchers and learned that she had to wait until the twins were four years old. When she enrolled the twins in the study, she hadn't known that the twins needed to give a DNA sample. As soon as Kim learned this, she took the twins out of the study. Kim thought that taking a DNA sample was an invasion of her children's privacy.

B *Pair Work* Discuss why the past perfect is used in each case in A. Then find a sentence with a time clause that describes two events that happened at the same time or almost the same time. What is the form of the verbs in this sentence?

Exercise 3.2 Time Clauses

Complete the article about siblings[1] who were separated as children. Circle the correct time word. Write the simple past or past perfect form of the verbs in parentheses. Sometimes more than one answer is possible.

There are many stories of non-twin brothers and sisters who are separated for one reason or another and meet again as adults. Here are a couple.

Glenn Mint and Bruce Mathews are brothers. They had never met **(until)/ after** Glenn ___*started*___ (start) working
       (1)   (2)
at the same company as Bruce. Bruce was surprised because the new employee looked just like him. They started asking each other questions. **Before / After** they
                                     (3)
met, each man _____ (know) that he
               (4)
had a sibling. **Before / As soon as** Glenn _____ (discover)
              (5)   (6)
Bruce's birth date, he knew Bruce was his long-lost brother.

Quin Mara, 82, knew that she was adopted and that she had siblings, but she had never met them. **After / Until** a relative _____ (find) a family tree,[2] Quin
              (7)   (8)
learned the names of her siblings and started looking for them. **Until / By the time**
                                                    (9)
she saw the family tree, she _____ (not / know) that she was
                              (10)
the youngest of nine children. **As soon as / Before** she _____
                                 (11)   (12)
(discover) that, she began to look for her brothers and sisters. She was very happy because five of her siblings were still alive. **Before / After** she _____
                                       (13)   (14)
(meet) them, she didn't know that they had spent the last several decades looking for each other.

[1]**sibling:** a brother or sister | [2]**family tree:** a drawing that shows all the members of a family, usually over a long period of time, and how they are related to each other

Exercise 3.3 Combining Sentences

Read the story about how environment affects personality. Combine the sentences with the time words in parentheses. Use the past perfect for the earlier event and the simple past for the later event.

1. Diego and Shannon were married for a few years. Then they decided to have a baby.

   (when) *When Diego and Shannon had been married for a few years, they decided to have a baby.*

2. Diego and Shannon did not think much about the nature versus nurture debate. Then their first child, Mario, was born.

   (until) _____

   _____

3. Diego and Shannon didn't have much experience with music. Then they became parents.

   (before) _____

   _____

4. Three-year-old Mario saw an electronic keyboard in a shop. Then he asked his parents to buy him one.

   (after) _____

   _____

5. Diego and Shannon heard Mario playing the keyboard. Then they realized their son's musical talent.

   (as soon as) _____

   _____

6. Diego and Shannon realized Mario's talent. Then they enrolled him in piano classes.

   (as soon as) _____

   _____

7. Diego and Shannon enrolled Mario in piano classes. Then Mario became an excellent musician.

   (after) _____

   _____

8. Mario took a few years of piano classes. He started composing music.

   (by the time) _____

   _____

4 Past Perfect Progressive

▶ Grammar Presentation

The past perfect progressive emphasizes the ongoing nature of a past activity or situation leading up to a more recent past time.	*Living with a roommate was hard for me in the beginning. I **had been living** alone for years.*

4.1 Forming Past Perfect Progressive

Form the past perfect progressive with *had + been + -ing* form of the verb. Form the negative by putting *not* between *had* and *been* or using the contraction *hadn't*.	*She knew Boston well when I visited her. She'**d been living** there for years.* *When my brother visited me, I **had not / hadn't been living** there long.*

4.2 Using Past Perfect Progressive

a. Use the past perfect progressive for an action or situation that continued up to an event or situation in past time. This can show a reason or give background information.	*He looked tired because he **had been working** all night.* *My eyes were sore because I **hadn't been wearing** my contacts.*
b. With some verbs such as *live, play, teach, wear,* and *work,* use either the past perfect or past perfect progressive. The meaning is similar.	*The twins **had lived** in different cities before they **discovered** each other.* OR *The twins **had been living** in different cities before they **discovered** each other.*

▶ Grammar Application

Exercise 4.1 Past Perfect Progressive

Complete the story about brothers who reconnected after many years. Use the past perfect progressive form of the verbs in parentheses.

Mark and Peter were brothers. Their parents could not take care of them. One family adopted Mark, and another family adopted Peter. Mark and Peter __had been dreaming__ (dream) of finding
(1)
each other since 2005. When they finally met, they were surprised by how much they had in common. For most of their adult lives, their jobs had been

related, even though they _____ (not / work) in the
(2)
same business. Mark _____ (make) furniture, and Peter
(3)
_____ (sell) furniture. Mark _____
(4)   (5)
(interview) for jobs in furniture stores and decided to take a new position at Mark's store. Peter _____ (talk) to a friendly customer when he
(6)
saw a man who looked like him walk into the store. Peter quickly stopped what he
_____ (do) and introduced himself. That first day, Peter and
(7)
Mark talked for hours. They found out that they _____
(8)
(not / live) in the same city, but they had attended schools in the same district for most of their childhood. They _____ (cross) paths for many years
(9)
without ever meeting. They had never expected to have so much in common.

Exercise 4.2 Past Perfect Progressive, Past Perfect, or Simple Past?

A Complete the interview with a woman who found her three siblings after many years. Use the past perfect progressive, the past perfect, or the simple past form of the verbs in parentheses. Use contractions when possible. Sometimes more than one answer is possible.

Vijay Tell us how you found your family.

Paula I _'d been looking_ (look) for my sister all my life. I _____
(1)   (2)
(not / have) much luck, though. Then one day, I turned on the TV. A talk show was

on. The host of the show was interviewing three siblings – two brothers and a half

sister.[1] Different families _____ (adopt) the siblings many
(3)

years before.

Vijay And?

Paula They _____ (talk) about me before I turned on the program.
(4)

The siblings had recently reunited, and they _____ (search)
(5)

for a fourth sibling for the past several months. I called the TV station, and we all

finally _____ (meet).
(6)

Vijay So, you _____ (look) for a sister all your life, and you found
(7)

three siblings!

Paula Yes, it was wonderful! We all met at one of the network offices the following week.

After we _____ (speak) for a while, it was obvious to me that
(8)

they _____ (look) for me all their lives, too.
(9)

[1]**half sister:** a sister who is biologically related by one parent only

B *Pair Work* Discuss these questions with a partner.

- Choose a sentence in A in which you can use either the past perfect or the past perfect progressive. Why are both possible here?

- In which sentence in A is only the past perfect correct?

C *Over to You* Do an online search for twins, siblings, or other family members who reunited after many years. Write five sentences about their experiences. Use the past perfect and the past perfect progressive.

5 | Avoid Common Mistakes ⚠

1. **Use the past perfect or past perfect progressive to give background information for a past tense event.**

   had
   I ~~have~~ never seen my sister in real life, so I was nervous the first time we met.

   had been dreaming
   I ~~have dreamed~~ about meeting her, and I finally did.

2. **Use the past perfect or past perfect progressive to give a reason for a past event.**

   had been crying
   Her eyes were red and puffy because she ~~cried~~.

3. **Use the past perfect (not the past perfect progressive) for a completed earlier event.**

   arranged
   They had ~~been arranging~~ a time to meet, but both of them forgot about it.

4. **Use the past perfect (not present perfect) to describe a completed event that happened before a past event.**

   had
   I ~~have~~ visited her in Maine twice before she came to visit me.

Editing Task

Find and correct seven more mistakes in the paragraphs about sibling differences.

had
    I ~~have~~ never really thought about sibling differences until my own children were born. When we had our first child, my husband and I have lived in Chicago for just a few months. We have not made many friends yet, so we spent all our time with our child. Baby Gilbert was happy to be the center of attention. He depended on us for everything.

5   By the time our second son, Chase, was born, we have developed a community of friends and a busier social life. We frequently visited friends and left the children at home with a babysitter. As a result of our busy schedules, Chase was more independent. One day I had just been hanging up the phone when Chase came into the room. Chase picked up the phone and started talking into it. I thought he was pretending, but I was wrong. He

10 had been figuring out how to use the phone!

    When my husband came home, he was tired because he worked all day. When I told him about Chase's phone conversation, though, he became very excited. Gilbert has never used the phone as a child. At first, we were surprised that Chase was so different from Gilbert. Then we realized that because of our busy lifestyles, Chase had learned to be

15 independent.

6 | Grammar for Writing ✎

Using Past Perfect to Provide Background Information and Reasons

Writers use the past perfect to provide background information and reasons for past situations and actions. Read these examples:

I had always thought that I was an only child, but I recently discovered that I have a sister. My parents had given me up for adoption. When I was 15, I decided to find my biological parents.

Pre-writing Task

1 Read the paragraph. What does the writer believe about the influence of the environment on relationships? What example does the writer use to explain this?

The Effects of Friends on Sibling Relationships

I believe that the experiences that a person has outside the home can be as influential as experiences inside the home. Examples of this are siblings who start out very similar but become very different from one another as they grow older. For example, Andy and Frank are two brothers who are only two years apart. They did everything together
5 and were best friends until they started junior high. After Andy had been in seventh grade for a little while, he started to change. He had made new friends at school, so he and Frank did not see each other much during the day. Frank had made new friends, too. In fact, Andy's new friends did not like Frank very much, so Andy did not feel comfortable asking Frank to spend time with them. By the time Andy and Frank were in high school, they had
10 grown very far apart. They had made different friends and they had developed different interests. They had been similar when they were young, but Andy and Frank had very little in common as young adults.

2 Read the paragraph again. Underline the sentences that contain both simple past and past perfect verbs. Double underline the sentences with verbs only in the past perfect. Circle the time clauses. Notice how the time clauses help clarify the earlier time period.

Writing Task

1 *Write* Use the paragraph in the Pre-writing Task to help you write about different conditions that influence people's behavior. Give examples from events and situations you have observed to support your opinion.

2 *Self-Edit* Use the editing tips to improve your paragraph. Make any necessary changes.

1. Did you use the past perfect to give background information and provide reasons?
2. Did you use time words and time clauses to clarify the time periods in your sentences or emphasize that some events happened earlier than others?
3. Did you avoid the mistakes in the Avoid Common Mistakes chart on page 59?

UNIT 5
Be Going To, Present Progressive, and Future Progressive

Looking Ahead at Technology

1 Grammar in the Real World

A How is technology used today? Read the web article about technology use in the future. What is one way that technology use will develop?

Looking Ahead at Technology

Technology has become an essential part of everyday life for many people. We depend on the Internet, for example, for easy access to information and communication. Computers, cell phones, and other handheld gadgets provide constant
5 entertainment. No one knows for sure what technology **is going to bring** us in the future. However, there is no doubt that it **will continue** to drastically affect how we live and work.

Market research[1] suggests that in the future we **will be depending** on the Internet even more than we are now.
10 According to British writer Tim Walker, the world **will be** "blanketed[2] by Wi-Fi."[3] This **will allow** us to connect to the Internet almost anywhere. However, people **will not want** to carry around bulky laptops. Instead, computers **will be** wearable. Computers **will be** combined with watches, glasses, shirts, or backpacks. Some people are already using glasses which project the Internet onto the glass lenses. People **will be** able to see the Internet but also
15 see the rest of the world. Combining computers and glasses **is going to become** even more popular in the future.

Other people **will use** fabric-based computers. This technology, called "smart clothing," **will combine** computers with clothing. With smart clothing, people **will be** able to look at their shirt sleeve and see the news or the weather, which people **will download**
20 directly from the Internet. Researchers predict that the use of laptops and computers **will decrease** as the availability of smart clothing increases.

In the future, there **will be** many advances in technology and many changes in the ways technology affects our lives. As technology changes, devices such as smart clothing **will become** more and more popular. In short, it is clear that almost everything we do **will**
25 **happen** with the help of technology.

[1]**market research:** the study of consumer behavior | [2]**blanket:** cover | [3]**Wi-Fi:** a system of wireless networks, especially used for the Internet

B Comprehension Check Answer the questions.

1. What are some ways technology will change in the future?
2. How will people in the future access the Internet?
3. What is "smart clothing"?

C Notice Find the sentences in the article and complete them.

1. Market research suggests that in the future we _____ on the Internet even more than we do now.

2. Combining computers and glasses _____ even more popular in the future.

3. Other people _____ fabric-based computers.

How many different verb forms in items 1–3 did the author of the reading use to talk about the future?

2 Be Going To, Present Progressive, and Simple Present for Future

▶ Grammar Presentation

Be going to and the present progressive are used to describe future plans. The simple present is used to describe a scheduled future event.	I **am going to buy** a new smartphone. The store **is offering** free Wi-Fi all next week. The new movie **comes out** next week.

2.1 Be Going to vs. Present Progressive for Future Plans

a. Use *be going to* + base form of the verb to express general intentions and plans for the future.	I**'m going to buy** a 3D TV someday.
You can use expressions like *probably, most likely, I think,* and *I believe* with this form.	My parents <u>probably</u> **aren't going to buy** one. <u>I think</u> they **are going to save** their money for a trip instead.
b. Use the present progressive to express definite plans and arrangements for the future, especially when a time or place is mentioned.	I**'m buying** a 3D TV tomorrow. The class **is taking** a trip to the science museum next week.
c. In many cases, both forms can be used to express the same idea.	I**'m watching** a movie this evening. I**'m going to watch** a movie this evening.

2.2 Simple Present for Scheduled Events

Use the simple present for scheduled events in the future and for timetables. Some common verbs for this use include *arrive*, *be*, *begin*, *finish*, *leave*, and *start*.

The conference **begins** on Monday and **ends** on Friday.

Beginning June 10, all trains to New England **leave** *from platform 14.*

▶ # Grammar Application

Exercise 2.1 *Be Going To* or Present Progressive?

A Complete the conversation about e-readers. Use *be going to* or the present progressive and the verbs in parentheses. Sometimes more than one answer is possible.

Mei   I <u>'m going to buy</u> (buy) an e-reader one of these days. Any suggestions?
            (1)

Kyle   Look at this ad. Big Buy _____ (have) a sale on the iRead next week.
                                           (2)

Mei   How much is it?

Kyle   They _____ (lower) the price to $69.
                     (3)

Mei   That's great. I _____ (visit) a friend near that area next week.
                          (4)
         I'll stop by.

Kyle   That's a great price.

Mei   Yes, it's quite a deal. You know, I think companies _____ (give)
                                                (5)
         e-readers away someday. They're getting less and less expensive. Soon they'll

         be free!

Kyle   I've got to go. I _____ (meet) some friends for dinner. What
                              (6)
         _____ you _____ (do) tonight?
          (7)   (7)

Mei   I _____ (go) straight home. I'm tired.
             (8)

B *Pair Work* Compare your answers with a partner. Discuss the reason for each of your answers.

In the first sentence, one of these days *made the plan seem like an intention because he wasn't really sure, so* be going to *is correct.*

Exercise 2.2 *Be Going To*, Present Progressive, or Simple Present?

Look at the clues. Then complete the sentences about a new phone. Use *be going to*, the present progressive, or the simple present form of the verbs in parentheses.

1. Clue: definite plan

   BestProduct _is launching_ (launch) a new YouPhone next week.

2. Clue: scheduled event

   The new YouPhone _____ (become) available in stores on Friday, January 15.

3. Clue: definite plan

   All employees _____ (prepare) for a busy first day of sales.

4. Clue: definite plan

   All stores _____ (open) at 8:00 a.m. that day.

5. Clue: definite plan

   The stores _____ (give) away water and free coffee to customers in line.

6. Clue: scheduled event

   School _____ (close) early that day because of a holiday.

7. Clue: future intention

   The newspaper _____ (interview) Anne Green, a representative from BestProduct.

8. Clue: future intention

   Ms. Green _____ probably _____ (speak) for a few minutes and then answer some questions.

Exercise 2.3 More *Be Going To*, Present Progressive, or Simple Present?

A Complete the article about a social networking site. Use *be going to*, the present progressive, or the simple present form of the verbs in parentheses. Sometimes more than one answer is possible.

Changes Ahead for Youth Network

Youth Network, Inc., announced today that it ___is buying___ (buy)
(1)
FacePlace, the popular social networking website. FacePlace
has already accepted Youth Network's offer of $3.1 billion. The
company has not made any definite plans, but it _____ probably
(2)
_____ (start) asking people to pay for the
(2)
site. It won't be free anymore. In addition, some people think that the
network _____ (put) ads on the site. Another
(3)
possibility is that Youth Network _____ (show)
(4)
its TV programs on FacePlace. Next week, FacePlace technicians
_____ (meet) with Youth Network technicians
(5)
to help with the changes. They _____ (plan) to
(6)
shut down the old FacePlace website at 1:00 a.m. on Saturday,
August 10. The new Youth Network site _____ (go)
(7)
live at 6:00 a.m. the next day.

B *Pair Work* Compare your answers with a partner. Discuss the reason for each of your answers.

In item 1, the plan seems definite because the company made an announcement to the press, so the company arranged the action. The present progressive is correct.

3 | *Will* and *Be Going To*

▶ Grammar Presentation

Will and *be going to* can both express future plans and predictions. They can also be used in other ways, for example, to make a promise or to express an expectation.	Wi-Fi **will allow** us to connect to the Internet almost anywhere. Technology **is going to become** easier to use. I**'ll help** you with your computer.

3.1 *Will* and *Be Going to* for Predictions and Expectations

a. Use *will* and *be going to* for predictions, expectations, or guesses about the future.	People **will connect** to the Internet from almost anywhere. I**'m not going to** have Internet access while I'm on vacation.
b. You can use *certainly, definitely, likely, maybe, perhaps,* and *probably* to show degrees of certainty.	Technology **will** <u>certainly</u> **be** more sophisticated in the future.
Use *certainly, definitely, likely,* and *probably* after *will* or after *be*.	There **will** <u>probably</u> **be** many people at the concert next week. People **are** <u>definitely</u> **going to wear** computers in the future.
Use *maybe* and *perhaps* at the beginning of sentences.	<u>Maybe</u> I**'ll get** an e-reader this year.
c. Use *be going to* to predict the future when there is present evidence.	My computer is behaving strangely. I think it**'s going to crash**.
d. Generally, in speaking, *be going to* is used for intentions and plans. However, in academic writing, *will* is used much more frequently.	By 2020, people throughout the world **will access** the Internet.

3.2 *Will* for Requests, Offers, and Promises

Use *will* for requests, offers, and promises.	**Will** you **help** me buy a computer? I**'ll research** the best buys for you.

3.3 *Will* for Quick Decisions

Use *will* for decisions made at the time of speaking.	*"We need someone to take notes for our group."* *"I'll do it."* (quick decision)
The same verb with *be going to* expresses a previous decision.	*"Bob is going to do it."* (previous decision)

▶ Grammar Application

Exercise 3.1 *Will* or *Be Going To*?

A Complete the phone conversation between an employee and a technician in the tech department. Circle *will* or *be going to*. If both are possible, circle both.

Bill Tech Department, Bill speaking.

Kate Hi, Bill. This is Kate in Business Development. My laptop is behaving very strangely

this morning. It **will /'s going to** crash at any minute. **Will you / Are you going to**
          (1)   (2)

send someone to look at it?

Bill Of course, I **will / am going to** .
                       (3)

Kate Soon?

Bill I promise. I'**ll /'m going to** send Dave in five minutes.
                         (4)

Kate Bill, **will you / are you going to** send Silvia instead, please? She's fixed this same
                           (5)

problem before.

Bill Oh, OK. Then Silvia **will / is going to** be there in about 5 minutes.
                           (6)

Kate Thanks, Bill. Bye.

A few minutes later:

Silvia Hi, Kate. Are you having problems with your laptop again?

Kate Uh-huh. This is the fourth time! I think I'**ll /'m going to** ask for a new computer.
                           (7)

Silvia I'**ll /'m going to** look at it for you.
                   (8)

Kate Thanks, Silvia.

B *Pair Work* Compare your answers with a partner. Discuss the reason for each of your answers.

I chose be going to *for item 1 because the speaker is making a prediction based on evidence. She said her computer was behaving strangely. That's evidence that it might be crashing.*

Exercise 3.2 More *Will* or *Be Going To*?

A 🔊) Listen to a discussion about education and technology. Complete the sentences with the form of the verbs you hear.

Ms. Ng _____Will_____ everyone please ___be___ quiet? The noise
     (1)   (1)

_____ it hard to hear our speaker. And _____
                    (2)   (3)

someone please _____ the windows? The air
                                    (3)

conditioner isn't working well.

Alex I _____ it.
                        (4)

Ms. Ng Thanks. And _____ you all please _____
                              (5)   (5)

your cell phones? I promise I _____ you
                                              (6)

to do anything else except enjoy today's presentation. OK, today,

we _____ from an expert on education, Dr. Paul Bell.
              (7)

I'm sure you _____ all _____ him very interesting.
                  (8)   (8)

Dr. Bell Thank you. Well, it's clear that the world of the college student

_____ very different in a matter of a few years. For
                (9)

example, we already know that colleges _____ more
                                                          (10)

courses online. This _____ money for schools and for
                                (11)

students. Students _____ money on transportation
                                (12)

costs because they can learn anywhere. Online learning also means that

schools and individuals _____ fewer resources such
                                        (13)

as paper and fuel. But what _____ the consequences of online education
                                    (14)

_____?
                (14)

B Find an example of each meaning, and write the number of the item next to it.

___1___ a request   _____ a promise

_____ a prediction based on evidence   _____ an offer

C *Group Work* Make predictions or share expectations about the future of phones, TVs, movies, schools, cars, or something else. As a group, write five sentences. Use *will* and *be going to*. Share your sentences with the class.

4 Future Progressive

▶ Grammar Presentation

The future progressive emphasizes an action that will be in progress at a specific time in the future.	We **will be reading** most books electronically in five years. Everyone **is going to be using** computers to watch TV in 2020.

4.1 Forming Future Progressive

a. Form the future progressive with *will* or *be going to* + *be* + verb + *-ing*.

People **will be working** on smartphones instead of laptops in 10 years.
Consumers **are not going to be using** coins and paper money by the year 2025.

b. Use the future progressive to describe or ask about an action in progress at a time in the future.

Will you **be working** tomorrow at noon?

Use *certainly*, *definitely*, *likely*, and *probably* after *will* or *be going to* to show degrees of certainty. Use them before *won't*.

I **definitely won't be watching** TV tonight.
I**'ll probably be working** on my project all afternoon.

c. Sometimes *will* + base form and future progressive are very similar in meaning, especially when the future event will occur at an indefinite time.

I think the computer specialist **will arrive** later. I don't see her.
I think the computer specialist **will be arriving** later. I don't see her.

4.2 Future Progressive and *Be Going To* Contrasted

The future progressive and *be going to* can both express plans and intentions.
Use the future progressive for a more formal tone.
Use *be going to* for a less formal tone.

Mr. Lee, **will** you **be coming** with me to the lecture on technology tomorrow? (more formal)
Marie, **are** you **going to come** with me to the lecture tomorrow? (less formal)

▶ Grammar Application

Exercise 4.1 Future Progressive

Complete the interview about the future of TV. Use the future progressive form of the verbs in parentheses.

Claire   Mr. Reyes, you've been involved in the television industry for well over 30 years. We know that the TV industry is changing rapidly. Tell us about its future.

Mr. Reyes   Certainly. The television industry _will be creating_ (create) its own
(1)
shows in the future. It _____ (save) a lot of money
(2)
this way because it _____ (not / buy) the shows from
(3)
other producers. In addition, people _____ (watch)
(4)
TV using many different types of media.

Claire   What do you mean?

Mr. Reyes   I mean that we _____ (use) computers, phones,
(5)
e-readers, and other gadgets to watch TV shows more and more. People

_____ (not / watch) by themselves, either. They
(6)
_____ (socialize) through social networks as they
(7)
watch TV.

Claire   How will that work?

Mr. Reyes   Viewers _____ (send) or texting messages, and they
(8)
_____ (chat) with others while they watch. In fact,
(9)
they have already started to do so. This will affect marketing, too.

Claire   In what way?

Mr. Reyes   Advertisers _____ (ask) viewers to share their
(10)
opinions of the things they are viewing, such as products in ads or clothes

worn by actors.

Claire   It sounds as though advertising will become interactive.

Mr. Reyes   Exactly.

Claire   Thank you very much, Mr. Reyes, for taking the time to talk to us.

Exercise 4.2 Future Progressive or *Be Going To*?

A Complete the formal announcement of a lecture on the future of movies. Use the future progressive form of the verbs in parentheses. Sometimes more than one answer is possible.

The Future of Movies
Presented by Dr. Maria Sanderson
Michaels Hall
8:00 p.m., Friday, January 7

What __*will*__ people __*be seeing*__ (see) at the movies 10 years from
　　　(1)　　　　　　　(1)
now? _____ we _____ (watch) only 3D movies? _____
　　　(2)　　　　　　(2)　　　　　　　　　　　　　　　　　　(3)
people _____ (view) movies in theaters, or will theaters
　　　　　　(3)
disappear? Dr. Sanderson _____ (discuss) the future
　　　　　　　　　　　　　　　(4)
of the movie industry and the movie-going experience in general. She
_____ (give) examples of past, present, and future film
　　(5)
technology, and she _____ (take) questions from the audience.
　　　　　　　　　　　(6)

B Complete the conversation between two students about the lecture in A. Use *be going to* or the future progressive and the verbs in parentheses. Sometimes more than one answer is possible.

Chao __*Are*__ you __*going to go*__ (go) to the lecture?
　　　　　(1)　　　　(1)
Verónica Yes, I _____ definitely _____ (attend). What about you?
　　　　　　　　(2)　　　　　　　　(2)
Chao No, I _____ (not / go). I'm not interested. Why _____ you
　　　　　　　(3)　　　　　　　　　　　　　　　　　　　　　(4)
_____ (go)?
　　(4)
Verónica I'm taking film history, so it will help me with my class. I _____ (take)
　　　　　　　　　　　　　　　　　　　　　　　　　　　　　　　　　　(5)
notes. I _____ also _____ (ask) questions.
　　　　　(6)　　　　　　(6)

Exercise 4.3 More Future Progressive

Over to You What will you be doing 20 years in the future? Where will you be living? What will you be doing for entertainment? Write five sentences about the way you imagine the future. Use the future progressive. Share your sentences with a partner.

5 Avoid Common Mistakes ⚠️

1. **Use the future progressive to talk about actions that will be in progress at a future time.**

   be working
   You won't see me next week because I will ~~work~~ in Seoul.

2. **Use the simple present for scheduled events.**

   starts
   The teleconference ~~will~~ always ~~start~~ at 4:00 p.m.

3. **Remember to use *be* with *be going to*.**

   am
   I ∧ going to give a presentation on the twenty-fifth of next month.

4. **Use the present progressive (not *will*) when talking about definite plans.**

   are traveling
   We ~~will travel~~ to the home office at the end of the month.

Editing Task

Find and correct the mistakes in the e-mail about travel plans.

| Send | Attach | Save Draft | Spelling ▾ | Cancel |

Hi Layla,

be presenting
    Thanks for agreeing to take this trip on short notice. Vinh can't go because he'll ~~present~~ at a conference in Chicago, and your name came up immediately as a replacement. We know you are familiar with the software, so we feel confident that you going to do a great job.

5   Your first flight leaves Newark Liberty International Airport at 9:00 a.m. on the twenty-second and arrives in London late in the afternoon. That evening you are having dinner with James and Eleanor Wilson. They going to be driving you around during your stay.

    On Monday, your first presentation starts at 9:00 a.m. at the headquarters of Logan and Lowe. We have scheduled three presentations that day. You are going to be very busy!

10   You leave London on the 8:00 p.m. flight to Beijing. In Beijing you won't have much free time because you will give your presentation at several companies. Alan going to send you the details in a separate e-mail. You are flying when he sends it.

Best of luck,

Antoine

6 | Grammar for Writing ✏

Using *Will* + Base Form and Future Progressive to Write About Future Plans

When writers describe changes that will happen in the future, they usually introduce a main idea, state a situation, or provide a context using the future progressive. They use the future with *will* + the base form of the verb to provide more details about that idea, situation, or context. Read this example paragraph:

> We will be making several improvements to our classrooms over the next few months. First, we will provide each classroom with a web cam. The web cams will allow students to watch lectures online when they cannot come to class.

Pre-writing Task

1 Read the paragraph. What is changing, and who is planning these changes?

Hillspoint College's Plans for Progress

Claire Gabriel, director of the Hillspoint College Language Center, will be making some exciting changes to the college's Language Center (LC) classrooms over the next two years. First, Ms. Gabriel will be transforming all the classrooms into smart classrooms. Each room will have computers, projectors, and an Internet connection. Teachers and
5 students will be able to access the Internet at any time. They will work with students and teachers all over the world using video conferencing. Next, Ms. Gabriel will be installing moveable walls. These walls will allow teachers to change one classroom into several small classrooms with the touch of a button. This will be useful when students are working in groups. Toward the end of the two-year period, Ms. Gabriel will be making more changes.
10 She will purchase smart desks with touch screens for students. Touch screens will allow students to take part in interactive activities. Several students will be able to do an activity together at the same time. According to Ms. Gabriel, the touch screens will encourage even shy students to participate in class. Surprisingly, all these changes will not increase student fees. The money for the upgrades will come from generous members of the Hillspoint
15 community.

2 Read the paragraph again. Circle the future with *will* (*not*) + the base form. Underline the verbs in the future progressive. Identify the main ideas that the writer introduces with the future progressive.

Writing Task

1 *Write* Use the paragraph in the Pre-writing Task to help you write about plans for change. You can write about one of these topics or use your own ideas.

- cars
- education
- home computers
- home entertainment centers
- houses
- movie theaters
- smartphones
- workplaces

2 *Self-Edit* Use the editing tips to improve your paragraph. Make any necessary changes.

1. Did you use the future progressive to introduce main ideas or provide contexts?
2. Did you use *will* + the base form to provide details about the ideas presented in the future progressive statements?
3. Did you avoid the mistakes in the Avoid Common Mistakes chart on page 73?

UNIT 6

Future Time Clauses, Future Perfect, and Future Perfect Progressive

Business Practices of the Future

1 Grammar in the Real World

A What personal information do you have online? Read the web article about cloud computing. What are the pros and cons?

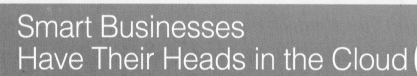

Smart Businesses Have Their Heads in the Cloud

More and more people are accessing their personal electronic data from their phones and other devices using cloud computing. *Cloud computing* is the term for computer work on the Internet. Instead of storing files on your own computer or mobile device, you pay a cloud services provider[1] to keep everything on a computer
5 in another location.

In addition to storing information, cloud computing sometimes offers software and management tools that can help companies cut costs. According to a recent survey on
10 cloud computing, by 2020, many companies **will have eliminated**[2] their technology departments and **saved** large sums of money because they **will have been using** the cloud. In addition, **when these businesses move**
15 **their work to the cloud**, they will not need to spend money on software updates because the cloud will provide access to the most current technology.

[1]**provider:** a business that provides access to a service, such as the Internet or the cloud | [2]**eliminate:** remove or take away

76

Cloud computing has risks, however. Some people say that cloud services are not secure. Also, experts say that there are a growing number of attacks by hackers[3] on
20 secure sites. Many companies will not use cloud services **until they are confident that their data will be secure**.

Nonetheless, companies will save a lot of money and will attract more customers by using the cloud. One study suggests that cloud computing **will have generated** more than $45.5 billion by 2015. However, Internet services are not always reliable,
25 and connection breakdowns are costly. Furthermore, the increasing number of hackers will pose a risk. Are these risks worth it?

[3]**hacker:** a person who breaks into computer networks and steals private information

B *Comprehension Check* Answer the questions.

1. What will happen to many technology departments in the future? Why?
2. What are some risks of cloud computing?

C *Notice* Complete these sentences from the article.

1. According to a recent survey on cloud computing, by 2020, many companies

_____ their technology departments and saved large

sums of money because they _____ the cloud.

2. Many companies _____ cloud services until they are

confident that their data will be secure.

Look at the verbs that you wrote. There are three different forms for describing the future. Which form describes completed future events?

2 Future Time Clauses

▶ Grammar Presentation

Future time clauses show the order of future events.	*Our business will increase **as soon as we improve our marketing**.* *We won't use a social networking site **until we hire someone to monitor it**.*

2.1 Using Time Clauses for Future Events

a. Use the simple present in the time clause. Use the future with *will* or *be going to* in the main clause.	*After I **buy** my new phone, I**'ll use** the cloud to store my data.* *We**'re going to research** cloud services before we **choose** one.*
You can also use the present perfect in the time clause to emphasize the completion of the event.	*Until business **has improved**, the company won't hire new employees.*
b. Use time clauses with *after, as soon as, once,* and *when* when the event in the time clause happens first.	FIRST EVENT ***As soon as / Once** they get cloud services, their* SECOND EVENT *business will improve.* SECOND EVENT　　　FIRST EVENT *I'll find a good job **after** I graduate.*
c. Use time clauses with *before* and *until* when the event in the time clause happens second.	FIRST EVENT　　　SECOND EVENT *I'll finish the report **before** I leave.*
Use *until* to show when the event in the main clause will stop or change.	 *I'll continue working on the report **until** she calls.*
In time clauses with *not ... until*, the action in the time clause happens first.	SECOND EVENT *We won't start using the software **until** all* FIRST EVENT *employees are trained.*

2.1 Using Time Clauses for Future Events *(continued)*

d. The time clause can come first or last in the sentence. Use a comma when the time clause comes first.

Once we start using the cloud, *we'll save money.*
*She is going to move **as soon as she finds a better job.***

2.2 Using Time Clauses with *When* and *While* for Ongoing Events

a. Use *when* or *while* with the simple present in the time clause and *will* or *be going to* in the main clause to show two events that are happening at the same time.

I'll be taking *my vacation **while** the company **moves** to its new office.*

You can also use the present progressive in the time clause to express an ongoing event.

*The staff **is going to wait** outside **while/when** we're **discussing** our budget.*

b. Use the simple present in the *when* clause to interrupt an ongoing event in the main clause.

*We'**ll be meeting when** he **arrives.** (The meeting will be happening. He will arrive during the meeting.)*

Grammar Application

Exercise 2.1 Using Future Time Clauses

A Read the sentences about cloud computing. Underline the time clauses, and circle the conjunctions in each clause. Double underline the main clauses.

1. (Once) a company starts using the cloud, it will have access to more customers.

2. Companies will start saving a great deal of money as soon as they move their work to the cloud.

3. Companies are going to have difficulty competing until they begin advertising on social networking sites.

4. After companies have moved to cloud computing, they will receive technological support and updates on new technology.

5. Once companies believe that the data is secure with cloud services, more companies are going to move their data to the cloud.

B Complete the sentences from a meeting about cloud computing. Circle the correct form of the verbs.

1. I think we (are going to attract)/ attract more international customers once we **are going to start** /(start) using cloud computing.

2. I'm concerned that our data **will not be / is** safe once we **begin / will begin** to use cloud computing.

3. As soon as our company **will start / starts** using the cloud, we **are going to save / save** a lot of money. We will be able to eliminate our technology department.

4. We **are going to save / have saved** up to $10,000 annually after we **will change / have changed** to using only electronic forms.

5. I'm pretty worried that the company **isn't going to save / hasn't saved** money until cloud services **will become / become** more reliable and secure.

6. As soon as the company marketing department **will create / has created** a social networking site, we **have / will have** free advertising.

7. We **won't approve / approve** using cloud services until the manager **has approved / will approve** the budget.

Exercise 2.2 Time Clauses with *When* and *While*

Complete the conversation about social networking and blogs in advertising. Use the correct form of the verbs in parentheses. Sometimes more than one answer is possible.

Erin OK, everyone. We're going to have to find cheaper ways to market our

products.

Bo I'm sure that while we _'re discussing_ (discuss) the new budget next week,
(1)

we'll think of some inexpensive ways to market our products.

Erin I think we should use social networking sites and blogs.

Bo I agree. Let's prepare a presentation. Lisa can write some descriptions of

our new products. I'll do research on the most popular social networking

sites while you _____ (find) some interesting blogs.
(2)

Erin Sounds good. While we _____ (do) that, the art department
(3)

will work on some drawings for our profile page.

Bo OK. I'll investigate how other food companies market themselves on social

networking sites while the art department _____ (work) on
(4)

the drawings.

Erin Look for Dan's Imported Food. That's our biggest competitor.

Bo Right. I'm sure that when I _____ (study) Dan's page, I'll get
(5)

some good ideas. I'll take notes while I _____ (look) at it.
(6)

Erin While you _____ (analyze) Dan's page, I'll think about how
(7)

we can use blogs for marketing as well.

Bo Great idea. While you _____ (think) about blogs, I'll get
(8)

some information on the impact e-mail can have.

Erin Good plan! Let's get moving!

Exercise 2.3 Time Clauses with *When*

Look at Jared's meeting agenda. Then complete the sentences about what is going to
happen. Pay close attention to the sequence of events. Use *will* or the future progressive
of the verbs in parentheses. Sometimes there is more than one correct answer.

Agenda

8:00–8:20	Introduce new employees
8:15	Sara arrives; introduce Sara
8:20–10:00	Brainstorm for new budget
10:00–10:20	Take break
10:00	Photocopy worksheets
10:20	Return from break; hand out worksheets; put everyone into small groups
10:20–11:30	Small-group discussions; walk around and take notes
11:30	Vice president arrives; reassemble group

1. I _will be introducing_ (introduce) the new employees when Sara arrives.

2. When Sara arrives, I _____ (introduce) her.

3. I _____ (photocopy) the worksheets when the group takes a break.

4. I _____ (hand out) the worksheets when the group returns from the break.

5. When people return from the break, I _____ (put) them into small groups.

6. When people work in small groups, I _____ (walk) around and _____ (take) notes.

7. When the vice president arrives, the groups _____ (finish) their discussions.

8. I _____ (reassemble) the group when the vice president arrives.

Exercise 2.4 More Future Time Clauses

A Combine the sentences from Marta and Aaron's "to-do" list. Note that *M* is Marta and *A* is Aaron. Use *after*, *until*, or *when* with the present perfect in the time clauses. Sometimes more than one answer is possible.

1. Jan.–Feb. (M & A): Research and plan the business
   Mar. (M): Get a loan
   After Marta and Aaron have researched and planned the business, Marta will get a loan./Marta will get a loan after Marta and Aaron have researched and planned the business.

2. Mar.–Apr. (M & A): Get business training
   May–Jun. (M & A): Get management training

   _____

3. Apr. (A): Think of a name for the business
   May (M): Find a location for the business

   _____

4. Sept. (M): Get a tax identification number
   Oct. (M & A): Buy equipment for the business

   _____

5. Nov. (M & A): Promote the business
   Dec. (M & A): Open the business

   _____

6. First week of Dec. (M & A): Have a sale
   Dec. 25–31: Close for one week

   _____

B *Pair Work* Compare your sentences with a partner. What are some different ways to express the same ideas?

   A I wrote "After Marta and Aaron have done some research, they will get a loan."

   B I wrote "Marta and Aaron won't get a loan until they have done some research."

3 | Future Perfect vs. Future Perfect Progressive

▶ Grammar Presentation

The future perfect is used to describe events that will be completed at a time in the future. The future perfect progressive describes events that will be in progress at a time in the future. These forms are much more common in speaking than in academic writing.

By 2020, many companies **will have moved** their work to online servers.

By 2020, our company **will have been using** online servers for 10 years.

3.1 Forming Future Perfect

Form the future perfect with *will* + *have* + the past participle of the main verb. Form the negative by putting *not* between *will* and *have*, or use *won't have*.

By May, we **will have opened** the new office.

Will the team **have finished** the project by next week?

By next week, the team **won't have finished** the project.

3.2 Forming Future Perfect Progressive

Form the future perfect progressive with *will* + *have* + *been* + the *-ing* form of the main verb. Form the negative by putting *not* between *will* and *have*, or use *won't have*.

By May, I **will have been working** here for a year.

How long **will** you **have been working** here by next month?

We **won't have been working** here for very long.

3.3 Future Perfect and Future Perfect Progressive Contrasted

a. Use the future perfect for an event that will be completed by a time in the future.

I **will have made** my decision before tomorrow.

Will she **have told** you her decision by noon?

b. Use the future perfect progressive for an event that will be in progress at a time in the future.

How long **will** he **have been working** in the computer industry on his fortieth birthday?

c. You can introduce a particular future time with a preposition such as *before* and *by* (*by that time, by then*) or a time clause in the simple present.

He**'ll have been working** for us for 10 years <u>by next June</u>.

They just moved to Dallas, so they **won't have been living** there long <u>when you visit next month</u>.

You can use *already* to express certainty about future situations.

We can't change the plan. The managers **will** <u>already</u> **have had** their meeting by Monday.

They**'ll have** <u>already</u> **made** a decision by the time we get there.

3.3 Future Perfect and Future Perfect Progressive *(continued)*

d. Use the future perfect, not the future perfect progressive, with stative verbs such as *have*, *hear*, and *know*.

*She **will have known** about it by then.*

NOT *She ~~will have been knowing~~ about it by then.*

▶ Grammar Application

Exercise 3.1 Future Perfect

Look at the schedules. Then complete the sentences with the future perfect. Use the negative when necessary.

10:45 a.m.: Katie will finish the report.
11:00 a.m.: The meeting will start.
11:15 a.m.: Kyle will arrive.

1. Katie _will have finished the report_ by the time Kyle arrives.

2. The meeting _____ by the time Kyle arrives.

3. By 11:00 Kyle _____ .

12:30 p.m.: The meeting will end.
  1:30 p.m.: Kyle and Katie will go out to eat lunch.
  2:30 p.m.: Kyle and Katie will return from lunch.

4. By 12:40, the meeting _____ .

5. By 1:40, Kyle and Katie _____ .

6. By 2:15, Kyle and Katie _____ .

5:30 p.m.: Kyle's wife arrives home.
6:00 p.m.: Kyle leaves work.
7:30 p.m.: Kyle and his family will eat dinner.

7. Kyle's wife _____ before Kyle leaves work.

8. Kyle _____ by 6:15.

9. At 6:45, Kyle and his family _____ .

Exercise 3.2 Future Perfect Progressive

Read Eric's work schedule. Then complete the sentences with the information in the schedule. Use the future perfect progressive and *for*.

Tuesday	Wednesday	Thursday–Friday
8:30: Be at work 12:00: Lunch meeting with Mark at restaurant 1:00–4:00: Discuss new project 5:00: Meet with Japanese tutor; cancel tutoring sessions for Wed.– Fri. 6:15–7:15: Call from Japan	8:00: Pick up laptop from IT 9:00–5:00: Attend software training; bring lunch from home	9:00–5:00: Attend software training; bring lunch from home 6:00–8:00: Work out at the gym

1. By 4:30 on Tuesday, Eric / work / hours

   By 4:30 on Tuesday, Eric will have been working for 8 hours.

2. By 4:00 on Tuesday, Eric / discuss the new project / hours

   _____

   _____

3. By 6:45 on Tuesday, Eric / talk on the phone / hour

   _____

   _____

4. By 4:00 on Wednesday, Eric / attend a software training / hours

   _____

   _____

5. By 5:00 on Friday, Eric / attend a software training / days

   _____

   _____

6. By 7:15 on Friday, Eric / work out at the gym / minutes

   _____

   _____

Exercise 3.3 Time Clauses with Future Perfect and Future Perfect Progressive

A 🔊 A company is making its building energy-efficient and healthier for its employees. Read the time line. Then listen to questions about the time line. Circle *Yes* or *No*.

Time Line

February 2015	Approve the building plans
March 2015	Find a temporary site for workers
April 2015	Move into the temporary site
May 2015	Construction firm starts construction; installs solar heating system
October 2015	Finish all construction; "green" interior designer arrives; install new workstations
February 2016	Move back into the building
June 2016	Water department inspects water quality
August 2016	Send report on building improvements to finance department
March 2017	New law starts that requires all buildings to have energy-saving features
August 2017	OSHA[1] (Occupational Safety and Health Administration) visit

[1]**OSHA:** a U.S. government agency that inspects companies' workplaces to make sure that the companies follow health and safety laws

1. Yes (No)	3. Yes No	5. Yes No	7. Yes No
2. Yes No	4. Yes No	6. Yes No	8. Yes No

B 🔊 Listen again and check your answers.

C *Over to You* Answer the questions. Then share your answers with a partner.

- What year will it be in two years?
- What will you have accomplished by that time?
- What will you have been doing until then?

4 Avoid Common Mistakes

1. Use future forms in the main clause and present forms for the time clause.

We will buy it after we ~~will~~ get back from our trip.

2. Remember to use the future perfect when describing a future event that occurs before another future event.

will have
They∧ left by the time we get there, so we won't see them.

have moved
By that time, you will ~~move~~.

3. Make sure you do not confuse the future perfect progressive with other forms.

living
In June, we will have been ~~lived~~ in Texas for 2 years.

4. Remember to use *will* when forming the future perfect.

will
By this time next year, she∧ have gotten a better job.

Editing Task

Find and correct seven more mistakes in the paragraph about the future of health care.

have changed
Experts say that by 2020, the health-care industry will ~~change~~ in many ways because of technology and the Internet. I plan on working in this industry, so it is fascinating for me to know that by the time I graduate, the job market has changed dramatically. One change that interests me is in the doctor-patient relationship. By that time,

5 technology will empower patients because they will have been used the Internet to gather information and discuss information with others. Also, health-care companies will have been used cloud computing for a few years, so a patient's medical files will always be available to both the patient and the doctor. This means that, for example, when a patient will arrive for his appointment, he will not have to fill out forms, and the doctor have

10 already seen the patient's information. By the time a patient decides on a treatment, the doctor and patient will have been discussed many options. The whole health-care system will have improved, so more people will live in a state of health.

5 Grammar for Writing

Using Future Perfect and Future Perfect Progressive to Write About Completed and Ongoing Events in the Future

Writers use a combination of future forms to describe something that will happen in the future. They use the future perfect for events that will be completed in the future. They use the future perfect progressive for ongoing events in the future. Read these examples:

You'll have become an expert in cloud computing by the time you get your degree.
Once I get my degree, I will have been in the program for three years.
I'll have been studying for a year before I really understand cloud computing.
By next May, he will have been working in cloud computing for eight years.

Writers also often use the words *before, by, by the time,* and *once* to indicate the time of an event. *By* can be followed only by a time or noun phrase, such as *by 1981* or *by the end of the year. Before* can be followed by a time or noun phrase or by a clause such as *before he arrives. By the time* and *once* can be followed only by a clause.

Pre-writing Task

1 Read the paragraph about getting an IT certificate. Who do you think is the writer of this paragraph? Where would you find a paragraph similar to this one?

Getting an IT Certificate

Westport City College (WCC) has become a well-respected institution in the

Westport community over the past several decades. By the end of this spring, WCC will

have been educating students for 50 years. Once summer break begins, we will have served

over 1 million Westport residents. WCC has always offered programs in leading fields

5 of industry, and we are constantly updating our programs to teach the most up-to-date

information. Right now, we have exciting news for students with an interest in computers.

By next fall, WCC will have been offering a certificate program in Information Technology

for over 30 years, but we are planning many important changes to the program for

September. For example, we will offer a specialized certificate in cloud computing next

10 fall. Two new professors will be joining our team of excellent instructors to help make this

happen. Professor Gordon Jones will be teaching several basic courses, including Cloud

Computing 101. By the time he joins us, Professor Jones will have been working in cloud

computing for 10 years. Professor Margaret Chan will have trained employees to use cloud computing in over a dozen successful technology companies by the time she begins

15 teaching at WCC. If you are interested in enrolling in our new and improved IT certificate program, please send your application right away. A lot of students are interested, and at this rate, we will have received over 200 applications by the end of the month!

2 Read the paragraph again. Circle the uses of the future perfect. Underline the uses of the future perfect progressive. Which actions will be completed in the future and which will be ongoing in the future? Double underline the expressions with *by*, *by the time*, and *once*. Which expressions are followed by a time or a noun phrase? Which are followed by clauses?

Writing Task

1 *Write* Use the paragraph in the Pre-writing Task to help you write about a new program of study you might be interested in. Imagine you are writing this paragraph for a brochure. Write about what the program will offer.

2 *Self-Edit* Use the editing tips to improve your paragraph. Make any necessary changes.

1. Did you use the future perfect to write about events that will be complete at a specific time?
2. Did you use the future perfect progressive to write about events that will be ongoing at a specific time?
3. Did you use the expressions *before*, *by*, *by the time*, and *once* to indicate times? Did you use time words and clauses after the appropriate expressions?
4. Did you avoid the mistakes in the Avoid Common Mistakes chart on page 87?

Social Modals

Learning How to Remember

1 Grammar in the Real World

A Have you ever forgotten something important? Read the article about memory improvement. Which memory-improvement technique do you think works best?

How to Improve Your Memory

Some people have excellent memories, but most of us struggle to remember at times. You know the feeling: You **have to give** a class presentation,
5 and you are terrified. As you wait your turn, you repeat the information over and over in your mind, but you keep forgetting a key point. You **should have brought** your notes with you, but where
10 are they? You **can't remember**. If you are more forgetful than you would like to be, you **might want to follow** the advice of memory-improvement experts. Whether you want to memorize a speech
15 or simply remember where you left your cell phone, these experts offer tips to jumpstart[1] your brain.

Gini Graham Scott, PhD, is the author of *30 Days to a More Powerful Memory*.
20 She points out that if you want to remember something, it is necessary that you pay attention. You **must observe** what you want to learn. People often

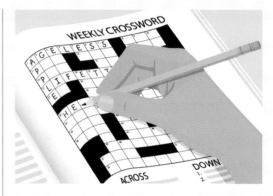

forget things simply because they weren't concentrating. Scott says that you **have** 25 **to** first **take in** information in order to save it in your memory. Other experts agree that visualization is an effective technique forgetful people **should try**. Create a mental picture – a picture 30 in your mind – of what you want to remember. The more unusual the image, the easier it will be to recall. For example, if you want to remember the due date for a final project, you **could visualize** 35 that date flashing in bold colors on a

---

[1]**jumpstart:** start something more quickly by giving it extra help

giant television screen. The scene **has to be** unusual and animated for the memory to stick. Memory specialists agree that
40 the more you exercise your brain, the better you will be able to remember information. How can you give your brain a workout?[2] You **might want to tackle** the daily crossword puzzle. Changing a
45 daily routine **is** also **supposed to work**. In addition, you **could challenge** your brain by writing with your nondominant[3]

hand or by taking a different route to school or work.

In today's multitasking[4] world, a good 50 memory is crucial. Without it, you **cannot maintain** order and priorities in your life. Fortunately, there are remedies[5] for forgetfulness. Practice careful observance, creative visualization, and mental exercise 55 to improve your memory.

---

[2]**workout:** a period of exercise │ [3]**nondominant:** not as important, strong, or noticeable │ [4]**multitask:** work on several tasks at the same time │ [5]**remedy:** a substance or method for curing an illness, or a way of dealing with a problem or difficulty

B Comprehension Check Answer the questions.

1. What must you do to remember something, according to Gini Graham Scott?
2. What is visualization?
3. What are some ways to exercise your brain?

C Notice Find the sentences in the article and complete them.

1. You _____ **give** a class presentation, and you are terrified.

2. You _____ **brought** your notes with you, but where are they?

3. Scott says that you _____ first **take in** information in order to save it in your memory.

Which sentences tell you it is necessary to do something?

2 Modals and Modal-like Expressions of Advice and Regret

▶ Grammar Presentation

The modals and modal-like expressions *could, had better, might, might want to, ought to,* and *should* can be used to express advice and regret.	You **should try** to improve your memory. I **should have** followed your advice.

2.1 Modals and Modal-like Expressions of Present and Future Advice

a. Use *could* and *might* to offer advice and suggestions or to give choices.	He **could do** some puzzles to improve his memory. You **might try** some tips for improving your memory.
Might (*not*) is often used with *want to* to give suggestions.	You **might not want to** start with the most difficult math problem. Try this one – it's easier.
b. Use *should* to say something is a good idea. Use *shouldn't* to say something is a bad idea.	Greg **should improve** his memory. Kate **shouldn't spend** so much time doing crossword puzzles.
Ought to is also possible, but less common. *Ought not* (*to*) is rare.	We **ought to take** a memory class together.
c. Use *had better* (*not*) only in informal conversation to give strong advice, especially as a warning.	You**'d better pay** attention now. (Or you will be in trouble.)
There is often a negative consequence if the advice or warning is not followed.	She **had better not forget** my book again tomorrow. (Or I will never lend her anything again.)
Had is almost always contracted, and often omitted, in informal conversation.	He**'d better** remember to bring his ID next time.

▶▶ Modals and Modal-like Expressions: See page A3.

2.2 Modals and Modal-like Expressions of Past Advice and Regret

a. Use *ought to have* or *should have* + the past participle for past events or situations that were advisable but did not happen.	She **ought to have been** at the lecture, but she was sick. (Being at the lecture was a good idea, but she wasn't there.) You **should have made** an effort to improve your memory. (Improving your memory was a good idea, but you didn't do it.)

2.2 Modals and Modal-like Expressions of Past Advice and Regret *(continued)*

b. Use *shouldn't have* + the past participle for past situations in which bad decisions were made. It is often used to express regret.

He **shouldn't have taken** that difficult class. (But he did, and now he's frustrated.)

We **shouldn't have listened** to him. (But we did, and now we're sorry.)

c. *Should (not) have* may be used to criticize.

You **should have followed** his advice. (But you didn't, and now look at the trouble you're in.)

▶ Grammar Application

Exercise 2.1 Present and Future Advice

A Complete the class discussion about improving memory. Circle the correct words or expressions.

Ms. Yost So, let's review our discussion about improving memory. What advice do experts give students? Sara?

Sara You (should)/ **'d better not** pay
(1)
attention to what you're learning.

Ms. Yost Right. So, for example, what's one good way to pay attention?

Sara Um, you **'d better / could** take notes
(2)
while you're reading.

Manuel Or you **might / 'd better** take notes during lectures.
(3)

Ms. Yost Right. Do you have any other advice?

Manuel I think students **'d better / shouldn't** use a computer to take notes. They
(4)
might not / should use a pen and a piece of paper.
(5)

Ms. Yost Good idea. In fact, studies show that writing information by hand – instead of using a keyboard – helps you remember it better.

B *Pair work* Compare your answers with a partner. Discuss the reason for each of your answers.

I use had better not *for warnings. This isn't a warning. It's advice. So I chose* should *in number 1.*

Exercise 2.2 More Present and Future Advice

A Read the study tips from a web article. Then complete the e-mail to a friend. Use the tips and the modals in parentheses.

Study Tips

1. Try visualizing to remember dates and names.
2. Read your textbook two or three times.
3. Try teaching someone else the material.

4. Don't wait until the last minute to study.
5. Get plenty of sleep before a test.

Send   Attach   Save Draft   Spelling ▾   Cancel

Hi _____ ,

I know you're having trouble studying for tests. I just read some study tips online. Here's some advice:

1. (could) *You could try visualizing to remember dates and names.*

2. (ought to) _____

3. (might) _____

4. (should not) _____

5. (had better) _____

I hope this helps! Talk to you soon.

Best,

_____

B *Pair Work* Tell a partner which tips you use. Then think of two more study tips and share them with another pair.

Exercise 2.3 Past Advice and Regret

A Complete the conversation about Phoebe, a student who plagiarized. Use the correct form of the words in parentheses.

Jake What happened to Phoebe? I heard she left college.

Sofia She committed plagiarism. She really

shouldn't have copied those articles from the
(1. not / should / copy)
Internet.

Jake I know. She _____
(2. should / take)
notes on the web articles. Then she

_____ her notes.
(3. ought to / summarize)

Sofia You're right. She _____
(4. should / give)
credit to the sources of the ideas, too. Why do you think she did this, anyway?

Jake Maybe she was under pressure or waited too long to start her paper. She

_____ earlier.
(5. ought to / start)

Sofia I agree. She _____ until the last minute.
(6. should / not / wait)

Jake Or she _____ to the teacher if she was
(7. should / talk)
having problems. Maybe we _____ her.
(8. should / help)

Sofia Yes, let's try to be more helpful the next time a classmate is stressed!

B *Pair Work* Compare your answers with a partner. Do you agree with the students' advice about Phoebe? What other advice would you give Phoebe?

C *Group Work* Think about a time when you made a decision you regret, or a time when a friend made a bad decision. What should you (or your friend) have done to make the situation better? Write five sentences with *should not have* + the past participle.

3 | Modals and Modal-like Expressions of Permission, Necessity, and Obligation

▶ Grammar Presentation

The modals and modal-like expressions *be allowed to, be required to, be supposed to, can, have to,* and *may* are used to express permission, necessity, and obligation in the present, past, and future.	We **weren't supposed to see** the answers for the memory test. They **will have to take** the test again. Students **may not take** the memory improvement class more than once.

3.1 Modals and Modal-like Expressions of Permission

a. Use *can* (*not*) and *may* (*not*) to talk about permission in the present and future.	Students **can register** for the class now. You **may wait** until next week to register. I **can't miss** more than two classes. You **may not join** after the first class.
Use *could* (*not*) as the past form of *can* (*not*).	We **could ask** questions at the end of the lecture, but we **couldn't interrupt** the lecture.
b. You can also use *be* (*not*) *allowed to* for permission in the present, past, and future. For the future, add *will* before *be* (*not*) *allowed to*.	We **aren't allowed to talk** during the test. He **was allowed to talk** during the test, but he **was not allowed to use** his books. They **will be allowed to use** their notes tomorrow. She **won't be allowed to use** her notes.
You can use *permitted* instead of *allowed* in formal speech and writing.	Students **are not permitted to refer** to notes during examinations.

3.2 Modals and Modal-like Expressions of Necessity and Obligation

a. Use *be required to, be supposed to, have to, must,* and *need to* to express necessity or obligation in the present and future. *Must* and *be required to* are more formal and are not often used in speaking.	You **are required to take** the class. Teachers **are supposed to hand out** the syllabus on the first day of class. Everyone **is required to work** hard. Applicants **must have** experience for this job.
Use *will be required to, will have to,* and *will need to* for future time.	You **will need to write** an essay for this course.

3.2 Modals and Modal-like Expressions of Necessity and Obligation *(continued)*

b. Use *be not supposed to* or *must not* for the present and future to say that something is inappropriate or to express prohibition.

Students **are not supposed to take** their books into the exam room. (It is inappropriate.)
You **must not talk** during the exam. (There is no choice.)

c. Use *were required to, were supposed to,* or *had to* to describe necessity and obligation in the past.

The applicant **was required to take** a test.
I **was supposed to stay** after class last week.
We **had to arrive** at 7:00 a.m. for the exam.

There is no past form of *must*. Use *had to* instead.

He **had to** reschedule his exam yesterday.
NOT He ~~must~~ reschedule his exam yesterday.

d. The negative forms of *be required to, have to,* and *need to* describe choices or options.

You **are not required to show** your ID. (It is optional.)
You **didn't have to remain** in the exam room after you finished. (It was your choice.)
Students **won't need to bring** their own pencils next time. (It will be your choice.)

▶ Grammar Application

Exercise 3.1 Present and Future Permission

A Complete the rules for a college Spanish class. Use the present or future form of the words in parentheses. Sometimes more than one answer is possible.

Spanish 101: Classroom Rules

Dictionaries

Students _can bring_ monolingual dictionaries along to class, but they
   (1. can / bring)

_____ any bilingual dictionaries at all. Students
   (2. not / may / use)

_____ print dictionaries during tests. However, they
   (3. can / use)

_____ online dictionaries during tests.
   (4. not / be allowed to / access)

Laptops

You _____ laptop computers to class for note taking
      (5. be allowed to / bring)

only. You _____ laptops for web browsing during class.
         (6. not / must / use)

Computer Lab

Students _____ the lab until they have purchased
           (7. not / may / use)

the book.

B Rewrite the sentences about the students in the Spanish class. Use the rules in A and the correct form of the words in parentheses.

1. Emily wants to bring a bilingual dictionary to class. (be permitted to)

   She isn't permitted to bring a bilingual dictionary to class.

2. Eric wants to use an online dictionary during a test. (be allowed to)

   _____

3. Ann wants to use a print dictionary during tests. (may)

   _____

4. Maria wants to bring a laptop to class. (can)

   _____

5. James wants to check his e-mail on his laptop during class. (be permitted to)

   _____

6. David hasn't bought the textbook yet. He wants to go to the lab. (can)

   _____

Exercise 3.2 Past Permission

A Complete the conversation about classroom rules. Use the correct past form of the words in parentheses.

Ming Last semester, I _could bring_ a monolingual dictionary to class.
(1. can / bring)

Danielle Yes, but you _____ it during tests.
(2. not / can / use)

Ming That's right. And we _____ laptops to class,
(3. be permitted to / bring)

but we _____ the Web during class.
(4. not / be allowed to / browse)

Danielle No, but we _____ on the Web in the computer
(5. be allowed to / go)

lab after we finished our work.

Ming _____ we _____ our own language at all during
(6)   (6. be allowed to / speak)

English class? I can't remember.

Danielle No. We _____ that. We even had to ask our
(7. not / be allowed to / do)

classmates questions in English.

B *Over to You* Think about a test or exam you took in the past. What could or couldn't you do? Write five sentences with *could* (*not*), (*not*) *be allowed to*, or (*not*) *be permitted to*. Then share your sentences with a partner.

Exercise 3.3 Present and Future Necessity and Obligation

Read the teacher's classroom rules and suggestions. Then rewrite the rules with the words in parentheses. Use the negative when necessary.

1. Read articles in English every day. It is an option. (have to)

   You don't have to read articles in English every day.

2. Don't be afraid to ask questions in class. (must)

   _____

3. Turn in all your homework. I expect this. (be supposed to)

   _____

4. Bring a flash drive next week. (must)

   _____

5. Write an essay at the end of the semester. (be required to)

   _____

6. Don't text during class. I expect this. (be supposed to)

   _____

7. Send your writing assignments electronically. It is an option. (need to)

   _____

Exercise 3.4 More Present and Future Necessity and Obligation

A 🔊 Listen to the psychology department announcement about a memory study. Circle *S* if the meaning of the sentence you read is the same as the one you hear. Circle *D* if the meaning of the sentence you read is different from the one you hear.

1. (S) D Participants must attend two sessions.
2. S D Sessions are not supposed to take more than one hour.
3. S D Participants are not supposed to be younger than 18 years of age.
4. S D Each participant must not have poor vision.
5. S D Each participant is supposed to have normal hearing.
6. S D Participants do not have to speak Mandarin.
7. S D Participants are required to be students at the university.
8. S D Participants must e-mail the researcher by July 31.

B 🔊 Listen again and check your answers.

Exercise 3.5 Past Necessity and Obligation

A Complete the story about an older person's learning experience. Use the correct forms of the words in parentheses.

When my grandmother was in high school, she _had to follow_ a lot of rules
                                                    (1. have to / follow)
and regulations, and she _____ very hard. There
                                    (2. have to / work)
were no computers, so she _____ notes by hand. She
                                        (3. have to / take)
_____ hundreds of textbook pages a week and write
        (4. be required to / read)
several papers each semester. She _____ any classes. She
                                        (5. not / be supposed to / miss)
_____ class every day in order to pass. Of course, there was
        (6. have to / attend)
no Internet then, so she _____ to the library to do research.
                                    (7. have to / go)
High school in her time was very different from how it is today!

B *Over to You* Write five sentences about some rules and regulations that you remember in a learning environment in the past, for example, in another school you attended. Share your sentences with a partner and discuss this question: How did the rules and regulations help you to learn?

4 Modals and Modal-like Expressions of Ability

▶ Grammar Presentation

The modals *be able to* and *can* are used to express ability in the present, past, and future.	*I **couldn't** remember anything the professor said. I **won't be able to** pass the test. She **can** remember dates well.*

4.1 Modals and Modal-like Expressions of Present and Future Ability

a. Use *be able to* and *can* to describe ability in the present.	*I **am able to remember** faces well, and I **can** usually **remember** names as well.*
Use *be not able to* and *can't / cannot* for negative statements in the present. *Be not able to* is more formal than *can't*.	*He **isn't able to meet** us today.*

4.1 Modals and Modal-like Expressions of Present and Future Ability *(continued)*

b. Use *can* and *will be able to* to describe ability in the future.	*We **can meet** the professor at noon tomorrow.* *He **will be able to see** us then.*
Use *can't* and *will not / won't be able to* for negative statements in the future. Notice that *not* comes before *be* in the future form.	*I **can't go** to the lecture on Friday.* *We **won't be able to take** the memory test until next month.*

4.2 Modals and Modal-like Expressions of Past Ability

a. Use *could (not)* to describe general ability in the past. *Was / were (not) able to* is also possible, especially to talk about a particular ability or talent.	*When I was younger, I **could be** very persuasive.* *I **could understand** the lecture, but I **couldn't remember** all of the information.* *She **was able to read** by the time she was four.*
Use *was / were able to*, not *could*, to describe ability on a particular occasion in the past.	*Once, I **was able to** convince my friend to memorize 100 new words in a week.* NOT *Once, I ~~could~~ convince my friend to memorize 100 new words in a week.*
b. Use *could have* + the past participle to describe situations in which a person had the ability to do something but did not do it.	*I **could have taken** the memory test last Saturday, but I didn't sign up for it.*
Use *couldn't have* + the past participle to describe situations in which a person didn't have the ability to do something.	*Eric **couldn't have known** the answer to that question. He didn't study at all.*

▶ Grammar Application

Exercise 4.1 Past, Present, and Future Ability

Complete the story about memory loss. Use the past, present, or future form of the words in parentheses.

A few years ago, Alicia was a successful physician. She was very popular with her

patients because she __*could diagnose*__ their problems quickly and accurately.

(1. can / diagnose)

Alicia's favorite pastime was riding her bike. She _____

(2. can / ride)

her mountain bike for hours in the hills around her town. Then one day last year, a car

came up behind Alicia while she was riding on a narrow road, and it hit her. The accident

caused a serious brain injury, even though she was wearing a helmet.

Alicia is in full-time therapy now. Today, she _____

many things. However, when she finishes therapy, she _____

(3. be able to / do)

(4. not / be able to / return)

to her old job because of her memory loss. Therefore, Alicia is planning to help other people

with her condition. Once Alicia is ready, she _____ of other

(5. be able to / take care)

patients.

Exercise 4.2 Past Ability

Complete the sentences about Diana. Use *could have* and the correct form of the verbs
in parentheses.

1. Diana had an accident like Alicia's. She was riding
   a bike in the hills when a car hit her. The driver
   could have avoided (avoid) hitting her, but he was
   driving too fast.

2. She went to a doctor, but he didn't think her
   injuries were serious. Diana didn't think the doctor
   _____ (make) a mistake
   about her diagnosis.[1]

3. Diana went to work after the accident, and
   her behavior seemed normal. Her co-workers
   _____ (not / imagine)
   that she had a brain injury.

4. The first clue that Diana was not well was when she
   went to a nearby store. She forgot how to get home.
   A neighbor had to help her. She _____ (not / remember)
   the way without help.

5. Finally, Diana found a specialist, Dr. Lee, who diagnosed her correctly and helped her
   get a service dog. Diana probably _____ (manage) fine
   by herself, but she was very thankful for the service dog because it made her life easier.
   Now she is in a memory rehabilitation program and doing well.

[1]**diagnosis:** when a doctor says what is wrong with someone who is ill

5 | Avoid Common Mistakes ⚠️

1. **When talking about advice and regret in the past, remember to use _have_ + the past participle after a modal, not the simple past form of the verb.**

   have
   I should ⌄remembered her name, but I didn't expect her to be at the party, and I got confused.

2. **Remember to use a form of _be_ in _be allowed to_ and _be supposed to_.**

   was
   The president ⌄supposed to attend the 2 o'clock meeting, but he didn't show up.

3. **Use _did not have to_ when talking about a choice in the past.**

   did not have to e-mail
   I ~~must not have e-mailed~~ the office manager, but I wanted to be sure he was aware of the problem.

Editing Task

Find and correct six more mistakes in the paragraphs about multitasking.

_is_
Technology ⌄supposed to simplify life; however, in reality, it has led to people trying to

do too many things at once. One example is driving while texting or talking on a cell phone.

After an accident, drivers who are caught by the police admit that they should turned off

their phones when they got in the car, but they did not. They must not have called someone

5 while driving, but they did.

Another issue is multitasking in the classroom. Many of my teachers have had a

difficult time dealing with students who surf the Web while listening to lectures. One of

my instructors said he ought to required a password last semester to log onto the Internet

during class. Students must not have gone online, but they sometimes checked e-mail or

10 visited websites instead of listening to the lecture. As a result, students were often distracted.

In contrast, my friend had an instructor who had the opposite view. My friend did

not worry about taking notes because students not allowed to – even on paper! The

professor thought all note taking was a form of multitasking; instead, he handed out

worksheets with highlights of his lecture. At the end of the semester, some students

15 complained. They argued that the professor should not banned computers in class

because students today are used to multitasking.

6 | Grammar for Writing

Using Modals to Write About Problems and Solutions

Writers often use modals and modal-like expressions of ability (*be able to, can, could*) to discuss the possible effects of a problem or difficult situation. They use modals of advice to give suggestions for helping someone deal with the situation. Read this example paragraph:

> *Studies show that students who sleep well before taking tests get better grades. When students do not get enough sleep after studying, their brains <u>cannot</u> process the information they read. Therefore, students <u>should</u> study over a period of a few days and get a good night's sleep before a test.*

Pre-writing Task

1 Read the paragraph. What are the effects of stress on academic achievement? What advice does the writer give to solve this problem?

Memory and Stress

Research shows a strong relationship between high levels of stress and low levels of academic achievement. Stress causes the body to produce high levels of the hormone cortisol. This hormone can limit the brain's ability to process information. Therefore, high levels of stress can have a negative effect on memory and could lead to poor test scores.

5 For this reason, colleges and universities should address the problems of stress in their new-student orientations. First, they should teach new students to recognize the signs of stress, such as headaches, anxiety, and trouble sleeping. The orientation schedule might include relaxation classes and deep-breathing lessons. Counselors could also tell students about the importance of exercise. In addition, colleges and universities should provide

10 stress reduction workshops for students during the school year. Students who learn how to manage their stress will remember what they learn, and will therefore have a better chance at success in their studies.

2 Read the paragraph again. Underline the modals and modal-like expressions that are used to describe the possible effects of stress. <u>Double underline</u> the modals and modal-like expressions that are used to describe ways of dealing with stress.

Writing Task

1 *Write* Use the paragraph in the Pre-writing Task to help you write about the effects of a problem or difficult situation that students may encounter. Explain the causes of the problem and suggest possible solutions. You can write about one of these topics or use your own ideas.

- difficulties with class participation
- problems understanding the teacher
- problems with homework
- trouble with tests or quizzes

2 *Self-Edit* Use the editing tips to improve your paragraph. Make any necessary changes.

1. Did you use modals and modal-like expressions of ability to describe possible effects of the problem?
2. Did you use different modals and modal-like expressions to give strong and less strong advice?
3. Did you avoid the mistakes in the Avoid Common Mistakes chart on page 103?

Modals of Probability: Present, Future, and Past

Computers and Crime

1 | Grammar in the Real World

A How do you protect personal information like computer passwords? Read the web article about hacking. What are some ways to prevent hackers from stealing personal information?

Hacking: A Computer Crime on the Rise

Cyber[1] hacking **may be** the most common computer crime today. Cyber hacking occurs when a person accesses someone else's computer without permission and steals
5 information. It **can happen** to anyone. It **might** even **have happened** to someone you know.

The truth is that hacking is not difficult to learn. In fact, it **might be** too easy. Young adults tend to be skilled at using computers, so it **may not be** surprising to learn that a large number of computer hackers are teenagers. They **might hack** into other computers
10 for the challenge – to see if they can do it and get away with it. There are other hackers, however, who **must have** more malicious[2] intentions because they steal credit card numbers and other personal information.

Severe[3] penalties for these cyber crimes **should have stopped** hacking by now, but they have had little effect. It does not look like cyber hacking **will go** away
15 anytime soon. For protection against hacking, anyone who uses a computer or other technological device **should be** aware of hackers and **should be using** antivirus software. Another safety measure is to use complex[4] passwords, which **could prevent** attacks from being successful.

In short, if you act safely and responsibly, hackers **will** likely **have** a hard time
20 breaking into your computer. However, even these safety measures cannot guarantee that your information is safe.

[1]**cyber:** related to computers | [2]**malicious:** intended to harm or upset other people | [3]**severe:** extreme |
[4]**complex:** having many connected parts, making it difficult to understand

B *Comprehension Check* Answer the questions.

1. What age are many hackers?
2. What information do some hackers steal?
3. Is anyone's computer completely safe from hackers?

C *Notice* Read the sentences. Check (✓) the box next to each sentence to show if the action or situation is possible or very certain.

	Possible	Very Certain
1. Cyber hacking **can** happen to anyone.	☐	☐
2. In fact, it **might be** too easy.	☐	☐
3. There are other hackers who **must have** more malicious intentions because they steal credit card numbers and other personal information.	☐	☐
4. In short, if you act safely and responsibly, hackers **will** likely **have** a hard time breaking into your computer.	☐	☐

Which bold words in the sentences tell you that an action or situation is possible?

2 Modals of Present Probability

▶ Grammar Presentation

Modals of present probability are used to express how likely it is that something is happening now.	*Your computer **may be** at risk of being hacked.* *He **must not be** worried about data security.*

2.1 Modals of Present Probability

a. Choose a modal depending on how certain you feel about something.

most certain ↑	*can't, couldn't, have to, must (not)*	*Hackers **can't be** interested in my data.* *Your password **must not be** secure.*
certain	*ought to, should (not)*	*Antivirus software **should protect** you.* *It **shouldn't be** difficult to find good software.*
least certain ↓	*could, may (not), might (not)*	*Good antivirus software **could cost** a lot.* *That software **might not be** good enough.*

2.1 Modals of Present Probability (continued)

b. Use *can't* and *couldn't* when you are almost certain something is not likely or not possible.

He **can't be** online now. His computer is broken.
Meg **couldn't be shopping** for a new laptop. Her old computer works perfectly.

You can also use *can't* and *couldn't* to express disbelief or surprise.

Your brand-new computer is broken? You **can't be** serious!

c. Use *have to* and *must* (*not*) when you are mostly certain or when you think there is only one logical conclusion.

As a lawyer, he **has to know** that hacking into computers is illegal!
Large companies **must worry** about the security of their data.

In formal speaking and writing, *must* is much more common than *have to*.

People without antivirus software **must believe** they are not at risk.

d. Use *ought to* and *should* (*not*) when you have an expectation based on experience or evidence. *Should* is more common than *ought to*. *Ought not to* is rare.

That computer **should be** available in the store because I saw it on the store's website.
You **shouldn't have** trouble figuring out my password because it's an easy one.

e. Use *could*, *may* (*not*), and *might* (*not*) when you are unsure or when you don't have much evidence.

I **could have** a virus on my computer because it isn't working normally.
I **might not buy** a new computer this year because my old one still works fine.

⌧ Modals and Modal-like Expressions: See page A3.

▶ Grammar Application

Exercise 2.1 Present Probability

A Complete the interview about hacking. Use the correct modals and the information in parentheses to help you. Sometimes more than one answer is possible.

Jason Today we are asking people: How secure is your computer or smartphone?
Could you be the victim of a hacker?

Emily It's impossible. Hackers ___can't / couldn't___ be
(1)
interested in my computer. I don't have anything
valuable on it. (**impossible**)

Jason But you _____ have some valuable
(2)
information on your computer. Everyone does.
(**a logical conclusion**)

Emily What do you mean?

Jason I'm sure you've bought things online at some point. Your credit card

information _____ be on your computer. (**a logical conclusion**)
        (3)

Carlos Well, I'm certain that my phone is safe. It

_____ be of interest to anyone,
     (4)

especially a hacker. (**unlikely**)

Jason Oh, you _____ have GPS – global
          (5)

positioning software – on your phone, then.

Because if you did, you'd feel different. (**a logical conclusion**)

Carlos But I do have GPS on my phone . . .

Jason Well, that _____ make you a little less sure, then, because GPS
           (6)

is one of the things that hackers are interested in. It lets them see where you

go every day. (**expectation based on evidence**)

Carlos My GPS? That _____ be true! (**surprise**)
             (7)

Belén You know, my computer _____
                  (8)

be of interest to a hacker for some reason,

I guess. (**unsure**)

Jason I'm afraid that's true.

B *Pair Work* Compare your answers with a partner. Take turns saying the sentences
with other modals that have the same meaning.

Hackers can't be interested in my computer.

Exercise 2.2 More Present Probability

A *Over to You* Read the statements. Then respond with information that is true
for you. Use modals of present probability to show how certain you feel that the
statements are true for you. Explain why.

1. A person can hack into your computer or smartphone at any time.

    That can't be true. I have excellent security software.

2. It is very likely that a thief will steal your identity.

_____

3. Your credit card number is not safe.

_____

4. Your home is very safe. It's unlikely that a burglar can enter and take valuable items from you.

_____

5. The downtown area of your city or town is dangerous at night. It's a bad idea to walk there alone at night.

_____

6. It's very safe for children to walk to school alone in your neighborhood.

_____

B *Pair Work* Take turns asking questions about each other's statements.

You say that it can't be true that a person can hack into your computer because you have good security, but good security is sometimes not enough. For example, banks tend to have good security, but hackers get into their computers.

3 | Modals of Future Probability

▶ Grammar Presentation

Modals of future probability with *could, may, might, ought to, should,* and *will* express the probability of something happening in the future.	*Your new computer* **should be** *here next week.* *I* **won't buy** *a new computer next year because my current one is still fairly new.*

3.1 Modals of Future Probability

a. Choose a modal depending on how certain you are about something.

most certain ⬆	*will (not)*	*Hackers* **will be** *interested in our company's financial data.*
certain	*should (not), ought to*	*Our new website* **should be** *ready by next week.* *The secure web page* **ought to be** *available soon.*
least certain ⬇	*may (not), might (not), could*	*She* **could learn** *a lot about Internet security in her course next month.*

b. Use *will* and *won't* to express strong certainty.

The company **will hire** *very few people this year.*

You can add words like *probably* and *likely* to weaken the certainty.

The company probably **won't hire** *any students.*

3.1 Modals of Future Probability *(continued)*

c. Use *should* (*not*) and *ought to* when you have an expectation based on experience or evidence.

*The software **should be** ready by Friday. (Because it is almost ready now.)*

*We **shouldn't expect** new passwords until Monday. (Because it usually takes a few days.)*

d. Use *could*, *may* (*not*), and *might* (*not*) when you are unsure or when you don't have much evidence.

*The company **could start** storing personal data as early as next month.*

*A manager **might join** us next week.*

You can also use these modals with a progressive form of the verb.

*The class **may be starting** soon. There are a lot of students in the room.*

▶ Grammar Application

Exercise 3.1 Future Probability

A Complete the ad with *will* and the verbs in parentheses.

I-safe Home Security System

The home of the future ___will be___ (be) safer.
(1)

Homeowners _____ (be) able
(2)

to control everything in the home with the new

I-safe Home Security System.

Here are just a few of I-safe's features:

- You _____ (not/need) to worry about the new babysitter. I-safe
  (3)

  _____ (let) parents use their computers or smartphones at work to
  (4)

  watch the babysitter.

- I-safe _____ (allow) you to control appliances and heating and cooling
  (5)

  systems from wherever you are.

- I-safe _____ (lock) the doors to your home for you.
  (6)

- The I-safe Home Security System _____ (be) available this spring.
  (7)

B Complete the conversation about the I-safe. The speakers are not very certain about the claims in the ad. Circle the correct words.

Customer Are you going to sell the I-safe system next spring?

Sales clerk It (will likely) / will be available next spring, but the manager isn't sure.
          (1)

Customer Can I use the I-safe to control the TV from my smartphone?

Sales clerk You **will / should** be able to control the TV, but I'm not really sure.
          (2)

Customer I have a babysitter. If I install I-safe cameras to watch her from time to time,

          she **should / may not** be happy about being on camera.
                  (3)

Sales clerk You're right, there **shouldn't / could** be some concerns about privacy.
                            (4)

Customer I use a tablet computer while I commute to work on the train. I haven't

          read anything about using the I-safe with my tablet. I-safe probably

          won't / shouldn't work with it, right?
               (5)

Sales clerk I'm not quite sure, but it **ought to / will** send images to your tablet.
                          (6)

Customer OK. Thanks for your help.

C *Pair Work* Imagine that the I-safe company is going to give away its product for free for one month. Will you get an I-safe? Why or why not? Use modals in your answers.

    A I probably won't get an I-safe because I'm not very worried about home security.
    B I might get one. I'm not sure because there could be some privacy issues with it.

Exercise 3.2 More Future Probability

A 🔊 Listen to the conversations about future probability. Write the missing words.

Conversation 1

    Anne Someone broke into the Lees' apartment, and now they're moving.

    Martín That's awful. Where are they going to go?

    Anne I'm not sure. *They'll* probably move to the suburbs.
                     (1)

    Martín But Joe Lee has a good job here in the city. _____ be able to
                                                          (2)

          move very far away.

    Anne I know. And the children are in school in the city. _____ want to
                                                          (3)

          change schools.

    Martín Well, I wish them luck.

Conversation 2

Truong I spoke with Andrew Martinez yesterday. Guess what? _____
(4)
buy a home security system.

Ben I know. We went to a home security show last week. He liked the system with
the cameras that send images to your phone. _____ be the
(5)
system he's going to buy.

Truong _____ learn a lot from Andrew when he puts in his system.
(6)

Conversation 3

Reporter The airport commissioner announced today that Bay City Airport will start
using cameras with sensors that will detect heart rate and body temperature.
_____ be ready by next year.
(7)

Josh I read about the cameras online as well. In fact, I heard that
_____ start using the cameras by the end of this year.
(8)

Katie _____ be interesting to see what happens.
(9)

B 🔊 Listen again and check your answers.

4 Modals of Past Probability

Grammar Presentation

Modals of past probability with *can, could, may, might,* and *must* are used to make inferences or guesses about the past.	A hacker **couldn't have accessed** this computer! I have the best protection available. A hacker **might have found** a way to break into it.

4.1 Forming Modals of Past Probability

Form modals of past probability with modal + *have* + the past participle of the main verb. Form the negative by putting *not* between the modal and *have*. Only use contractions with *could* and *can*.	The company **may have been** careless with security. I **must not have turned off** my phone. She **could have changed** her password, but I'm not sure. It **couldn't have been** Joe's fault. He wasn't here.

4.2 Using Modals of Past Probability

a. Choose a modal depending on how certain you are that something happened.

most certain	*couldn't, can't*
certain	*must (not)*
least certain	*may (not), might (not), could*

You **couldn't have chosen** a strong password. Kim guessed it immediately!

Someone **must have stolen** all the passwords because hackers have gotten into every computer.

The computer **may not have had** strong antivirus software because it was older.

b. Use *can't have* or *couldn't have* when you are absolutely certain something was impossible or unlikely.

I **can't have entered** the wrong password! I've had the same one forever.

He **couldn't have hacked** our computers. He doesn't know how.

c. Use *must (not) have* when you feel certain about something or when you believe there is only one logical conclusion.

I **must not have written** the password down. I can't find it anywhere.

You **must have received** the security e-mail. Ms. Liu sent it to everyone.

d. Use *could have, may (not) have,* or *might (not) have* when there isn't much evidence or when you are guessing.

He **may not have followed** the security advice because he didn't believe it was important.

He **might have changed** his password. I don't think he is still using his old one.

Data from the Real World

May (not) have, could (not) have, and *might (not) have* are the most common modals used for speculating about the past in speaking and writing. *Must (not) have* is less common. *Cannot/can't have* is relatively rare.

may (not) have	
could (not) have	
might (not) have	
must (not) have	
cannot/can't have	

▶ Grammar Application

Exercise 4.1 Past Probability

Complete the article about credit card fraud. Use the correct form of the words in parentheses.

Credit Card Fraud: How Does It Happen?

There was a $10,000 charge from a jewelry store on Claudia's credit card

statement. She didn't buy any jewelry, so someone _must have stolen_ her credit
(1. must / steal)

card number.

Claudia said, "I _____ the victim of credit card theft."
(2. not / could / be)
However, someone obviously _____ her card information.
(3. must / obtain)
How _____ that _____ ? There are many ways a
(4)　　　　　　　(4. could / happen)
person _____ Claudia's credit card information. Someone
(5. might / steal)
_____ Claudia's credit card number when she used her card
(6. may / steal)
in a store or a restaurant. In addition, a thief _____ a credit card
(7. could / take)
account statement or a bill from her mailbox or her trash.

Exercise 4.2 More Past Probability

Write a response for each situation. Use the words in parentheses with modals of past probability to write guesses or logical conclusions. Sometimes more than one answer is possible.

1. Isabela can't find her wallet.
   She may/might/could have lost it.
   (**guess:** she / lose / it)
2. There was a charge on Bo's bill that he didn't recognize.

   _____
   (**logical conclusion:** someone / steal / his credit card number)
3. Bo paid his credit card bill, even though he didn't recognize some of the charges.

   _____
   (**logical conclusion:** he / not / call / the credit card company)
4. The waiter took a long time to bring Hong's credit card back.

   _____
   (**guess:** he / copy / the card number)
5. Terry threw an unopened letter from her credit card company into the trash.

   _____
   (**logical conclusion:** she / not / think / it was important)

Exercise 4.3 Using Modals of Past Probability

Read the web article about tips for avoiding identity theft. Then complete the sentences about examples of identity theft. Use the tips to write logical conclusions or guesses about what has happened. Sometimes more than one answer is possible.

How to Avoid Identity Theft

1. Write to credit card companies. Tell them to remove your name from their mailing lists.
2. Check your credit card bill carefully each month. Make sure there are no incorrect charges on it.
3. Don't carry all of your credit cards with you.
4. Make photocopies of important documents, such as your passport, and keep the copies in a safe place in your home.
5. Check that e-mails from your bank and other businesses are authentic. Never give personal information in an e-mail.

1. Fred gets a lot of credit card offers in the mail. He never opens them.
   He must not have called the companies and asked them to remove his name from their mailing lists.

2. Sarah paid her credit card bill, but there were charges on it for things she did not buy.
   _____

3. A pickpocket stole Luis's wallet while he was riding the bus. Now Luis has to cancel all of his credit cards.
   _____

4. Wei went to Canada on a business trip and lost his passport. It took longer than usual for him to leave the country because he didn't know his passport number.
   _____

5. Nicole responded to an e-mail that she thought was from her bank, and now she is missing money from her account.
   _____

5 | Avoid Common Mistakes ⚠

1. **Do not use _must_ to talk about future probabilities.**

   will / may

   It ~~must~~ be even more difficult to catch cyber criminals in the future.

2. **Remember to use _be_ + verb + _-ing_ when using the progressive with modals.**

   be

   He might ∧ working.

3. **Use the correct word order when using modals of probability to talk about the past.**

   not

   He must ∧ have ~~not~~ locked the computer because the thief was able to get his information.

Editing Task

Find and correct four mistakes in the paragraph about computer hackers.

What happens to computer hackers who decide to stop hacking? They might find that cyber crime can lead to interesting careers. For example, some companies hire a computer hacker with the hope that the former cyber criminal ~~must~~ *will* become a brilliant security consultant in the future. Although some say that these companies might taking a

5 risk by hiring these former criminals, the companies seem to believe that the risk is worth it. Adrian Lamo was breaking into computer systems for fun in high school. However, when he hacked into the *New York Times* in 2002, the newspaper must have not thought it was funny, because he was arrested. He now uses his skills for a different purpose and works as a consultant. Robert Tappan Morris might have ended his chances for a good job

10 when he created the Morris worm, a particularly bad computer virus, in 1988. However, he is now on the faculty of the famous Massachusetts Institute of Technology (MIT). Apparently, they believe that a reformed hacker must be able to stop future cyber crimes. In short, while computer hackers sometimes go to prison for their crimes, these days their career opportunities may increasing.

6 | Grammar for Writing ✎

Using Modals to Hedge

Can, could, and *may (not)* make your writing sound less certain. This is especially helpful when you are stating opinions. Using modals to sound less certain is called *hedging.* Hedging is more common in academic writing than in other kinds of writing, such as editorial pieces. Read these examples:

Strong laws <u>will</u> reduce cyber crime.
Strong laws <u>may</u> reduce cyber crime.

The first sentence expresses strong certainty. The second sentence expresses less certainty. It shows that other opinions are possible, too. The writer of the second sentence is hedging.

Pre-writing Task

1 Read the paragraph. What type of crime is the paragraph about? What is the writer's opinion of these criminals?

New Types of Criminals

Cyber crime is a serious problem throughout the world for many reasons. Cyber criminals are extremely difficult to find. They may be the hardest criminals to catch. Cyber criminals can commit their crimes from anywhere in the world. Also, it can be impossible to know if they are working alone or with other cyber criminals. They do not need to be

5 in the same place. Also, cyber criminals may be more educated and know more about computers than most other criminals. They may know more about the Internet than the police or even many computer specialists. Furthermore, no one knows how many cyber crimes have been committed. Some victims of cyber crimes may not have reported the crimes because they did not realize that a cyber crime happened to them. Another problem

10 is that the laws against cyber crimes are changing all the time. In addition, some countries may not even have any clear laws against cyber crime yet. In the future, people will make more and more purchases and do more and more business using e-mail and the Internet. This could become riskier as cyber criminals continue to get smarter and harder to catch.

2 Read the paragraph again. Circle the uses of *can, could,* and *may* as hedging expressions. Underline the hedging modal that refers to the past. <u>Double underline</u> the hedging modal that refers to the future.

Writing Task

1 *Write* Use the paragraph in the Pre-writing Task to help you write about why many employers read their employees' e-mails and track their Internet use. Use these sentence starters.

- Employers may read their employees' e-mail in order to _____ .
- Some employees could be _____ .
- Reading employees' e-mails could lead to _____ .

2 *Self-Edit* Use the editing tips to improve your paragraph. Make any necessary changes.

1. Did you use hedging modals to show that other opinions are possible?
2. Did you use *cannot, could not, have to, must* (*not*), *ought to,* and/or *should* (*not*) to express probability in the present when you were fairly certain?
3. Did you use *will* and other modals with time words to express probability in the future?
4. Did you avoid the mistakes in the Avoid Common Mistakes chart on page 117?

UNIT

9

Nouns and Modifying Nouns

Attitudes Toward Nutrition

1 | Grammar in the Real World

A What makes a person healthy? Read the article about health habits today. Are people as healthy today as they were in the past?

∂ A Health Crisis ∂

Obesity has become **a major problem** in the United States. According to recent National Institutes of Health studies, less than one-third of **Americans** over the age of 20 are at a healthy weight. That means that two-thirds of the **adult population** is overweight, and one-third of all **adults** are obese.[1]

5   **Modern U.S. society** is partially responsible for this **alarming health trend**. Processed, prepared, and packaged **food** has very little nutritional value. Michael Pollan, author of *Food Rules*, argues that **many modern food products** are not truly **food** at all. They contain a great deal of **fat** and refined[2] **sugar** but very little – or no – nutrition.

One other cause of obesity is the unhealthy choices people are making in **their** 10 **lifestyles**. **Exercise** used to be part of everyday **life**. It was a necessary part of a society where work depended mostly on farming and physical labor.[3] Today, people often sit at a computer all day, watch hours of TV, use personal cars, and have little daily exercise.

Health experts have been studying ways to reduce obesity because there is a link between obesity and other serious **diseases**, such as **diabetes**[4] and **heart disease**. **One** 15 **way** is to eat more **green and brown food**, such as green **vegetables** and brown **rice** and **grains**. These foods help people use calories, and they aid digestion.[5] In contrast, people who have a **diet** of mostly fast food, white sugar, white flour, and **fat** are at greater risk of obesity. **These diets** contain calories that easily become **fat** when people do not use them for **energy** and exercise.

20   Experts recommend fewer **servings of** unhealthy food, bigger **portions of** healthy food, and a more active lifestyle.

---
[1]**obese:** extremely fat | [2]**refined:** made more pure by removing unwanted material | [3]**physical labor:** work that involves effort from the body | [4]**diabetes:** a disease in which the body cannot control the amount of sugar in the blood | [5]**digestion:** the ability of the body to create energy from food

120

B *Comprehension Check* Answer the questions.

1. Why does Michael Pollan argue that many modern food products are not truly food?
2. How did people stay active in the past?
3. What are some diseases related to obesity?

C *Notice* Look at the nouns in bold. Write *C* next to each noun that you can count and *NC* next to each noun that you can't count. Then look at the words that modify some of the nouns. Are they all adjectives? Circle the ones that are not adjectives. What part of speech are they?

1. green and brown **food**
2. heart **disease**
3. food **products**
4. the **elderly**
5. **obesity**

2 | Nouns

▶ Grammar Presentation

There are two types of common nouns in English: count and noncount.	COUNT NOUN ***Vegetables*** *are good for you.* NONCOUNT NOUN *Good **nutrition** is essential for good health.*

2.1 Count Nouns

Count nouns are nouns that you can count and make plural. Use a singular or plural verb with count nouns.	*This **apple** tastes great.* ***Vegetables** are very important and keep us healthy.*
Use a determiner such as *a/an*, *the*, *this*, and *his* with singular count nouns.	*Is a **tomato** a **vegetable**?* *There's an **onion** in the **refrigerator**.* *This **banana** doesn't taste ripe.* *His **sandwich** looks delicious.*
You can use a plural count noun with or without a determiner such as *a few*, *many*, *some*, *these*, and *those*.	*Some **diets** don't work very well.* ***Diets** often don't work very well.*

2.2 Irregular Plural Nouns

a. Some plural nouns have irregular forms. These are the most common irregular plural nouns in academic writing.

man – men	*woman – women*
child – children	*person – people*
foot – feet	*tooth – teeth*

b. Some nouns have the same form for singular and plural.

one fish – two fish   *one sheep – two sheep*

c. Some nouns are only plural. They do not have a singular form.

clothes	*headphones*	*pants*
glasses	*jeans*	*scissors*

2.3 Noncount Nouns

a. Noncount nouns are nouns that cannot be counted. Use a singular verb with noncount nouns.

Here are some common categories of noncount nouns.

Abstract concepts: *health, nutrition*

Good **health** is very important.

Activities and sports: *dancing, exercise, swimming, tennis, yoga*

Yoga has been my favorite activity for years.

Diseases and health conditions: *arthritis, depression, diabetes, obesity*

Obesity has become a serious problem.

Elements and gases: *gold, hydrogen, oxygen, silver*

Oxygen is the most common element in the body by weight.

Food: *beef, broccoli, cheese, rice*

Broccoli isn't popular with my family.

Liquids: *coffee, gasoline, oil, tea*

Tea has many health benefits.

Natural phenomena: *electricity, hail, lightning, rain, thunder*

Hail consists of small balls of ice.

Particles: *pepper, salt, sand, sugar*

Too much **salt** isn't good for you.

Subjects: *economics, genetics, geology*

I wasn't very good at **economics** in college.

Areas of work: *construction, business, medicine, nursing*

She's studying **nursing**.

b. You can use a noncount noun with or without a determiner. Use a determiner after you have already mentioned the noun and wish to give more information.

Cheese is one of my favorite foods, but I don't like the **cheese** on this pizza. It's too stringy.

c. You can use *the* + certain adjectives to describe a group of people with the same characteristic or quality: *the dead, the disabled, the educated, the elderly, the living, the poor, the rich, the unemployed.*
Use a plural verb.

The elderly sometimes don't eat well.
The poor are often not able to buy nutritious food.
The unemployed are especially affected by the poor economy.

▸ Noncount Nouns and Measurement Words to Make Noncount Nouns Countable: See page A5.

Data from the Real World

Some common noncount nouns in speaking and writing are:

advice	equipment	information	music	research	stuff
bread	evidence	knowledge	news	rice	traffic
cash	fun	luck	permission	safety	water
coffee	furniture	milk	progress	security	weather
damage	health	money	publicity	software	work

Grammar Application

Exercise 2.1 Count Nouns

A Complete the excerpt from a web article about nutrition. Circle the correct verbs.

A healthy diet **include / (includes)** a lot of fresh fruit and vegetables. Vegetables
(1)
is / are especially low in calories and high in nutrients such as vitamins and
(2)
minerals. Therefore, it's a good idea to add more fruit and vegetables to your diet
if you want to improve your health.

Current nutrition guidelines **suggest / suggests** eating about four or five
(3)
servings of fruit and vegetables a day. One serving **is / are** about a half cup.
(4)
Nutrition experts also **suggest / suggests** choosing fruit and vegetables by color –
(5)
dark green, yellow, red, and so on – and eating a variety of colors each day.
This is because fruit and vegetables with a lot of color often **contain / contains**
(6)
the highest amounts of nutrients. Half a cup of broccoli, for example, **has / have**
(7)
50 milligrams of vitamin C and only about 15 calories.

Low-calorie fruit, such as tomatoes and berries, **is / are** also a good choice. A
(8)
medium tomato **has / have** only about 20 calories and 15 milligrams of vitamin C.
(9)
Blueberries **has / have** 80 calories and 15 milligrams of vitamin C per cup.
(10)
Intensely colored fruit and vegetables often **contain / contains** antioxidants,
(11)
chemicals that protect cells from disease. Antioxidants also **enhance / enhances**
(12)
the effects of vitamin C and protect the heart and your health!

B *Over to You* What else do you know about the benefits of fruit and vegetables? Write five sentences about fruit and vegetables. Share your sentences with a partner.

Exercise 2.2 *The* + Adjective

Complete the statements about nutritional issues that affect different groups of people. Rewrite the words in parentheses with *the* + adjective.

1. _The wealthy_ (People who are wealthy) tend to have a better diet than poor people do because they can easily shop for and buy whatever they need.

2. _____ (People who are poor) often do not have convenient access to fresh fruit and vegetables because there are few good supermarkets in poor neighborhoods.

3. There often are free food programs for _____ (people who are homeless) in large urban areas.

4. _____ (People who are elderly) sometimes have poor nutrition because they might suffer from diseases that cause a loss of appetite.

5. _____ (People who are young) are becoming less healthy in America because of too much junk food and a lack of exercise.

6. In Minneapolis and in many other parts of the country, farmers' markets are opening in areas that are easier for _____ (people who are disabled) to access.

7. _____ (People who are unemployed) in the United States can get help buying food by applying for SNAP, the government-sponsored Supplemental Nutrition Assistance Program.

8. We usually assume that _____ (people who are educated) make wise choices when they eat, but this is not always true.

Exercise 2.3 Count or Noncount Noun?

A Complete the magazine article about health. Add plural endings to the nouns in bold where necessary. If a noun does not have a plural, write ✗ on the line.

～～～ Tips for a Healthy Life ～～～

Due to the worldwide epidemic of obesity, many people are concerned about their

health ✗ (1) . **Specialist** _____ (2) who study how the body works have some **advice** _____ (3) for you: exercise more and eat healthier food.

The Harvard School of Public Health recommends adding more exercise to your daily life.

With the exception of some people who work in very active **occupation** _____ (4) such as

construction _____ (5) or landscaping, many of us simply do not move enough throughout the day.

Exercise _____ (6) not only helps burn calories, it also lowers the risk for many **illness** _____ (7) such

as **heart disease** _____ (8) and diabetes. One way to increase activity is through aerobic exercise

such as **swimming** _____ (9) . Aerobic exercise increases your intake of **oxygen** _____ (10) , which

helps you burn fat faster. However, many physical activities count as exercise, including

dancing _____ (11) and **gardening** _____ (12) .

The next step is changing our diet. Some **research** _____ (13) shows that a plant-based diet

is a good choice. People who eat less meat tend to be healthy. They do not usually eat

processed food that is high in fat, sugar, and **salt** _____ (14) . The Harvard School of Public

Health suggests that we follow a plant-based diet. They suggest eating fresh fruit and

vegetable _____ (15) and whole grains such as brown **rice** _____ (16) . They also recommend preparing

your food from fresh **ingredient** _____ (17) .

There is a lot of confusing **information** _____ (18) about nutrition, but exercise and simple,

unprocessed food are all you really need to live a healthy life.

B *Pair Work* Make a list of the noncount nouns in A. Then work with a partner and identify which category the nouns in A are from: abstract concepts, activities and sports, diseases and health conditions, food, subjects, particles, or areas of work. Then think of one more noun for each category.

A Health *is an abstract concept.*

B Right. And kindness *is another abstract concept.*

3 Noncount Nouns as Count Nouns

▶ Grammar Presentation

When we refer to noncount nouns as individual items, they can sometimes have a count meaning. They may also be made countable with measurement words describing specific quantities.

NONCOUNT NOUN
Light *makes plants grow.*

MEASUREMENT+ COUNT NOUN
*A bunch of **lights** were visible in the distance.*

3.1 Making Noncount Nouns Countable

a. Some noncount nouns can have a count meaning when we refer to individual items within a general category.

*I always put **cheese** on my pasta.* (general category)
*English **cheeses** are very strong.* (individual kinds)
***Food** is essential to life.* (general category)
*Some **foods** contain a lot of sugar.* (individual food items)

b. Use measurement words to make noncount nouns countable. Here are common measurement words and expressions.

Abstract concepts: *a bit of, a kind of, a piece of*
Activities or sports: *a game of*
Food: *a drop of, a grain of, a piece of, a serving of, a slice of*
Liquids: *a cup of, a gallon / quart of, a glass of*
Natural phenomena: *a bolt of, a drop of, a ray of*
Particles: *a grain of, a pinch of*
Subjects and occupations: *an area of, a branch of, a field of, a type of*
Miscellaneous: *an article of* (clothing), *a bunch of* (people, objects), *a crowd of, a group of, a pack of* (wolves, dogs, wild animals), *a piece of* (furniture, equipment, news)

*Eight glasses of **water** are on the table.*
*There is a piece of **cake** in the refrigerator.*

*A bit of **kindness** goes a long way.*
*I play five games of **tennis** a week.*
*Would you like a piece of **pie**?*

*The recipe calls for two cups of **oil**.*
*A few drops of **rain** are enough to ruin a picnic.*
*A pinch of **salt** makes food taste good.*
*Two branches of **medicine** are cardiology and neurology.*
*There were a bunch of **people** at the store.*

▸▸ Noncount Nouns and Measurement Words to Make Noncount Nouns Countable: See page A5.

▶ Grammar Application

Exercise 3.1 Noncount Nouns with Count Meanings

A Complete the conversation about purchasing food through the Internet. Use the correct form of the nouns in parentheses. Sometimes more than one answer is possible.

Jake Do you have any __experience__ (experience) buying food online?
(1)

Emily Yes, I've bought different kinds of imported _____ (cheese),
(2)

a variety of _____ (coffee), and different sorts of
(3)

_____ (tea).
(4)

Jake I didn't know you liked _____ (cheese) so much.
(5)

Emily I don't. I bought all of those _____ (cheese) as gifts.
(6)

Jake Anyway, how was the shopping?

Emily I've had many good _____ (experience) with online shopping.
(7)
The prices were reasonable, and the items arrived in good condition.

Jake Did it take a long _____ (time) for the items to arrive?
(8)

Emily Not usually. Two _____ (time) they were late.
(9)

Jake Do you ever buy _____ (fruit) online?
(10)

Emily I don't think that's a good idea, but I have friends who buy

_____ (fruit) like *cherimoya* and *durian* online without any
(11)
problems.

Jake It's probably safe to buy _____ (coffee) and
(12)

_____ (tea) online, right?
(13)

Emily Sure. I've also bought items like _____ (sugar) and
(14)

_____ (flour) online.
(15)

Jake Why would you do that?

Emily I buy hard-to-get _____ (sugar) such as *demerara* and
(16)
turbinado online because I can't find them in my local store.

Jake And there are special types of _____ (flour), too?
(17)

Emily Well, I have a friend who is allergic to wheat, so I get a few different

gluten-free _____ (flour) from a special diet site.
(18)

B *Pair Work* Compare your answers with a partner. Discuss the reasons for each of your answers.

I chose the noncount noun experience *in item 1 because the speaker is talking about an abstract concept.*

Exercise 3.2 Measurement Words with Noncount Nouns

Complete the sentences with the correct quantifier from the box. Add determiners and any other necessary words. Sometimes more than one answer is possible.

bit	cup	gallon	glass	piece	serving
can	drop	game	grain	pinch	slice

1. Let me give you _*a bit of*_ advice: Stop worrying about calories, and just eat food that's good for you.

2. Should we play _____ chess after dinner?

3. Please cut a very thin _____ bread for me.

4. _____ fruit is about a half a cup.

5. _____ tea has less caffeine than a cup of coffee.

6. Doctors recommend drinking 32 ounces of water a day, but it's hard to remember to drink four _____ water each day.

7. This sauce needs just _____ salt – not too much!

8. The cupboard is empty. There isn't even _____ rice left there!

9. Here's a bottle of soy sauce. Just put a tiny _____ soy sauce on the fish. We're trying to cut down on sodium.

10. The chocolate cheesecake that you baked looks absolutely delicious! Could you cut _____ for me?

11. I've brought you _____ chicken soup to help with your cold. It's not homemade, but I think it will help you feel better.

12. If you're going to the supermarket, could you pick up _____ milk? The children drink so much of it and we need a lot.

Exercise 3.3 More Measurement Words with Noncount Nouns

A Write the correct quantities of food in Luis's blog. Use the words in the box. Add any other necessary words.

1 / bottle / water	~~quart / olive oil~~	2 / piece / fish
1 / box / pasta	2 / loaf / bread	wedge / cheese

The Wandering Gourmet
by Luis Martinez

The highlight of my trip to San Francisco was the Ferry Plaza Farmers' Market. I spent a lot of money! My chef friend, Lisa, came with me. She made a delicious dinner from the ingredients. Here's what we bought:

1. _a quart of olive oil_   2. _____   3. _____

4. _____   5. _____   6. _____

B *Pair Work* Compare your answers with a partner. Then work together to think of more noncount nouns that you can use with each measurement word.

A *You can also say* a quart of water.
B *Or* a quart of milk.

4 Modifying Nouns

▶ Grammar Presentation

Adjectives that modify nouns, including nouns acting as adjectives, follow a specific order.	That was a **delicious green Washington** apple! (opinion + color + origin) I saw a **shocking government** report on nutrition. (opinion + type)

4.1 Order of Modifiers

The order of modifiers is as follows:

Opinion / Evaluation	Size	Age	Shape	Color	Origin	Material	Type
delicious traditional useful	large short small tall	antique new old two-year-old young	round square triangular	black green yellow	French imaginary scientific	cotton leather metal	dog government shoulder

▶▶┤ Order of Adjectives Before Nouns: See page A6.

4.2 Using Modifiers

a. Do not use commas between two adjectives from different categories

> OPINION ORIGIN
> That was a **delicious French** cake.
> OPINION TYPE
> It was a **disappointing medical** report.
> SIZE MATERIAL
> You'll need a **big metal** pan.

b. Use *and* or a comma between two adjectives of opinion.

> OPINION OPINION
> The food has an **interesting** <u>and</u> **memorable** taste.
> The food has an **interesting, memorable** taste.

Use *and* between two colors or two materials used as adjectives.

> COLOR + COLOR
> She bought a **red** <u>and</u> **yellow** dress.
> MATERIAL + MATERIAL
> The **cotton** <u>and</u> **silk** tablecloth is new.

▶ Grammar Application

Exercise 4.1 Order of Adjectives

Complete the sentences with the adjectives in parentheses. Remember to use the correct order.

1. Wei got a _new French glass_ (French / glass / new) coffeemaker for his 25th birthday.

2. Every other week, Mei's Kitchen will feature _____ (easy / Asian / new) recipes for you to try at home.

3. SNAP is a _____ (government / useful) food program for people who are out of work.

4. We went to the farmers' market in the city last Saturday and bought a lot of _____ (small / purple) potatoes.

5. The _____ (Thai / new) restaurant downtown has a _____ (rectangular / lovely) dining room area with _____ (red / beautiful) walls.

6. There were _____ (lovely / white) flowers in some _____ (glass / antique / tall) vases on the tables.

Exercise 4.2 More Order of Adjectives

A On a separate sheet of paper, write five sentences about things in the picture. Use two or three adjectives in each sentence. Choose adjectives from the box, or think of your own adjectives.

antique	large	silver
beautiful	long	small
clean	metal	square
cotton	oval	tall
delicious	rectangular	white
enormous	round	wooden

There are clean white napkins in the tall clear glasses.

B *Over to You* Think of a party or wedding that you attended. Write five sentences to describe the decorations and the food. Use two or three adjectives in each sentence.

Exercise 4.3 More Order of Adjectives

A ◄)) Listen to a restaurant review. Complete the sentences with the missing words. Pay attention to punctuation and adjective order.

Last week, we ate at Le Bambou, an _elegant new_ Vietnamese restaurant
                                                    (1)
in town. We ordered several _____ dishes. We highly
                                            (2)
recommend the _____ spring rolls. They were
                            (3)
a _____ appetizer, and they were perfect
                (4)
for the _____ evening. The main course
                    (5)
was a _____ chicken dish served with
                (6)
_____ vegetables.
                (7)
    We were especially impressed with Le Bambou's atmosphere. It has a

_____ dining room. The tables were covered
                (8)
with _____ tablecloths, and they were all lit by
                    (9)
_____ candles in _____
                (10)   (11)
holders. The walls were painted a lovely shade of blue, and the color gave the restaurant

a sense of calm. The serving dishes looked like _____
                                                                    (12)
antiques. There were _____ dragons on the plates.
                                    (13)
    All in all, Le Bambou was a _____ experience.
                                                    (14)

B ◄)) Listen again and check your answers.

C *Over to You* Choose a restaurant that you know. Write a review of the restaurant similar to the review in A. Share your sentences with a partner.

*Last month we went to the lovely, popular neighborhood restaurant called
Buon Appetito...*

5 | Avoid Common Mistakes ⚠

1. **When a noun modifies another noun and a number comes before it, use the singular form of the noun.**

   eight-year-old
   An ~~eight-years-old~~ child should be able to pronounce all of the ingredients.

2. **When a noun is followed by a prepositional phrase, the verb agrees with the noun, not the object of the preposition.**

   advertises
   The company behind these products ~~advertise~~ to young children.

3. **Do not make noncount nouns plural.**

   advice
   The author has ~~advices~~ for shoppers.

4. **Remember to use the plural form of count nouns.**

   vegetables
   These ~~vegetable~~ taste good when they are served raw with salad dressing.

Editing Task

Find and correct seven more mistakes in the paragraphs about children's eating habits.

   ten-year-old
   What does a ~~ten-years-old~~ child eat in a day? Specialists in nutrition is finding out
   that the news is not good. As a result, they are looking for ways to improve children's
   eating habit. They are also involved in trying to help families make healthier choice.

   Most experts suggest that a few key practices can help families. One of these
5 practices are common sense: people should eat unprocessed food. When there is a choice
   between canned corn and fresh corn, people should choose the fresh corn. Secondly,
   people should read labels carefully. Because labels contain a lot of informations, people
   should familiarize themselves with the nutrition and calorie content of their favorite
   products. Finally, people can boost the health content of certain kinds of food. For
10 example, it is possible to substitute whole-grain flours for white flour in most recipes.

   Parents and children live busy lives, but research shows that when a healthy child
   becomes a 40-years-old adult, that person can look forward to a healthy old age.

6 Grammar for Writing ✎

Using Precise Nouns and Adjectives to Make Your Writing Clearer

Using precise nouns and precise adjectives will make your writing clearer. For example, instead of using the general noun *people* to say what type of people you are writing about, instead use *adults*, *children*, *senior citizens*, or *students*. Read these examples:

Many <u>people</u> aren't aware of the nutritional value of food.
Many <u>Americans</u> aren't aware of the nutritional value of food.

Note that an easy way to be specific is to use adjectives, such as <u>young</u> adults, <u>middle-aged</u> people, and <u>sugary</u> desserts.

Pre-writing Task

1 Read the paragraphs. What kinds of changes is the writer suggesting? How many suggestions does the writer give?

Small Changes for Better Health

Doctors say that most of their overweight patients know that they would benefit from some lifestyle changes. However, many of these same patients are quick to tell their doctors about their own personal reasons for not making these changes. Overweight children may prefer to play indoors rather than go outside and play. Overweight adults

5 often say they are too busy at work.

Doctors and nutritionists have studied this problem. They have found that many overweight adults and children think they need to do a lot of vigorous exercise to get any benefit. This false belief discourages them, and so they end up doing nothing at all. Recent studies show that a little light exercise can help. Some suggestions for small changes

10 include parking the car at the far end of a parking lot or getting off the bus one stop early. Another practical suggestion is taking stairs instead of elevators. Doctors also suggest that when watching TV, people walk or run in place during the commercials. Another clever idea for working adults and busy teens is to stand up and walk around when using the phone. Big changes can be scary and overwhelming, but small changes are not, so it is

15 more likely that people will try them.

2 Read the paragraph again. Underline the nouns that refer to people. Which ones seem especially precise? Circle the adjectives.

Writing Task

1 *Write* Use the paragraph in the Pre-writing Task to help you write about a health problem or issue people have. What suggestions do you have for changes? You can write about one of these topics or use your own ideas.

- healthy or unhealthy eating habits
- healthy or unhealthy exercise habits
- healthy or unhealthy lifestyle habits (getting too little sleep, watching too much TV, etc.)

2 *Self-Edit* Use the editing tips to improve your paragraph. Make any necessary changes.

1. Did you replace any general nouns with precise nouns?
2. Did you use adjectives to make your nouns more precise?
3. Did you avoid the mistakes in the Avoid Common Mistakes chart on page 133?

UNIT
10

Articles and Quantifiers
Color

1 | Grammar in the Real World

A How does color affect your mood? Read the magazine article about the effects of color on mood. What is your favorite color? How does it affect your mood?

The Effects of Color on Mood

Research has shown that colors have **a** direct impact on our feelings. Therefore, it makes sense for people to surround themselves with colors
5 that make them feel good. Successful decorating depends on making **the** right color choices.

It is beneficial to choose colors that make people feel comfortable, happy,
10 relaxed, energized, or whatever mood is desired. Bright orange walls in **a** bedroom, for instance, may keep **a** sensitive person awake, whereas light blue seems to have **a** relaxing effect. Maya Romero of Omaha,
15 Nebraska, suffered from chronic insomnia. **A** friend suggested that **the** orange walls in her bedroom might be contributing to **the** problem. Maya listened to her friend's advice and painted **the** walls light blue. Since then, she has had much less trouble 20 sleeping.

Color affects moods in **a** variety of ways. Yellow is **a** cheerful, uplifting color for **most** people. However, strong shades of yellow can be overwhelming when used 25 for **an** entire room. Light yellow, on the other hand, can lift **a** person's mood like **a** room filled with sunshine. Similarly, green can revive **the** spirit. This may be because green reminds us of nature. 30

Typically, people experience **the** color blue as comforting. However, it is better to avoid using too much blue in one room. **A** room with blue walls and blue furniture can seem cold and overly formal. 35 Christopher and Marie Wang of Duvall, Washington, moved into **a** new home and painted **the** walls in their living room blue. Then they filled **the** room with furniture of varying shades of blue. They loved it, 40 but they noticed that conversation died when they sat in **the** room with guests. They asked advice from **a** decorator to see if **the** problem was related to **the** decor.

45 **The** decorator suggested that they replace their icy blue carpet with **a** carpet in warm colors, such as dark red or warm beige. She also recommended replacing their classic-style furniture with more comfortable
50 pieces. **The** Wangs report that, after they made **the** changes, **the** living room quickly became their favorite room for entertaining.

Clearly, **the** colors in an environment have **a** tremendous impact on **the** people who live or work there. Certain colors can 55 improve moods dramatically, while others can actually bring on feelings of sadness or loneliness. It is crucial to carefully consider color choices when decorating **a** living space or office. 60

B *Comprehension Check* Answer the questions.

1. Why is it important to choose colors carefully when decorating a room?
2. What advice did the decorator give to the Wangs?
3. What are some examples of color-feeling associations?

C *Notice* Find the words in the article. Then circle the meaning of each set of words within the context.

1. bright orange walls
   a. a group of walls in general   b. specific walls

2. the orange walls
   a. a group of walls in general   b. specific walls

3. a sensitive person
   a. one example from a category or group   b. something in particular that was previously mentioned in the text

4. the problem
   a. one example from a category or group   b. something in particular that was previously mentioned in the text

Can you make a generalization about the use of *a / an, the,* and no article?

2 Indefinite Article, Definite Article, and No Article

Grammar Presentation

The indefinite articles *a* and *an* and the definite article *the* come before singular count nouns. The definite article *the* can come before plural count nouns and noncount nouns.

*The color blue in **a** bedroom may relax people.*
*Choosing colors is **an** important part of decorating.*
The orange walls contributed to her insomnia.

2.1 Indefinite Articles: *A / An*

a. Use *a/an* before a singular count noun when the noun is part of a category or if it is a profession.

Blue is **a** color.
The power of color is **an** issue that many researchers study.
Her sister is **an** interior decorator.

b. Use *a/an* to introduce a singular count noun when you first mention it.

A room with blue walls can seem formal.
An orange bedroom can keep you awake.

c. Use *a/an* before a singular count noun to give definitions or make generalizations.

A decorator is a person who chooses colors and furniture for a room.
A yellow room is more cheerful than **a** blue room.

2.2 Definite Article: *The*

a. You can use *the* before singular count nouns, plural count nouns, and noncount nouns.

Where is **the** chair?
The salespeople are very knowledgeable.
The furniture in her house looks new.

b. Use *the* before a noun when you mention it a second time.

FIRST MENTION   SECOND MENTION
I took **an** interesting class. **The** class was about the effects of color on people's moods.

c. Use *the* when a noun gives more information about a previously mentioned noun. The second noun is associated with the first noun.

This is **a** good study on colors. **The** research makes

some good points.

That is **a** very interesting article. **The** information in it

explains a lot about the power of color.

d. Use *the* when the listener or reader can physically see or visualize the noun.

Push **the** button in front of you.
Your class is in **the** room just below this one.

e. Use *the* when the noun is unique.

The students are learning about **the** sun, **the** Earth, and **the** solar system.

f. Use *the* before a singular noun used to represent a whole class or category. This is very formal.

The male robin is more colorful than the female.

2.3 No Article

Use no article when a noncount noun or a plural count noun is used to make a generalization.

Research has taught us many things about the ways that we are affected by colors.
Colors can affect our moods.

Grammar Application

Exercise 2.1 *A/An* or *The*?

Complete the textbook excerpt about color theory. Circle the correct articles.
Sometimes more than one answer is possible.

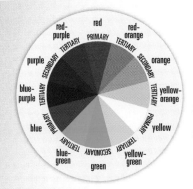

Color Theory

What is color theory? It is **a/the** tool and
(1)
a/the guide for understanding colors. There are
(2)
different versions of color theory, but in **a/the**
(3)
basic version, there are three primary colors.

A/The colors are blue, red, and yellow. As you
(4)
can see by looking at **a/the** color wheel, mixing equal parts of two primary
(5)
colors produces a secondary color. For example, if you mix blue and red,
you get purple. If you mix red and yellow, you get **a/the** color orange.
(6)

Tertiary colors are also created by mixing two primary colors. However,
to make **a/the** tertiary color, you use unequal amounts of two colors. By
(7)
doing that, you get colors like blue-green and yellow-orange.

Now, look at **a/the** color wheel again. **A/The** colors that lie opposite
(8)   (9)
each other on **a/the** color wheel are called complementary colors. For
(10)
example, **a/the** colors red and green are complementary colors. So are
(11)
a/the colors orange and blue. Look at **a/the** square below. It contains
(12)   (13)
a/the complementary colors red and green. Stare at it for 15 seconds,
(14)
then stare at **a/the** white wall or **a/the** piece of white paper.
(15)   (16)

Did you notice that the "ghost" image (the image
you see on the white wall or paper) has the opposite
colors? **A/The** green half of the square becomes red
(17)
and **a/the** red half becomes green. This is one
(18)
characteristic of complementary colors.

Exercise 2.2 A/An, The, or No Article?

A 🔊 Listen to the web article about color harmony. Write *a/an*, *the*, or Ø for no article.

Color Harmony

Some colors go together while some colors don't. Why? Is there a way to understand why some colors work better together than others? As many artists and designers know, <u>Ø</u> color harmony is based on _____ color theory.
(1)   (2)

Let's think about _____ ways color harmony works in a room. One main rule
(3)
of color harmony is that one color must be stronger than _____ other colors in
(4)
the room. In other words, one color must be more intense than the others or cover a larger area than the others.

Another rule of color harmony is that you should not put two very intense colors next to each other. For example, you should not have _____ bright red sofa on
(5)
top of _____ bright green rug. _____ human eye cannot focus on both
(6)   (7)
colors at the same time, and _____ colors may seem to vibrate.
(8)

A third rule of color harmony is that the colors in a room should be related to each other in some way. You can determine colors' relationships to each other by looking at _____ color wheel. Colors that are next to each other on the color
(9)
wheel, such as red and red-orange, will usually look good together. You can also put _____ complementary colors together. These are colors that are on
(10)
opposite sides of the color wheel, such as yellow and purple. Color triads go well together, too. These are three colors that are the same distance from each other on the color wheel. For example, _____ primary colors, red, blue, and yellow, form
(11)
a color triad. The secondary colors, green, purple, and orange, also form a color triad.

B *Over to You* What is your favorite color combination? Write five sentences describing why you like this color combination and describing things that you own in these colors. Use nouns with *a/an*, *the*, and no article in your sentences. Then share your sentences with a partner.

My favorite color combination is pink and orange. I like it because both colors are bright. I have a T-shirt with the colors pink and orange. The shirt was a gift from my sister. I also have a pair of pink and orange shoes.

3 | Quantifiers

Grammar Presentation

> Quantifiers are words such as *all* (*of*), *some* (*of*), and *a lot of* that describe an amount or number.
>
> **All of** the colors go well together.
> I have **some** information about colors.

3.1 Quantifiers with Count Nouns and Noncount Nouns

a. Quantifiers describe both large and small quantities or amounts. They are used with both count and noncount nouns.

More ↑
all (*of*)
many / a lot of
quite a few (*of*) */ a great deal of*
some (*of*)
a few (*of*) */ a little* (*of*)
few (*of*) */ little* (*of*)
not a lot of / not many (*of*) */ not much* (*of*)
Less ↓ *not any* (*of*) */ none of / no*

b. Use the following quantifiers only with count nouns:
quite a few (*of*), *few*, *a few* (*of*), *not many* (*of*)

Quite a few painters have studied at that art school.
A few painters shared the paint.
Few students have time for art classes.
Not many students have found a summer job.

c. Use the following quantifiers only with noncount nouns:
a great deal of, a little, little, not much (*of*)

We have **a great deal of** work to do.
I have **a little** information.
She has **little** patience.
There is **not much** time left to complete the work.

d. Use *a few* to say there are some but not many.

There are always **a few** students who want to major in art.

Use *few* for a very small number.

There are **few** scholarships for international students.

e. Use *a little* and *little* with noncount nouns.

Use *a little* to say there is some but not much.

I have **a little** money, so I can pay for it.

Use *little* for a very small amount.

I have **little** money. I don't have enough money.

3.2 Quantifiers That Are Used with Count Nouns and Noncount Nouns

The following quantifiers can be used with both count and noncount nouns:

COUNT NOUNS	NONCOUNT NOUNS
All of the <u>students</u> in my class work hard.	I gave him **all of** the <u>money</u>.
She used **a lot of** <u>colors</u> in her painting.	I don't have **a lot of** <u>time</u> today to study.
Most of the <u>answers</u> are clear.	I knew how to use **most of** the <u>software</u>.
Some of the <u>students</u> don't know a lot about art.	I painted **some of** the <u>time</u> while I was on vacation.
I did**n't** take **a lot of** <u>notes</u> in class.	He did**n't** have **a lot of** <u>help</u> on the project.
We do**n't** have **any** <u>solutions</u>.	They did**n't** put **any** <u>effort</u> into the job.
None of the <u>students</u> is absent.	**None of** the <u>work</u> is good.
There are **no** <u>excuses</u> for poor work.	That room has **no** <u>sunshine</u>.

3.3 Quantifiers and *Of*

a. Use a quantifier without *of* when a noun is used in an indefinite or general sense.

> **Some** students are late.
> I was interested in **a few** art classes.

b. Use a quantifier with *of* when the noun is specific and known to both the speaker and listener. Use *of* before a determiner such as *the, my, your, his, her, our, their, these,* or *those*.

> **Some of** <u>the</u> students at my school are very smart.
> **A few of** <u>the</u> activities in class require artistic ability.

c. The quantifiers *a great deal of, a lot of,* and *none of* always include *of*.

> **A lot of** people are interested in art.
> NOT A~~ lot~~ people are interested in art.

Grammar Application

Exercise 3.1 Quantifiers

A Complete the article about color blindness. Circle the correct quantifiers.

Color Blindness

Color blindness is a condition in which a person cannot see the difference between certain colors. **All of /Many** people think that color-blind people see
(1)
no /none colors at all and only see black and white. However, complete color
(2)
blindness is very rare. **Not much /Not many** people are completely color blind.
(3)
However, **many /much** people do have some degree of color blindness. A large
(4)
number of the men in the world are color blind. Very **few /little** women, however,
(5)
are color blind.

    A great deal of /Quite a few people who suffer from weak color vision have
(6)
red-green color blindness. They cannot tell the difference between red and green.
Think about the color purple. It is made up of two colors: red and blue. If you have
a little /a few red color blindness, and you look at a bright purple flower, you may
(7)
be able to see **a little /a few** red, but the flower will look almost blue. If you have
(8)
a more serious case of red color blindness, the flower may look completely blue to
you. You'll see **no /none of** the red at all.
(9)
    So why are some people color blind? We have red, blue, and green cones in our
eyes. You need to have **all /little** of the types in order to see colors correctly. If you
(10)
don't have **all /much** of the types of
(11)
cones, or if **few /some** of them are not
(12)
working right, you may see a red flower as
green or a green vegetable as brown.

    Look at this image. It is an Ishihara
plate. Ishihara plates are made up of
different-colored dots. Do you see a
number within the circle? If not, you may
have weak red-green color vision.

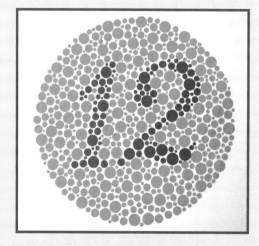

B *Pair Work* Work with a partner. Think about some activities (getting dressed, driving, watching TV, reading, using a computer) that people with color blindness might have trouble with. Write four sentences. Use different quantifiers in each sentence.

Many people with color blindness will have difficulty matching their socks.

Exercise 3.2 More Quantifiers

A Complete the report about car sales. Use the quantifiers in the box and the chart below. Use each quantifier only once. Sometimes more than one answer is possible.

| a great deal of | few | ~~little~~ | many |
| many of | most | no | quite a few |

Anderson Auto Sales
Percentage of Sales by Color 2010 & 2011

	White	Silver	Black	Grey	Red	Blue	Brown	Green	Yellow	Other
% of Total Sales 2011	23	19	14	15	3	7	9	5	1	3
% of Total Sales 2010	19	32	12	9	12	9	2	0	2	3

1. In 2011, there was _little_ demand for yellow cars.

2. In 2010, they had _____ success in selling green cars.

3. When Anderson Auto Sales created sales projections for 2012, they probably did not

   plan to sell _____ yellow cars.

4. _____ the cars sold in 2010 were white, silver, or black.

5. _____ of the cars sold in 2011 were white, silver, or black.

6. Compared to 2010, _____ the cars sold in 2011 were grey.

7. Compared to 2010, _____ customers favored red cars in 2011.

8. Compared to 2010, _____ customers bought brown cars in 2011.

B Rewrite five sentences from A using different quantifiers.

In 2011, there wasn't much demand for yellow cars.

1. _____

2. _____

3. _____

4. _____

5. _____

C *Over to You* Do Internet research to find out the most popular car colors this year or last year. Discuss your findings with a partner.

Exercise 3.3 ◄))) Using Quantifiers with *Of*

Listen to the interview with the students about changes to their school. Complete the sentences with *of* or ✗ when *of* is not used.

Changes at Bay City University

Mark Recently, our university hired some __✗__ interior designers and color
                 (1)
experts to redesign the interior of the library at Bay City University. I asked
a group of students at the college what they thought about this. Here's what
they said:

Josh Some __of__ my friends don't like it. They think the colors are too bright.
       (2)
Some _____ people don't like to study at the library because the bright
      (3)
colors make them uncomfortable.

Amy All _____ my friends love the new colors, but we know that some _____
     (4)   (5)
people don't like the color choices. You can never please all of the people
when you make a change, though.

Lynn A few _____ the people I know think it's great! They like being surrounded
      (6)
by a lot _____ bright colors. I think a few _____ students would probably
     (7)   (8)
prefer to have softer colors in the library, though.

Paulo None _____ my friends study in the library anymore. All _____ them study
      (9)   (10)
in the dorms because they don't like the colors in the library. But I like the
new design. There were no _____ students studying on the first floor of the
        (11)
library this morning, so I had the whole place to myself.

Exercise 3.4 More Quantifiers

A *Over to You* Interview some of your classmates. Have each student answer this question: *If you could make your room one color, which color would you choose and why?* Write the answers in the chart. Then write sentences about your classmates using quantifiers.

Name	Male (M) or Female (F)	Color
David	M	blue
Maria	F	beige (light brown)

Few of the male students chose blue. A lot of the female students chose beige.

B *Group Work* Share your sentences in a small group. What are the most popular colors for the women in your class? What are the most popular colors for the men in your class?

4 Avoid Common Mistakes

1. Do not use *much* with plural nouns.

many
We interviewed ~~much~~ interesting candidates, and we ended up hiring Ms. Stevens.

2. Use an article before a singular occupation.

an
I am‿assistant researcher.

3. Write *a lot* as two words.

a lot
I have ~~alot~~ of friends.

Editing Task

Find and correct six more mistakes in this paragraph about color and memory.

Color and Memory

According to recent research, natural colors can help people remember things better.

a
Felix A. Wichmann,‿research scientist, and two of his colleagues conducted experiments

on color and memory. In the first experiment, participants looked at 48 photographs

of nature scenes. None of the photographs were of people. Half of the photos were in

5 black and white, and half were in color. Afterward, they looked at the same 48 photos

mixed up with alot of new photos. They had to say which ones they had already seen.

They remembered the color scenes much better than the black-and-white ones. None of

the participants were sure about all of the photos. Another experiment involved much

artificially colored photos. When artificially colored photos were included in the set of

10 48 photos, participants forgot much of the photos. They did not remember the artificially

colored photos any better than they remembered the black-and-white photos. These

findings suggest that it is not just any colors that help to create alot of our memories. Only

natural colors have that power.

Why is this research important? For one thing, advertiser may find these results

15 interesting. If advertiser uses natural colors in ads, consumers may be able to remember

them better.

5 | Grammar for Writing ✎

Using Quantifiers and Pronouns to Hedge

Writers rarely use the absolute quantifiers *all*, *none of*, or *not any* or the pronouns *everybody*, *everyone*, *nobody*, or *no one* in academic writing. Instead, they use the quantifiers that fall between *all* and *none* in meaning, such as *little*, *many*, *not many*, and *quite a few*. They use these indefinite quantifiers to hedge, in other words, to indicate that the information is less certain because the writer knows that this information might not be true in all cases. Read these examples:

All people feel the effects of color without knowing it. (absolute quantifier)
People feel the effects of color without knowing it. (no quantifier)
Many people feel the effects of color without knowing it. (indefinite quantifier)

The first two sentences have the same meaning. The use of *many* rather than *all* or no quantifier in the third sentence makes the statement more likely to be true and more appropriate for academic writing.

Pre-writing Task

1 Read the paragraphs about color therapy. Do you believe that colors can heal?

Color Therapy

Many people agree that colors can affect the way we feel. But most of the time, we may not be aware of the effect. Colors can even cause physical reactions. For example, a person might feel cold in a room with blue walls. If that same room were painted red, the same person might feel warm. Because of these physical reactions, some people believe

5 that colors can heal. The use of colors to heal is called color therapy, or chromotherapy.

Only a few people believe in chromotherapy. Not many traditional scientists believe in it. In fact, quite a few of them call it a "pseudoscience," which means that it is not based on any real, proven science. These scientists also argue that colors have different meanings in different cultures, so the same colors are unlikely to have the same effect on

10 all patients. Furthermore, research has shown that the effects of a color are temporary. For example, people may feel happy while they are in a yellow room, but they will lose that feeling of happiness soon after they leave the room. The next time you feel warm or cold, happy or excited, look around you. Are colors affecting you?

2 Read the paragraphs again. Circle the use of *all*. Why does the writer use *all* here? Underline the quantifiers that describe a large or medium number. How does the meaning of each sentence change if you change these quantifiers to *all*? <u>Double underline</u> the quantifiers that describe a small amount.

Writing Task

1 *Write* Use the paragraphs in the Pre-writing Task to help you write about how colors affect people's lives. You can write about one of these topics or use your own ideas.

- color in advertising
- color in nature
- color in your home
- color in clothing
- color in video games
- color in your school

2 *Self-Edit* Use the editing tips to improve your paragraph. Make any necessary changes.

1. Did you use quantifiers to hedge?
2. Did you use quantifiers to avoid repeating yourself?
3. Did you avoid the mistakes in the Avoid Common Mistakes chart on page 147?

UNIT
11

Pronouns
Unusual Work Environments

1 | Grammar in the Real World

A What are the characteristics of a good workplace? Read the article about a unique workplace. How is this workplace unique?

The Company You Keep

Imagine **yourself** living the good life[1] and working at the same time. Employees of SAS do that every day. The SAS Institute is a software development firm[2] in North Carolina. In 2010 and
5 2011, it was number one on *Fortune* magazine's list of "Best 100 Companies to Work for in America."

In the late 1980s, SAS started giving its employees free candy. The perks[3] grew from there. There is now a long list of on-site services at SAS.
10 These include a fitness center, massage therapy, dry cleaning, and a beauty salon. **Anyone** can walk on the nature trails outside the offices at SAS and enjoy gourmet food in the cafeteria. The perks reduce distractions so **everyone** can focus on work. These innovations[4] also encourage employees to interact with **each other**.

The company benefits[5] are impressive as well. One benefit is a company child-care
15 center. **Another** is a free health care facility. For employees and their families, there is also counseling and support for issues such as parenting, financial planning, and stress management.

With a voluntary turnover rate[6] of only 2 percent, most employees seem satisfied with their jobs and are not considering leaving. This appears to show that the perks
20 and benefits are a success. While not all companies go to such extremes to keep their employees happy, it is clear that this strategy works well for SAS.

---

[1]**the good life:** a happy and contented life without financial problems | [2]**firm:** a company | [3]**perk:** a special, extra service that companies offer their employees, such as free or low-cost health club memberships | [4]**innovation:** something new or different | [5]**benefit:** a helpful service given to employees in addition to pay | [6]**turnover rate:** the percent of workers who leave a company

B *Comprehension Check* Answer the questions.

1. What are some of the perks that SAS gives its employees?
2. What are some reasons SAS gives its employees these perks?
3. What does the voluntary turnover rate at SAS seem to show?

C *Notice* Find the sentences in the article. What nouns do the words in bold refer to?

1. Imagine **yourself** living the good life and working at the same time.
2. **Another** is a free health care facility.
3. These innovations also encourage employees to interact with **each other**.

2 Reflexive Pronouns

▶ Grammar Presentation

Reflexive pronouns are used to talk about actions when the subject and object of a sentence are the same person or people. They are often used for emphasis to say that the action is performed by that person and nobody else.

We should enjoy **ourselves** at work.
Sue **herself** determines how she is evaluated.
(Sue determines this, not someone else.)

2.1 Forming Reflexive Pronouns

There is a reflexive pronoun for each subject pronoun.

I	*myself*	we	*ourselves*
you	*yourself*	you (plural)	*yourselves*
he	*himself*	they	*themselves*
she	*herself*		
it	*itself*		

2.2 Using Reflexive Pronouns as Objects

a. Use a reflexive pronoun when the subject and object of a sentence are the same.

SUBJECT   OBJECT
*They can get **themselves** treats during the workday.*

SUBJECT   OBJECT
*We introduced **ourselves** to the new staff.*

b. Use a reflexive pronoun after an imperative in which you are directly addressing the reader or listener. The implied subject of the sentence is *you.*

*Imagine **yourself** living the good life and working at the same time.*
*Give **yourselves** a day off!*
*Ask **yourself** if this company is right for you.*

c. Reflexive pronouns are often used with the following verbs:

be hard on	*She was always hard on **herself**.*
be proud of	*He was very proud of **himself** and his grades.*
believe in	*You have to believe in **yourself**. You can do it.*
blame	*They blamed **themselves** for what happened.*
enjoy	*We really enjoyed **ourselves** at the conference.*
feel good about	*Eating well helps you feel good about **yourself**.*
help	*Please help **yourselves** to some food.*
hurt	*I hurt **myself** carrying those heavy boxes.*
look at	*Look at **yourself** in the mirror.*
push	*She should push **herself** to work harder.*
remind	*He reminded **himself** to get to work early.*
see	*The company saw **itself** as an innovator.*
take care of	*Take care of **yourself**. You're working too hard.*
tell	*I tell **myself** that I am good at what I do.*

d. Use an object pronoun, not a reflexive pronoun, after prepositions when the meaning is clear without a reflexive pronoun. If the meaning isn't clear, use a reflexive pronoun.

*They took the candy home with **them**. (They couldn't take the candy home with someone else.)*
*I'm very proud of **myself**. (I could be proud of someone else.)*

▸▸ Verbs That Can Be Used Reflexively: See page A6.

2.3 Other Uses of Reflexive Pronouns

a. You can put the reflexive pronoun directly after a noun or pronoun for greater emphasis or at the end of the clause for less emphasis.

*The manager **herself** gave us candy. (more emphatic)*
*I interviewed the candidates **myself**. (less emphatic)*

b. Use *by* + a reflexive pronoun to mean "alone" or without help.

*I can work by **myself**, or I can work on a team.*
*John completed the whole project by **himself**.*

▶ Grammar Application

Exercise 2.1 Reflexive Pronouns

A Complete the statements about conditions at different companies. Circle the correct reflexive pronouns.

1. When the CEO and the head of Human Resources saw **himself /(themselves)** in the "100 Best Companies" article, they were surprised.

2. A pet cannot take care of **itself / ourselves** while its owner is on a business trip, so JM Corporation offers free pet care to its employees.

3. My company lets us take special days off, so I gave **itself / myself** a day off from work on my birthday.

4. The president helped to make the company a good place to work, so he was very proud of **herself / himself** when JM Corporation got the "100 Best Companies" award.

5. Susan and I own our company, so we can give **themselves / ourselves** a vacation anytime.

6. Before you go to your interview, you should ask **myself / yourself** why you want to work at JM Corporation.

7. Our new CEO introduced **ourselves / himself** to us at a meeting this morning.

8. Our manager said, "You and your team should congratulate **yourself / yourselves** . You all did a great job on the last project!"

B *Over to You* Answer the questions with information that is true for you. Use reflexive pronouns.

- How do you take care of yourself?

- What should people tell themselves before a job interview?

- Think about a time when a friend or family member felt good about himself or herself. What happened?

Exercise 2.2 Reflexive Pronouns as Objects

Complete the excerpt from the Careers page of a company website. Write the correct reflexive or object pronoun.

Work at JM!

Imagine _yourself_ working at JM Corporation! Read these comments from our
(1)
happy employees and their families:

Jane Recognition makes JM a great place to work. If we challenge

_____ and take on special projects, we get rewarded. Also,
(2)
I can give _____ a day off whenever I want.
(3)

Manuel We love the benefits, such as child care. My wife couldn't imagine

_____ leaving the twins all day while she worked. Now, she
(4)
takes the twins to work with _____ every day.
(5)

Lisa The work-life balance is great here. At JM Corporation, I never take my

work home with _____ . For example, I can get everything
(6)
done by Friday and enjoy _____ on the weekends. Just
(7)
ask _____ : If you could have all this and a great salary,
(8)
wouldn't you want to work here, too?

Exercise 2.3 Other Uses of Reflexive Pronouns

A Complete the sentences with reflexive pronouns. Use the information in parentheses to help you.

1. Bianca is a highly valued employee. She is able to handle difficult management crises

    by herself (alone).

2. Bianca _____ (emphasis) always takes responsibility for any problems on

    a project.

3. I _____ (emphasis) think she would be a good candidate for promotion.

4. Robert is on Bianca's team, but he prefers to work _____ (alone).

5. Only Robert _____ (emphasis) can learn to become a better team player.

6. Two other team members would also rather work _____ (alone).

7. Bianca recognized this issue and suggested team-building training

_____ (emphasis).

8. Only the employees _____ (emphasis) can fix this problem, in my

opinion.

B *Group Work* Ask and answer the questions with your group members. Use reflexive
pronouns. Then share your group's answers with the class.

- What kind of company do you imagine yourself working at someday?
- What kind of job do you see yourself doing someday?
- What kind of work tasks can you do by yourself?

*Paulo imagines himself working at a big international company someday. He sees
himself being the manager of a large group. He doesn't want to work by himself.*

3 Pronouns with *Other / Another*

Grammar Presentation

Another, others, the other, and *the others* are pronouns that refer back to a noun. *Each other* and *one another* are reciprocal pronouns. They are used when two or more people do the same thing.	Some employees are happy, but **others** are not. The fitness center is one benefit. **Another** is the dry-cleaning service. Employees help **each other**.

3.1 Pronouns: *The Other, the Others, Others, Another*

a. Use *the other* to describe the remaining member of a pair. Use *another* to describe an additional member of a group. It means "one more."	I have two favorite sports. One is swimming. **The other** is tennis. (There are only two sports.) Swimming is one of my favorite sports. **Another** is tennis. (There are more than two sports.)
Use third-person singular verb forms with *the other* and *another*.	One of my children goes to college and **the other** works.
b. Use *the others* for two or more remaining members of a specific group. Use plural verb forms with *the others*.	One of my children is in high school. **The others** are in college. (I have at least three children: the one in high school and at least two in college.)
c. Use *others* (without *the*) for additional members of a group or to contrast these members with previous ones. Use plural verb forms with *others*.	Some people without jobs look for work every day. **Others** look once a week. (Two contrasting groups of people.)

3.2 Reciprocal Pronouns: *Each Other, One Another*

a. *Each other* and *one another* are reciprocal pronouns. Use them when two or more people or groups do the same thing. There is no difference in meaning.

Each other is more common and more informal than *one another*.

The teacher and the student respect **each other**.

The teacher and the student respect **one another**. (The teacher respects the student. The student respects the teacher.)

The five employees in my company help **each other**.

The five employees in my company help **one another**. (Each employee helps the other four employees.)

Data in the Real World

Each other is more common than *one another* in conversation and academic writing. *One another* is slightly more common in academic writing than in conversation.

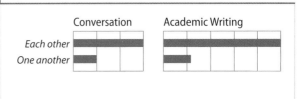

Reciprocal pronouns are less frequently used than personal pronouns (*I, you*, etc.).

▶ Grammar Application

Exercise 3.1 *The Other, the Others, Others, or Another?*

A Complete the article about the benefits at two companies. Circle the correct words.

Some Great Benefits

Vacation time is often a key benefit that attracts people to a company.

The others are/(Another is) child care. Although many companies today are cutting
(1)
these types of benefits, **others are/the other is** still providing them.
(2)
Two California companies offer great benefits for their workers. One is Amgen.

Others are/The other is Google. One of the benefits employees at Amgen enjoy is 17
(3)
paid days off and three weeks of paid vacation each year. **The others is/Another is** the
(4)
cafeteria. Many companies have on-site cafeterias, but **the others don't/the other doesn't**
(5)
tend to offer take-out breakfasts and lunches like Amgen does.

Free food is one of the perks that Google employees really love, and rightly so.

Another includes/Others include four gyms, free laundry machines, and on-site
(6)
doctors. Google also provides new parents with vouchers for take-out meals for three
months so they don't have to cook when they get home.

Some employees appreciate the free food and laundry services at companies like Google. **Others are / The other is** looking for long, paid vacations. When you are looking
(7)
for a job, be sure to consider the benefits offered by the company, and not just the salary.

B *Over to You* What benefits do you look for in a job? On a separate sheet of paper, complete the sentences. Then share your sentences with a partner.

There are two major benefits that I look for in a job. One benefit is

_____ . The other is _____ . There are

other benefits that I think would be nice. One is _____ . Others are

_____ and _____ .

There are two major benefits that I look for in a job. One benefit is health insurance.
The other is paid vacation days. There are other benefits that I think would be nice.
One is help with child-care costs. Others are flexible hours and a gym.

Exercise 3.2 *The Other, Another, Each Other, or One Another?*

Complete the information from a company website. Use *the other*, *another*, *each other*, or *one another*. Sometimes more than one answer is possible.

Do you want your employees to respect *each other / one another* ?
(1)
TeamBuilders has several programs to help you and your staff trust _____
(2)
more and work more productively together.

Read some of our reviews from our customers:

JM Corporation: My staff participated in five TeamBuilders activities, and we really

enjoyed them. One great activity was the Blindfold activity. _____ was
(3)
the "Say It Out Loud!" activity. With these activities, all 12 people on my team learned

how to communicate with _____ . Thanks, TeamBuilders, for giving us
(4)
the tools we need to help _____ get the job done!
(5)

Big Buy Stores: Our company did a couple of TeamBuilders activities. Even though we'd

only planned to do one activity called "Build-It," we had so much fun that we decided

to do _____ . We enjoyed both activities, but we preferred "Build-It" to
(6)
_____ activity.
(7)

4 Indefinite Pronouns

▶ Grammar Presentation

Indefinite pronouns (such as *everything, someone, anywhere, nobody*) are used when the noun is unknown or not important.

*The new boss wants to talk to **everybody.***
***Someone** is moving into our office.*

4.1 Using Indefinite Pronouns

a. Use *everybody, everyone, everything,* and *everywhere* to describe all members or things in a group. Use *everybody* or *everyone* for people. Use *everything* for things. Use *everywhere* for places.

***Everybody** loves working here.*
*Is **everyone** ready?*
*He knows **everything** about this company.*
*It seems you've looked **everywhere** for a job.*

b. Use *somebody, someone, something,* and *somewhere* to refer to an unnamed person, place, or thing.

***Somebody** is going to review our work today.*
*Can I ask you **something**?*
*I'd like to work **somewhere** really interesting.*

Use indefinite pronouns with *some-* in questions to offer things or ask for things.

*Would you like **something** to drink?*

c. Use *anybody, anyone, anything,* and *anywhere* to refer to an unnamed person, place, or thing.

*"Can **anybody** receive financial help here?"*
*"Sure. **Anyone** can ask for help."*
*Do you need **anything** from the cafeteria?*
*You can't take **anything** from this shelf.*
*Have they advertised the product **anywhere**?*
*I didn't go **anywhere** last night.*

Use indefinite pronouns with *any-* to ask questions and in negative sentences.

d. Use *nobody, no one, nothing,* and *nowhere* to mean "none" or "not one" in affirmative statements.

***No one** likes this company.* (= not one person)
*She said **nothing** important in the meeting.*
(= not one thing)
*There is **nowhere** I'd rather work.*
(= not one other place)

Grammar Application

Exercise 4.1 Indefinite Pronouns

Complete the interview between a career site and Ahn Nguyen, a corporate concierge for JM corporation. Circle the correct indefinite pronouns.

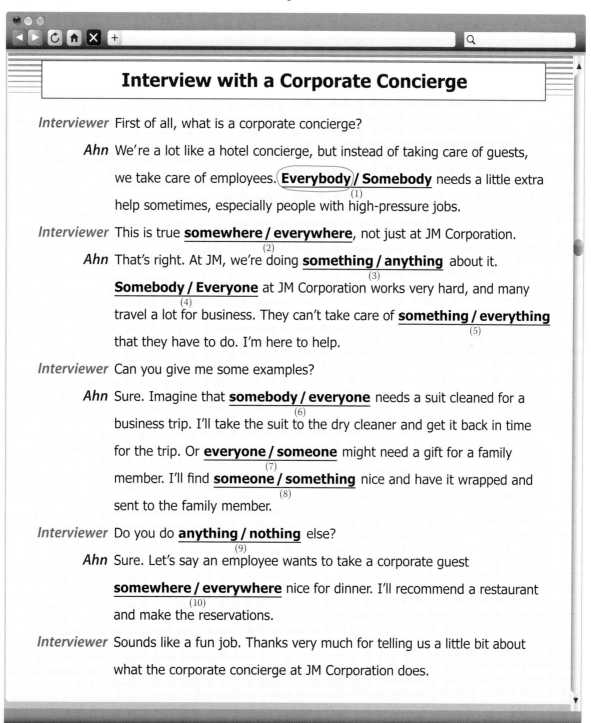

Interview with a Corporate Concierge

Interviewer First of all, what is a corporate concierge?

Ahn We're a lot like a hotel concierge, but instead of taking care of guests, we take care of employees. **Everybody** / **Somebody** needs a little extra
(1)
help sometimes, especially people with high-pressure jobs.

Interviewer This is true **somewhere** / **everywhere**, not just at JM Corporation.
(2)

Ahn That's right. At JM, we're doing **something** / **anything** about it.
(3)
Somebody / **Everyone** at JM Corporation works very hard, and many
(4)
travel a lot for business. They can't take care of **something** / **everything**
(5)
that they have to do. I'm here to help.

Interviewer Can you give me some examples?

Ahn Sure. Imagine that **somebody** / **everyone** needs a suit cleaned for a
(6)
business trip. I'll take the suit to the dry cleaner and get it back in time
for the trip. Or **everyone** / **someone** might need a gift for a family
(7)
member. I'll find **someone** / **something** nice and have it wrapped and
(8)
sent to the family member.

Interviewer Do you do **anything** / **nothing** else?
(9)

Ahn Sure. Let's say an employee wants to take a corporate guest
somewhere / **everywhere** nice for dinner. I'll recommend a restaurant
(10)
and make the reservations.

Interviewer Sounds like a fun job. Thanks very much for telling us a little bit about
what the corporate concierge at JM Corporation does.

Exercise 4.2 More Indefinite Pronouns

A Complete the conversation about vacations. Use *anyone, anything, anywhere, no one, nothing,* or *nowhere.*

Jane Are you going *anywhere* for your vacation this summer?
(1)

Adam No, we aren't doing _____ . We're too busy at this time of year.
(2)

_____ takes a vacation in the summer at my company.
(3)

Jane Wow! Does _____ complain about that?
(4)

Adam No. _____ complains because we get three weeks' paid vacation each
(5)

year. It's just that _____ can take it in the summer.
(6)

Jane Well, I wouldn't say _____ negative about that, either!
(7)

Adam What about you? Are you going _____ ?
(8)

Jane Well, _____ important happens at my company in the summer, so my
(9)

family is planning a two-week trip to the mountains. We went there last summer, too.

It's very beautiful and peaceful. There's _____ I'd rather be this summer
(10)

than in those mountains with my family.

Adam Sounds great!

B 🔊 Listen to a continuation of the conversation in A. Then answer the questions.

1. On average, how many paid vacation days do people in these places get?

   European Union: _____*25–30 days*_____

   Mexico: _____

   The United States: _____

   South Korea: _____

   Japan: _____

2. Where do people get the most paid vacation time? _____

3. Where do people get the least paid time off? _____

C *Pair Work* Ask and answer the questions with a partner.

• Are you going anywhere for vacation this summer?

• Did you go anywhere last summer? If so, where did you go?

• Are you doing anything special during your time off this year?

• Does everyone in your family take off work at the same time for vacation?

5 | Avoid Common Mistakes ⚠

1. Use the plural pronoun *others* when talking about two or more people or things.

others
Some managers value discipline; ~~other~~ believe in praise for good work.

2. Use the object pronoun to form the reflexive pronouns *himself, itself,* and *themselves*.

themselves
Valuable employees can solve problems ~~theirselves~~.

3. Indefinite pronouns with *any-*, *every-*, and *no-* (such as *anyone, everyone,* and *no one*) take singular verb forms.

gets
Everyone in the company ~~get~~ a performance review once a year.

Editing Task

Find and correct six more mistakes in the paragraphs about management styles.

Management styles can vary widely. At one end of the extreme are the authoritarian managers who make all the decisions and are very strict. At the opposite end, there

others
are ~~other~~ who permit their employees to solve problems and suggest ideas theirselves. Permissive managers are most effective when innovation and problem solving are part of

5 the work process, for example, in technology. Stricter ones are effective when people are inexperienced or need a lot of guidance, or where there is high turnover of staff.

Mr. Jones is an example of an authoritarian manager. He relies only on hisself to make decisions at the restaurant where he works. Everyone are expected to follow his orders exactly. His style works because employees are constantly changing, so nobody

10 need to understand the rules and regulations.

Ms. Taylor is more democratic. The agents at her real estate agency manage their client accounts theirselves. Some of her agents focus on business while other work with private real estate accounts. It would be impossible for her to know what each agent is doing at any given time, so Ms. Taylor's style works well for her company.

15 There are different kinds of management styles ranging from very controlling to very open. Effective managers have a style of managing that is appropriate to the needs of their companies.

6 Grammar for Writing

Using Pronouns for Emphasis and to Avoid Repetition

Using reciprocal pronouns helps explain the relationship between two nouns, and using pronouns such as *one* and *another* is a useful way for writers to avoid repeating a noun too often. These two kinds of pronouns make your writing clearer and help it flow better. Read these examples:

The employees appreciate the company's generosity. They often talk with <u>one another</u> about the benefits of working there.

One important benefit for employees is health insurance. <u>Another</u> is a discount on lunch in the company cafeteria.

Notice that in the second sentence of each pair, there is no confusion about what nouns the pronouns refer to. If there is any confusion, it is better to repeat the noun.

Pre-writing Task

1 Read the paragraphs. What are the three different rules that good teams follow?

Job Satisfaction

Job satisfaction means different things to different people. However, for many people, the most important thing is having good co-workers. For some people, working with employees they like and respect is crucial. These people feel the workday is much more pleasant when they enjoy the people around them. For others, having co-workers
5 they like and respect isn't enough. They want to be able to actually work cooperatively with other people. These people generally like to work with people who are good team players. Teams that work well follow important rules. One is that members must be able to communicate easily with one another. Another is that team members should be able to listen to each other. Finally, team members should be flexible enough to
10 compromise when they don't agree with one another.

On the other hand, there are people who work better alone. They don't want to have to deal with others all the time. They say it slows them down to have to explain themselves. They like to work with others who enjoy working alone, but who are supportive and friendly and like to talk once in a while. Whatever their preferred work
15 style, most people prefer working with people they like.

2 Read the paragraphs again. Circle the reciprocal pronouns. Draw arrows to the nouns the pronouns refer to. <u>Double underline</u> the reflexive pronoun. Is the reflexive pronoun there for emphasis or because it is an object of a sentence with the same subject?

Writing Task

1 *Write* Use the paragraphs in the Pre-writing Task to help you write about working with other people. This could be at work or at school. You can write about one of these topics or use your own ideas.

- problems with working alone
- problems with working with people
- tasks that are good to do in teams
- tasks that are better to do alone
- types of people you like to work with

2 *Self-Edit* Use the editing tips to improve your paragraph. Make any necessary changes.

1. Did you use *other*, *another*, *others*, and *the others* to refer to people and things?
2. Did you use reciprocal pronouns (*one another*, *each other*) to show that two nouns have a mutual relationship?
3. Did you use a reflexive pronoun when the subject and object in a sentence are the same?
4. Did you avoid the mistakes in the Avoid Common Mistakes chart on page 161?

UNIT 12 Gerunds

Getting an Education

1 Grammar in the Real World

A What can make attending college in the United States difficult? Read the web article about the cost of attending college. What are some ways to make college more affordable?

The Cost of U.S. Higher Education

In many countries, the cost of a college education is not very high. In France, for example, university students pay an affordable $220 a year. French students do
5 not have to **worry about paying** a lot for a college education because the government pays for it. In the United States, however, college tuition[1] is more expensive. Many students **have difficulty affording** it,
10 especially at private colleges[2] In 2010, the average cost per year of a private college in the United States was $35,000.

Public colleges[3] generally cost less because they depend on the government to help pay some of the expenses of education. However, if budget cuts reduce that money, tuition can increase.
15 This can **prevent** students **from attending** even a public college.

The tuition at community colleges is the least expensive, costing about $2,500–$3,000 a year. Community colleges offer two-year programs with an associate's degree.[4] Other colleges and universities offer four-year programs and a bachelor's degree.[5] **Not attending** a four-year college right away is one option students use to save money. Many students attend
20 a community college for the first two years of college and then transfer to a more expensive school for the last two years.

[1]**tuition:** the money students pay for education | [2]**private college:** a school that does not receive its main financial support from the government | [3]**public college:** a school that depends on some financial support from the government | [4]**associate's degree:** a two-year degree at a community college | [5]**bachelor's degree:** a four-year degree at a college or university

To help pay for college, many students apply for financial aid. Financial aid consists of loans, grants,[6] scholarships, and work-study programs. Students can apply for a student loan at a low interest rate. They must, however, **plan on repaying** the loan plus interest
25 after they graduate. Some students want to **avoid repaying** loans, so they apply for grants, which they do not have to repay. Scholarships are another form of financial aid that students do not have to repay. **Playing** a sport for a college team is one way to receive a scholarship. Finally, students can apply for work-study programs. In these programs, students work at jobs at their school and receive a small salary to help pay for expenses.

30 For students **interested in getting** a higher education in the United States, the cost can be high; however, there are ways to make it less expensive. Once students resolve the issue of money, they can **concentrate on having** the exciting experience of college life.

[6]**grant:** money that a university, government, or an organization gives to someone for a purpose, such as to do research or study

B *Comprehension Check* Answer the questions.

1. Why do public colleges cost less than private colleges?
2. What is the difference between a grant and a loan?
3. What are two ways students can reduce or eliminate tuition costs?

C *Notice* Find the sentences in the article and complete them.

1. French students do not have to worry about _____ a lot for a college education because the government pays for it.

2. Some students want to avoid _____ loans, so they apply for grants, which they do not have to repay.

3. _____ a sport for a college team is one way to receive a scholarship.

What do the missing words have in common? In which sentence(s) does the missing word act as a subject? In which sentence(s) does the missing word act as an object?

Gerunds as Subjects and Objects

Grammar Presentation

A gerund is the *-ing* form of a verb that functions as a noun. It can be the subject or object of a sentence.

Attending college is important these days.
I enjoy **learning**.

2.1 Using Gerunds as Subjects and Objects

a. Use a singular verb form when the gerund is the subject of the sentence.

Studying in the morning <u>is</u> difficult for me.
Completing my application <u>has</u> taken hours.

b. Use a gerund as the object after the following verbs:
Time: *delay, finish*
Likes and dislikes: *appreciate, dislike, enjoy, mind*

Effort and interest: *avoid, keep, practice*
Communication: *defend, discuss, propose*
Thinking: *consider, imagine, suggest*

I <u>finished</u> **working** on the project last night.
My sister <u>dislikes</u> **working** in a bookstore.
I <u>enjoy</u> **teaching**.
Practice **interviewing** with a friend.
<u>Discuss</u> **applying** for a loan with your parents.
He <u>considered</u> **transferring** to another school.

c. Use *not* before a gerund to make it negative.

Not attending a four-year college is one option for students with little money.

d. Do not confuse a gerund with the present progressive form of the verb.

PRESENT PROGRESSIVE   GERUND
I <u>am considering</u> **working** at home.

▶▌ Verbs Followed by Gerunds Only: See page A7.
▶▌ Verbs followed by Gerunds or Infinitives: See page A7.

▶ Grammar Application

Exercise 2.1 Gerunds as Subjects and Objects

A Students are commenting on the process of applying for college in the United States. Use the words to write sentences with gerund subjects and objects. Use the simple present for the main verbs.

1. complete the college application / take / a long time

   Completing the college application takes a long time.

2. find the money for college / be / a problem for me

   _____

3. my counselor / suggest / borrow money for college

   _____

4. not get into a good college / worry / me

   _____

5. I / enjoy / discuss my future plans with my friends

   _____

6. not have enough money for tuition / be / a concern

   _____

7. go to interviews at schools / make / me nervous

_____

8. teachers / suggest / start the application process early

_____

B *Pair Work* Discuss the gerunds in A with your partner. Which are subjects? Which are objects?

Exercise 2.2 Gerunds as Objects

A Complete the web article about tips for starting the college application process. Use the correct forms of the verbs in parentheses.

Tips for Getting a College Education

Do you want a college education? First,

consider looking (consider / look) for the
(1)

right college as soon as possible. If you are in

high school or attending community college,

_____ (keep / study)
(2)

hard so you'll have good grades. Some schools

require an essay on their college application. Many students in this position

_____ (dislike / write) the essay, but it's important, so
(3)

_____ (not delay / think about) it. Some schools require
(4)

an on-site interview, so _____ (practice / interview) with
(5)

your friends or family.

   Where will the money come from? Some students _____
(6)

(consider / pay) for college themselves. Other students _____
(7)

(not mind / borrow) money from their families, but not all families can afford to

pay for a college education. Sit down with your family, and discuss all the options.

_____ (discuss / work) at a part-time job while you go to
(8)

school, and _____ (imagine / work), studying, and adjusting
(9)

to a new lifestyle all at once. Is this really for you? If you think it is, then following

these tips will make the process easier.

B *Group Work* Answer the questions. Use gerunds in your sentences. Then share your ideas with the group.

- What should people in high school keep doing as soon as they decide to go to college?
- What should people consider doing when they need money for college?
- What should people try imagining before they make the final decision to go to college?

Exercise 2.3 More Gerunds as Objects

Use the words to write sentences about students and tuition costs. Use gerunds as objects and the present progressive form of the main verbs.

1. Jack / consider / go to a community college to save money

   Jack is considering going to a community college to save money.

2. Bo / think about / apply for financial aid instead of working

   _____

3. Jane / avoid / borrow money by getting a part-time job at school

   _____

   _____

4. My parents and I / not discuss / get a loan

   _____

5. Tom / not enjoy / work while he goes to college

   _____

6. My friend / delay / go back to school until he saves more money

   _____

   _____

7. Lisa and Henry / discuss / take part in a work-study program

   _____

   _____

8. Mei-ling / not consider / start college without a part-time job

   _____

   _____

9. Naresh / avoid / apply to too many different institutions

   _____

   _____

3 Gerunds After Prepositions and Fixed Expressions

► Grammar Presentation

The gerund is the only verb form used after prepositions and in certain fixed expressions.	*I **am interested in studying** art.* *I'm not **in favor of skipping** a year of college.*

3.1 Using Gerunds as Objects of Prepositions

Use a gerund as the object of prepositions after these common verb + preposition combinations:

Likes, dislikes, emotions: *be afraid of, care for, be excited about, be interested in, worry about* (or *be worried about*)	*Are you afraid of **failing**?* *Bryn is excited about **applying** to college.* *I worry about **not choosing** the right school.*
Interests and efforts: *be interested in, learn about, be responsible for, be successful at, take care of*	*Many students are responsible for **paying** their own tuition.*
Communication: *complain about, hear of, insist on, talk about, be warned of*	*Some parents complain about **having** more than one child in college at the same time.* *My friend insisted on **visiting** the school with me.* *Did anyone talk about **studying** together tonight?*
Thought: *be aware of, believe in, concentrate on, dream of, forget about*	*I believe in sometimes **staying** up all night to study for a test.* *My sister dreams of **winning** a scholarship.*
Blame and responsibility: *admit to, apologize for, confess to, be guilty of*	*We apologize for **not contacting** you sooner.*
Other: *apply for, depend on, plan on, be used to*	*I'm used to **taking** care of myself. I've lived alone for years.*

▸▸ Verbs + Prepositions: See page A9.

3.2 Using Gerunds with Common Fixed Expressions

a. Use a gerund after certain common fixed verb + noun expressions: *have a difficult time/have difficulty/have trouble, spend time/spend money, waste time/waste money*

She *had trouble* **finishing** her degree.
I *spent* a lot of *time* **helping** in the library.
Don't *waste time* **complaining**.

b. Use a gerund after certain common fixed noun + preposition expressions: *an excuse for, in favor of, an interest in, a reason for*

There's *no excuse for* **being** late.
He has *a reason for* **choosing** this school.

▸▸ Expressions with Gerunds: See page A8.

▶ Grammar Application

Exercise 3.1 Gerunds as Objects of Prepositions

A student is talking about his plans for going to college. Match the sentence parts.

1. Many students worry __*c*__
2. To pay for their education, they depend _____
3. I am very interested _____
4. I hope I will be successful _____
5. I'm not used _____
6. Fortunately, my parents want me to concentrate _____
7. They are planning _____

   a. in getting a college education.
   b. on applying for financial aid for me.
   c̶. about being able to afford college tuition.
   d. on receiving scholarships and loans.
   e. on having an exciting college experience and not worrying about finances.
   f. at getting into the school of my choice.
   g. to studying and working at the same time.

Exercise 3.2 More Gerunds as Objects of Prepositions

A Complete the presentation on grants. Use the correct prepositions for the verbs in bold and the gerund form of the verbs in parentheses.

I know many of you are **excited** _*about starting*_ (start) college soon. Also,
                                                            (1)

many of you are **worried** _____ (pay) for school. I'm sure you have been
                        (2)

warned _____ (take) out a lot of big loans. You have heard some people
            (3)

complain _____ (owe) money for the rest of their lives. Well, today, I'm
            (4)

going to **talk** _____ (apply) for three grants. Grants aren't loans. You
            (5)

aren't **responsible** _____ (pay) them back.
            (6)

The first type is the Pell Grant. The Pell Grant is for students who are going to college at least part-time and need financial aid. If you're **interested** _____ (ask) for a Pell Grant, **insist** _____ (talk) with a guidance counselor to find out more about this program.

(7)

(8)

Are any of you **planning** _____ (major) in the areas of science or mathematics? Then you might be **interested** _____ (try) for the National Smart Grant. **Forget** _____ (get) this grant unless you have maintained at least a 3.0 GPA in your first two years of college.

(9)

(10)

(11)

Finally, I know some of you are **dreaming** _____ (become) teachers. The TEACH Grant is for students who **plan** _____ (teach) at least four years in a low-income public or private school after graduation.

(12)

(13)

Now, are there any questions?

B Read about each person's situation and complete the advice. Use the words in parentheses with the correct preposition and the gerund form of the verbs.

1. Chelsea wants to be an engineer, but she doesn't have a 3.0 GPA. She should not
   depend on getting (depend / get) a National Smart Grant.

2. Michael has completed two years of community college, but he doesn't have enough
   money to go to a four-year college. He should not _____
   (be afraid / apply for) a Pell Grant.

3. Alison got a TEACH Grant, but she quit her teaching job after two years and got a
   high-paying job in computers instead. She must not _____
   (be worried / pay) back her loan.

4. Brandon goes to the community college, but he spends time partying and has a low
   GPA. He must not _____ (be interested / study).

5. Jorge got a TEACH Grant, taught for several years, and now is the head teacher at a
   private school. He must _____ (be successful / teach).

6. Sharon wants to major in computer science and get a National Smart Grant, but
   so far, her grades aren't that good. She should _____
   (concentrate / improve) her grades.

7. Rob's family can't help him pay for college, and he needs financial aid. He can probably
   _____ (depend / receive) a Pell Grant.

Exercise 3.3 Gerunds with Common Fixed Expressions

A Complete the conversations about college life. Use the correct forms of the fixed expressions in the box and the gerund forms of the verbs in parentheses.

(an) excuse for	have difficulty	in favor of	spend time
(an) interest in	have trouble	(a) reason for	waste time

Conversation 1

A I've heard some crazy _excuses for not handing in_ (not / hand in) papers.
(1)

B I don't think there's any good _____ (not / do) your
(2)
work once you're in college.

Conversation 2

A You _____ a lot of _____ (study). Does
(3)   (3)
it help?

B Yes, I would _____ (keep up) with my classes if I
(4)
didn't spend a lot of time studying.

Conversation 3

A A lot of people _____ (party) in college. What do you
(5)
plan on doing after you leave this school?

B I have _____ (get) a bachelor's degree, so I plan on
(6)
transferring to a four-year institution.

Conversation 4

A What type of student is the Joe Olinsky Foundation

_____ (give) grants to?
(7)

B We have money from a government fund that we use

for students who would otherwise _____ (afford) a
(8)
two-year college.

B 🔊 Listen and check your answers.

C *Group Work* Answer the questions. Use gerunds when appropriate. Then compare your sentences in your groups.

- What do you spend most of your time doing at school?
- What do you have the most trouble dealing with at school?
- What do you have an interest in doing after you leave this school?

Viet spends most of his time at school going to classes. I do, too. He has the most trouble dealing with parking. I have trouble dealing with the homework.

4 Gerunds After Nouns + *of*

▶ Grammar Presentation

Gerunds are often used after nouns + *of*.	**The cost of getting** an education is rising. I believe in the **importance of studying** hard.

4.1 Nouns + *of* + Gerunds

The following nouns are often used in noun + *of* + gerund combinations:

benefit of	A <u>benefit of</u> **going** to community college is cost savings.
cost of	The <u>cost of</u> **commuting** is rising because of gas prices.
danger of	There is a <u>danger of</u> **borrowing** too much money.
(dis)advantage of	What are some <u>disadvantages of</u> **taking** out loans for school?
effect of	The <u>effects of</u> **being** late are serious.
fear of	The <u>fear of</u> **being** jobless is what keeps me in school.
habit of	I'm in the <u>habit of</u> **not getting** up early.
idea of	The <u>idea of</u> **not going** to school is not an option.
importance of	It's impossible to underestimate the <u>importance of</u> **working** hard in school.
possibility of	The <u>possibility of</u> **not graduating** is worrisome.
problem of	The <u>problem of</u> **increasing** college costs affects a lot of students.
process of	He explained the <u>process of</u> **enrolling** in school.
risk of	She told me about the <u>risks of</u> **taking** out a loan.
way of	I'm thinking of a <u>way of</u> **paying** for school.

▶ Grammar Application

Exercise 4.1 Nouns + *of* + Gerunds

A Complete the conversations between Ms. Sparks, a community college counselor, and various families. Use the gerund form and the words in parentheses.

Conversation 1

Ms. Jones We are concerned about _the cost of paying_ (the cost / pay) for our
(1)
son's education.

Ms. Sparks I understand _____
(2)
(the fear / not be able to) afford college.

Ms. Jones Of course, I want my son to have _____
(3)
(the possibility / get) the best education there is, but it's expensive.

Conversation 2

Mr. Allen What are _____ (the advantages / go)
(4)
to a community college?

Ms. Sparks _____ (the benefits / attend) a
(5)
community college are numerous. It's especially helpful for students

who aren't sure of their major.

Mr. Allen Is there _____ (a possibility / get) in
(6)
this semester?

Ms. Sparks Yes, you can register today, if you like.

Conversation 3

Luisa _____ (the process / apply) to college is long!
(7)
Ms. Sparks I know it takes time, but you can reduce _____
(8)
(the risk / leave) something out by being organized. Here's a checklist to use.

B *Over to You* Write four sentences on a separate piece of paper about your family's and your thoughts about going to school. Use some of the noun + *of* expressions in the box with gerunds. Then share your sentences with a partner.

benefit of   effect of   habit of   idea of   possibility of   risk of   way of

One benefit of going to school when you are older is that you know what you want to do.

5 | Avoid Common Mistakes ⚠

1. Remember to use a gerund after a preposition.

getting
Students often worry about ~~get~~ into college.

2. As a general rule, when you use a verb as a subject, use a gerund.

Paying
~~Pay~~ for a private college can be very expensive.

3. Always use a singular verb with a gerund subject.

is
Interviewing at several colleges ~~are~~ time-consuming.

Editing Task

Find and correct seven more mistakes in the paragraphs about study habits.

studying
All students start the semester with the intention of ~~study~~ hard; however, find time to study can be challenging. Finding good places to study are one challenge. Another is finding enough hours in the day and creating a schedule. Successful students face these problems realistically.

5   Different people have different purposes and needs when it comes to doing college work. Study in a quiet library works well for some people. At the same time, a coffee shop or cafeteria can also be a good place to work for those who get energy from be in a stimulating environment.

     Then there is the question of time. Most students today are working, paying bills, 10 and taking classes at the same time, so they do not have the luxury of spend many hours with their books. However, research offers hope. Studying for a few minutes several times a day are a good way to learn new material.

     Learn what works for you is the key to academic success.

6 | Grammar for Writing

Using Noun + *of* + Gerund Constructions

Noun + *of* + gerund constructions are common in academic writing. These constructions can make your writing sound clearer and more precise. Read these examples:

A lot of learning can take place in the <u>process of making</u> mistakes.
The teachers tried to teach the <u>importance of getting</u> enough sleep before taking a test.

Pre-writing Task

1 Read the paragraphs. What type of student are the paragraphs about? How many advantages and disadvantages are listed?

Completing a College Degree

Many students at community colleges do not go to school full-time because the cost of getting a degree requires them to work while they are in school. There are both advantages and disadvantages of getting a degree while working. The disadvantages may be more obvious. First, students have to balance work, class, and homework. This can be

5 particularly difficult to do sometimes. Also, students can face the danger of losing interest. It can be hard to maintain interest in something that takes a very long time to complete. Another potential problem is that some classes are only offered at specific times. Students may not be able to change their work schedules to fit these classes into their schedules.

However, there are some advantages, too. Working students can usually finish their

10 studies without having any loans to pay back. Some employers might also help their employees with their educational fees. In addition, working students sometimes have the possibility of using what they learn in class at work. The experience of working and going to school at the same time can be difficult, but there are some important advantages of being a part-time working student, too.

2 Read the paragraphs again. Underline the noun + *of* + gerund constructions. Notice which of these gerund constructions are subjects and which are objects.

Writing Task

1 *Write* Use the paragraphs in the Pre-writing Task to help you write about the advantages and disadvantages of one aspect of being a student. You can write about one of these topics or use your own ideas.

- returning to school as an adult
- taking morning/afternoon/evening classes
- being in a big class or small class
- working on or off campus
- doing your homework in the evening or in the morning

2 *Self-Edit* Use the editing tips to improve your paragraph. Make any necessary changes.

1. Did you use gerunds as both subjects and objects?
2. Did you use any noun + *of* + gerund constructions?
3. Did you use any verb + preposition + gerund constructions?
4. Did you avoid the mistakes in the Avoid Common Mistakes chart on page 175?

UNIT

13

Infinitives

Innovative Marketing Techniques

1 | Grammar in the Real World

A What are some unusual types of advertising that you have noticed recently? Read the article on "guerrilla marketing." How do advertisers measure the success of a guerrilla marketing campaign?

Advertising, Guerrilla Style

Would you tattoo a website address on your body? One woman from Utah did just that. A company **got her to tattoo** its website address on her forehead for $10,000. She **wanted to do** it to raise money for her son's education. The company **wanted her to do** it for cheap advertising space. They also got free publicity[1] because the story was
5 on the news. This kind of extreme advertising – known as guerrilla marketing – uses surprising ways to advertise a product and get people's attention.

A **way to advertise** with guerrilla marketing is **to use** the environment in an unexpected way. For example, a few years ago, a popular candy company painted park benches so that they looked like giant chocolate bars. This creative ad[2] strategy got
10 consumers' attention in a positive way.

For guerrilla marketing to be successful, people must talk about the ads. In the 1990s, the company Half.com **persuaded** the town of Halfway, Oregon, **to change** its name to Half.com. People all over the United States heard about Half.com, and soon thousands of consumers went to the website.

15 Not all guerrilla marketing works. In 2007, an ad company **decided to place** signs with flashing lights around different cities to advertise a television show. However, in Boston, the police thought the signs were bombs. The police **tried to find** and **destroy** all of the signs.

Unlike those who use traditional advertising strategies, guerrilla marketers are not
20 **afraid to shock** people. The idea is to **convince people to talk** about the products. However, it is **important** for companies **to consider** how people will react. Not all publicity is always good publicity.

[1]**publicity:** the attention received as a result of an activity meant to attract interest | [2]**ad:** advertisement; advertising

178

B *Comprehension Check* Answer the questions.

1. What is guerrilla marketing? What is the purpose of guerrilla marketing?
2. How does guerrilla marketing get people's attention?
3. How is it different from traditional advertising?

C *Notice* Find the sentences in the article and complete them.

1. She wanted _____ it to raise money for her son's education.

2. The police tried _____ and destroy all of the signs.

3. A way to advertise with guerrilla marketing is _____ the environment in an unexpected way.

What do all the verbs you wrote have in common? Look at the words that come before these verbs. What kinds of words are they?

2 | Infinitives with Verbs

Grammar Presentation

An infinitive is *to* + the base form of a verb. Some main verbs in a sentence are followed by an infinitive, not a gerund.	*I decided **to learn** about advertising.* *The company planned **not to use** traditional advertising.*

2.1 Verbs + Infinitives

Use an infinitive after the following verbs: Time: *hesitate, wait* Likes or dislikes: *care* Plans or desires: *decide, hope, need, plan* Efforts: *attempt, help, learn, manage*	*We hesitated **to use** guerrilla marketing.* *I don't care **to see** boring ads on TV.* *The company is hoping **to buy** advertising space.* *Guerrilla marketers attempt **to get** your attention.*
Communication: *agree, offer, promise* Possibility: *appear, seem, tend*	*Our company promised **not to waste** money.* *Guerrilla ads tend **to shock** consumers.*
Use *not* before the infinitive to show the infinitive is negative.	

▶◀ Verbs Followed by Infinitives Only: See page A7.

2.2 Verbs + Objects + Infinitives

a. After some verbs, an object comes before the infinitive. The object performs the action of the infinitive. The following verbs are followed by an object + infinitive: *advise, allow, convince, encourage, get, persuade, prepare, teach, tell, urge,* and *warn.*

VERB + OBJ + INF
He <u>got us</u> **to try** a new advertising technique.
The company didn't <u>tell the salespeople</u> **to educate** consumers.
They <u>urged the advertisers</u> **not to surprise** people.

b. Some verbs can be followed by either an object + infinitive or an infinitive only. These verbs include *ask, choose, expect, help, need, promise, want,* and *would like.*

VERB + OBJ + INF
My department <u>chose Sally</u> **to create** the new ads. (Sally will create the ads.)
VERB + INF
My department <u>chose</u> **to create** the new ads. (My department will create the ads.)

▸▸ Verbs + Objects + Infinitives: See page A8.

Research shows that these are the most common verbs + infinitives in academic writing:

appear, begin, continue, fail, seem, tend, try, want	Sales of the new product **continued to rise** last month. The boss **failed to recognize** the company's problems.

▶ Grammar Application

Exercise 2.1 Verbs + Infinitives

Complete the online homework assignment about guerrilla marketing with the correct forms of the words in parentheses. Use the simple present form of the main verbs.

Guerrilla Marketing 101

Guerrilla marketing _attempts to reach_ (attempt/reach) consumers
(1)
in unexpected or unusual contexts, such as public places. Guerrilla marketers

_____ (hope/shock) or surprise potential consumers.
(2)
Why is guerrilla marketing so popular? One reason for this is that it

_____ (tend/cost) less than traditional marketing. Guerrilla
(3)
marketing usually _____ (manage/generate)
(4)

a lot of publicity for little money. It _____ (seem/be)
(5)

effective for most products; however, several experts think that people are getting

tired of it. I _____ (hesitate/admit) this, but I agree.
(6)

Exercise 2.2 Verbs + Objects + Infinitives

A Complete the conversation about a nontraditional type of advertising called reverse graffiti. Use the words in parentheses. Use the correct form of the main verbs according to the context.

Dae Ho Our advertising consultants _are advising us to try_ (advise / us / try) a type of
(1)
guerrilla marketing called reverse graffiti.

Erin What's reverse graffiti?

Luis It's a way to write an image on a dirty public surface by removing the dirt. It

_____ (get / consumers / notice) a product.
(2)
Do you think the managers will like the idea?

Erin Actually, I think the managers will _____
(3)
(tell / us / not do) it.

Dae Ho Why? I think we can probably _____
(4)
(convince / them / try) it because it's cheap.

Luis I bet we can _____ (persuade / them / do) it.
(5)

Dae Ho OK. We'll need help though.

Luis I'll _____ (tell / Mike / create) a presentation.
(6)

Erin OK, Luis, but you should _____
(7)
(warn / him / prepare) for a lot of questions. Some people think it destroys property,

so it's vandalism. It might not be legal.

B *Over to You* Answer the questions with information that is true for you. Include the verbs from A in your answers. Then share your sentences with a partner.

- What is your opinion of guerrilla marketing?
- Does it work for you and your demographic (that is, people who are your age and have similar likes and dislikes)? Why or why not?

Guerrilla marketing tends to work well with people my age because my generation likes innovative ideas.

Exercise 2.3 Verbs + Infinitives and Verbs + Objects + Infinitives

Complete the report on quick response (QR) codes.[1] Use the words in parentheses with the simple present or simple past form.

Last week, Steve Green *asked me to look into* (ask/me/look into) QR
                                                    (1)
codes, so I decided to interview people who use QR codes for marketing. One

way companies use QR codes is through smartphones. Consumers point their

smartphones at QRs, and the code takes them immediately to a company or product website.

I _____ (choose/interview) two different people. Steve
                   (2)
_____ (urge/me/interview) the manager from Dan's Gourmet
                   (3)
Food for this report because his company uses QR codes. Dan said the QR codes

_____ (help/inform) consumers about the nutritional content of
                   (4)
the product and _____ (help/them/use) the product correctly.
                            (5)
Dan also _____ (want/consumers/find out) about
                         (6)
new products, so the QR code contains a link to Dan's company's website. The QR code

_____ (promise/become) an important marketing tool.
                   (7)
After I interviewed the manager from Dan's, I _____
                                                            (8)
(prepare/visit) Liz Kurikova, the owner of a small flower shop. She was unable to meet

with me this week, but she _____ (encourage/me/contact)
                                       (9)
a friend of hers who runs a small ice cream shop. I spoke with Ned Searby at Astoria

Ice Cream. Currently, they _____ (not need/offer) this
                                       (10)
option to their customers. Once they start selling other products, however, they

_____ (expect/include) QR codes for products on the shelves.
              (11)
They _____ (would like/use) this technology to expand their
              (12)
business and promote their new products.

[1]**QR code:** an image like a bar code on products that contains links to text, web addresses, and other types of information

3 | Infinitives vs. Gerunds

▶ Grammar Presentation

Some verbs can be followed by an infinitive or a gerund. Much of the time, the meaning is the same or very close, but sometimes there is a difference in meaning.	The woman **stopped to read** the ad. (The woman saw the ad as she was walking and stopped. She read the ad.) *The woman **stopped reading** the ad.* (The woman was reading the ad. Then she stopped.)

3.1 Similar Meanings of Infinitives vs. Gerunds

After some verbs, you can use either a gerund or an infinitive without any change in meaning. Verbs that can be followed by either an infinitive or a gerund include *begin, can't stand, continue, hate, like, love, prefer,* and *start*.	Broadcasters <u>love</u> **to get** free publicity. Broadcasters <u>love</u> **getting** free publicity.
When *begin, continue,* or *start* are in a progressive form, use an infinitive.	I'm <u>beginning</u> **to work** on the assignment now. NOT *I'm beginning ~~working~~ on the assignment now.*

3.2 Different Meanings of Infinitives vs. Gerunds

a. The following verbs can be followed by either an infinitive or a gerund, but the meaning is different:

INFINITIVES	GERUNDS
Did you <u>forget</u> **to tell** your secretary you'd be late today? (You never told your secretary.)	Did you <u>forget</u> **telling** your secretary you'd be late today? (You told your secretary, but you do not remember it.)
I <u>regret</u> **to tell** you that our sales have dropped. (I'm sorry that our sales have dropped, but I'm telling you about it.)	I <u>regret</u> **telling** you that our sales have dropped. (I told you our sales had dropped, but I wish I hadn't.)
They <u>remembered</u> **to e-mail** the sales figures. (They almost forgot, but then they sent the e-mail.)	They <u>remembered</u> **e-mailing** the sales figures. (They sent the e-mail. Later, they thought about it again.)
People <u>stopped</u> **to look** at the colorful signs. (People stopped and looked at them.)	People <u>stopped</u> **looking** at the colorful signs. (People were looking at them but then stopped.)
The mayor <u>tried</u> **to change** the town's name, but the citizens didn't want to. (This was an experiment to see if he could do it. The mayor didn't succeed. He couldn't change the name.)	The mayor <u>tried</u> **changing** the town's name, but it didn't help tourism. (The mayor made an effort to do this, and he succeeded. He changed the name.)

b. Note that the meaning of *tried* is only different in the past.

I *tried* **to pay** with a credit card, but the store only accepted cash. (I wanted to pay with a credit card, but they wouldn't let me.) ≠ I *tried* **paying** with a credit card, but I didn't like it. (I did pay with a credit card.)	I will *try* **to call** you tomorrow. = I will *try* **calling** you tomorrow. (= Tomorrow I plan to call you, but it may not work.)

▸▸I Verbs Followed by Gerunds or Infinitives: See page A7.

▶ Grammar Application

Exercise 3.1 Meanings of Infinitives vs. Gerunds

A Rewrite the sentences about paying people to promote products through social media. Replace the infinitives in bold with gerunds. Replace the gerunds in bold with infinitives. Then label the sentence *S* (if the meaning is the same) or *D* (if the meaning is different).

1. Companies have begun **to pay** people to blog about their products.

   Companies have begun paying people to blog about their products.   *S*

2. LP Social Friends regrets **to tell** the media that they pay people to be "friends."

   _____   ____

3. I stopped **to read** the article about social media marketing.

   _____   ____

4. Alison forgot **mentioning** GamerWorld in her blog yesterday.

   _____   ____

5. Upside Energy Drinks continues **to pay** fans on social networking sites.

   _____   ____

6. People have started **questioning** Upside Energy Drinks' marketing strategy.

   _____   ____

7. A lot of people can't stand **reading** blogs that are full of ads.

   _____   ____

8. GamerWorld tried **to pay** me to write about them in my blog.

   _____   ____

9. I tried **changing** the privacy settings since I don't want messages from advertisers.

   _____   ____

B *Pair Work* In which sentences in A does the meaning change? Explain the difference in meaning to a partner.

Exercise 3.2 Infinitive or Gerund?

A ◀)) Listen to a discussion of the results of a focus group.[1] The focus group watched a reality TV show called *Jake's Life* and tried to remember a product that they saw in the show. Match the sentence parts.

1. Bo regrets   *e*
2. Bo tried _____
3. Jocelyn doesn't regret _____
4. Participant 1 stopped _____
5. Participant 2 stopped _____
6. Participant 3 didn't remember _____
7. Nobody forgot _____
8. Jocelyn told Bo _____

a. to push the button when Jake drank soda.
b. to get a snack.
c. to stop reading.
d. seeing Jake drink anything.
e̸. to say that the product placement isn't working.
f. watching after the third episode.
g. doing things differently this time.
h. hiring Bo.

[1] **focus group:** a group of people whose opinions help marketers

B ◀)) Listen again and check your answers.

4 Infinitives After Adjectives and Nouns

▶ Grammar Presentation

Infinitives can also follow some adjectives and nouns.	The consumers were **happy to see** some interesting advertising. The advertisers needed more **time to educate** the community.

4.1 *Be* + Adjectives + Infinitives

Use infinitives after the following adjectives: *afraid, amazed, difficult, easy, embarrassed, fun, interesting, lucky, necessary, ready, sad, shocked, sorry, surprised, (un)likely, upset.*	Some companies are <u>afraid</u> **to use** new marketing techniques. The police were <u>ready</u> **to destroy** the ads. The advertisers were <u>sorry</u> **to cause** a problem.
It + be is frequently used with many of these words.	<u>It would be fun</u> **to surprise** people with guerrilla advertising.

▸▸ᴵ *Be* + Adjectives + Infinitives: See page A9.

4.2 Nouns + Infinitives

Use infinitives after the following nouns: *ability, chance, decision, time, way.*	Some ads have the <u>ability</u> **to excite** the public. It was a great <u>chance</u> **to learn** something new. It's <u>time</u> **to be** more creative in advertising.

▶ Grammar Application

Exercise 4.1 *It* + *Be* + Adjective + Infinitive

Complete the article about tracking technology. Use the adjective + infinitive combinations in the box.

difficult / avoid	fun / go	necessary / use	~~surprising / know~~
easy / acquire	interesting / read	shocked / find out	unlikely / change

Who is watching you as you visit Internet pages? It may be

<u>*surprising to know*</u> that advertisers are following you as you surf the
(1)

Web. Many Internet users would be _____ how much
(2)

companies know about them through tracking technology such as cookies,

which allow websites to identify visitors and their web page preferences.

Today, because of tracking technology, it is _____
(3)

data on people's habits and tastes. Most websites have this technology,

so it is _____ . Companies believe that it is
(4)

_____ tracking because it helps consumers find out
(5)

about products that they like.

Here is an example of what companies can learn through tracking.

Maria thinks it is _____ to websites and comment
(6)

on movies she has seen. She also thinks it is _____
(7)

about health issues on several sites. She notices that ads pop up on topics

that she has done searches on, but she is _____ her
(8)

search habits because of this.

Exercise 4.2 Nouns + Infinitives

Complete the conversations about using nontraditional marketing. Use the words in parentheses to write sentences.

1. *A* We're going to do a survey on how well guerrilla marketing really works.
   B (that / be / a good way / get / information)

   That's a good way to get information.

2. *A* Our survey shows that product placement isn't working.
   B (it / be / time / do / something different now)

   _____

3. *A* Are you going to use QR codes or reverse graffiti?
   B (we / make / the decision / use / QR codes / yesterday)

   _____

4. *A* Why should I hire your advertising agency?
   B (we / have / the ability / attract / the 18- to 24-year-old demographic)

   _____

5. *A* Why are you considering paying sports bloggers to write about your product?
   B (it / be / a chance / introduce / our product to athletes)

   _____

6. *A* Why doesn't guerrilla marketing work, in your opinion?
   B (it / not / be / the best way / get / messages across / to older demographics)

   _____

7. *A* Why is the character holding the soda can so we can see the brand?
   B (it / be / a chance / sell / the product to viewers)

   _____

Exercise 4.3 Using Infinitives After Adjectives and Nouns

Group Work Think about the different types of marketing below. Evaluate each strategy in terms of how it works with children, teens, adults, and seniors (people over age 65). Compare and discuss your ideas with your group members. Use an infinitive + adjective and noun in each statement.

Guerrilla marketing may not be an effective way to attract seniors because it may be too shocking for some of them.

- Traditional advertising (TV commercials, magazine ads)
- Guerrilla marketing
- Product placement (placement of products in movies and TV shows)
- Viral marketing (paying bloggers and people with social networking sites)

5 | Avoid Common Mistakes

1. With the verb _want_, use verb + object + infinitive, not verb + _that_ clause.

The advertisers want ~~that~~ you $_\wedge$ buy their products. *[to]*

2. Use the correct word order when using the negative form of an infinitive.

The company decided $_\wedge$ to ~~not~~ pay bloggers to write about their products. *[not]*

3. Do not confuse the preposition _to_ with an infinitive _to_.

PREP + GERUND

I look forward to ~~see~~ the new dragon movie. *[seeing]*

VERB + INFINITIVE

Many people like to ~~seeing~~ familiar places and objects in a movie. *[see]*

4. Use an infinitive (_to_ + the base form of verb), not _for_ + base form of verb, where appropriate.

It is important ~~for~~ make sure the advertisement targets the right audience. *[to]*

Editing Task

Find and correct the mistakes in the paragraphs about advertising in movies.

Product placement in movies is a type of advertising that is popular today. Advertisers want ~~that~~ consumers $_\wedge$ see their products in movies so that their products will *[to]* seem more appealing. That's why advertisers pay filmmakers for place their products in movies. For example, in one movie, a director arranged to using a pair of famous

5 brand-name sunglasses for make his characters appear fashionable. In another movie, the plot required a certain type of luxury car. The filmmakers used the car in their film, but in this case they did not receive any money from the auto's manufacturers. For the automaker, it was an easy way to not pay for advertising. Filmmakers seem to not mind the advertising because they can earn extra money. Moviegoers do not seem to mind it, either.

10   In my opinion, product placement in movies is acceptable, but I want that advertisers use product placement carefully. If directors expect to making a film that is believable, then everything in the film must fit the story. Otherwise, the movie will seem more like an advertisement. This would be terrible. I hope that filmmakers continue to making wise decisions and use products that look natural on screen.

6 Grammar for Writing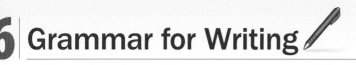

Using Verb + Infinitive and Adjective + Infinitive Constructions

Writers often use verb + infinitive and adjective + infinitive constructions in academic writing. Read these examples:

All advertising agencies <u>attempt to find</u> new ideas that will get the attention of consumers. At one time, it was <u>inappropriate to say</u> the name of your competitor in an ad.

Pre-writing Task

1 Read the paragraph. Are the advertising techniques discussed in the paragraph creative or not creative? Why do advertising companies continue to use them?

Tried and True Advertising Techniques

There are many new kinds of advertising techniques, such as guerrilla advertising and reverse graffiti, but it is wrong to think that the old techniques are gone. Advertising companies continue to use many of them. For example, ads have appeared inside buses and subways for a long time. They are effective because they give people on buses and subways something to look at, and the ads are inexpensive. Creativity with these ads is not necessary to grab the audience's attention. These techniques appear to be effective for certain products and in certain environments. However, if a company wants its ads to be very creative, these techniques are unlikely to be the answer.

2 Read the paragraph again. Underline the verb + infinitive constructions. Can any of these infinitives be changed to gerunds? If so, does the meaning change? Circle the adjective + infinitive and noun + infinitive constructions.

Writing Task

1 *Write* Use the paragraph in the Pre-writing Task to help you write about advertising techniques. You can write about one of these topics or use your own ideas.

- advertising techniques that appeal to you
- new advertising trends that you've seen
- advertising techniques that don't appeal to you
- T-shirt advertising and other free strategies

2 *Self-Edit* Use the editing tips to improve your paragraph. Make any necessary changes.

1. Did you use verb + infinitive constructions and adjective + infinitive constructions?
2. Did you include objects before infinitives when necessary?
3. Did you avoid the mistakes in the Avoid Common Mistakes chart on page 188?

Appendices

1. Irregular Verbs

Base Form	Simple Past	Past Participle	Base Form	Simple Past	Past Participle
be	was / were	been	hide	hid	hidden
become	became	become	hit	hit	hit
begin	began	begun	hold	held	held
bite	bit	bitten	hurt	hurt	hurt
blow	blew	blown	keep	kept	kept
break	broke	broken	know	knew	known
bring	brought	brought	leave	left	left
build	built	built	lose	lost	lost
buy	bought	bought	make	made	made
catch	caught	caught	meet	met	met
choose	chose	chosen	pay	paid	paid
come	came	come	put	put	put
cost	cost	cost	read	read	read
cut	cut	cut	ride	rode	ridden
do	did	done	run	ran	run
draw	drew	drawn	say	said	said
drink	drank	drunk	see	saw	seen
drive	drove	driven	sell	sold	sold
eat	ate	eaten	send	sent	sent
fall	fell	fallen	set	set	set
feed	fed	fed	shake	shook	shaken
feel	felt	felt	show	showed	shown
fight	fought	fought	shut	shut	shut
find	found	found	sing	sang	sung
fly	flew	flown	sit	sat	sat
forget	forgot	forgotten	sleep	slept	slept
forgive	forgave	forgiven	speak	spoke	spoken
get	got	gotten	spend	spent	spent
give	gave	given	stand	stood	stood
go	went	gone	steal	stole	stolen
grow	grew	grown	swim	swam	swum
have	had	had	take	took	taken
hear	heard	heard	teach	taught	taught

Base Form	Simple Past	Past Participle	Base Form	Simple Past	Past Participle
tell	told	told	wake	woke	woken
think	thought	thought	wear	wore	worn
throw	threw	thrown	win	won	won
understand	understood	understood	write	wrote	written

Stative (Non-Action) Verbs

Stative verbs do not describe actions. They describe states or situations. Stative verbs are not usually used in the progressive. Some are occasionally used in the present progressive, but often with a different meaning.

Research shows that the 25 most common stative verbs in spoken and written English are:

agree	dislike	hope	love	see
believe	expect	hurt	need	seem
care (about)	hate	know	notice	think
cost	have	like	own	understand
disagree	hear	look like	prefer	want

Other stative verbs:

appear	deserve	mean	smell
be	feel	owe	sound
belong	forgive	recognize	taste
concern	look	remember	weigh
contain	matter		

Stative verbs that also have action meanings:

be	have	look	taste
expect	hear	see	think
feel	hope	smell	weigh

Using the present progressive form of these verbs changes the meaning to an action.
*Can you **see** the red car?   (= use your eyes to be aware of something)*
*I**'m seeing** an old friend tomorrow.   (= meeting someone)*
*I **think** you're right.   (= believe)*
*Dina **is thinking** of taking a vacation soon.   (= considering)*
*I **have** two sisters.   (= be related to)*
*We**'re having** eggs for breakfast. (= eating)*
*He **is** in his first year of college.   (= exist)*
*She **is being** difficult.   (= act)*

3. Modals and Modal-like Expressions

Modals are helper verbs. Most modals have multiple meanings.

Function	Modal or Modal-like Expression	Time	Example
Advice less strong	*could* *might* (*not*)	present, future	*He **could** do some puzzles to improve his memory.* *You **might** try some tips on improving your memory.*
stronger	*ought to* *should* (*not*)	present, future	*We **ought to** take a memory class next month.* *Greg **should** improve his memory.*
	had better (*not*)	present, future	*You**'d better** pay attention now.*
Past Advice, Regret, or Criticism	*ought to have* *should* (*not*) *have*	past	*She **ought to have** tried harder to improve her memory.* *You **should have** made an effort to improve your memory.* *He **shouldn't have** taken that difficult class.*
Permission	*can* (*not*) *may* (*not*)	present, future	*You **can** register for the class next week.* *You **may not** register after the first class.*
	could (*not*)	past	*You **could** ask questions during the lecture yesterday, but you **could not** leave the room.*
formal →	*be* (*not*) *allowed to* *be* (*not*) *permitted to*	past, present, future	*He **was not allowed to** talk during the test, but he **was allowed to** use his books.* *Students **will not be permitted to** refer to notes during examinations.*
Necessity / Obligation	*have to* *need to* *be required to* *be supposed to*	past, present, future	*I **have to** study tonight.* *She **needs to** quit her stressful job.* *You **won't be required to** take a test.* *He **is supposed to** tell you his decision tomorrow.*
	must (*not*)	present, future	*You **must** have experience for this job.*
Obligation not to / Prohibition	*must not* *be not supposed to*	present, future	*You **must not** talk during the exam.* *Students **are not supposed to** take their books into the exam room.*

Modals and Modal-like Expressions (continued)

Function	Modal or Modal-like Expression	Time	Example
Lack of Necessity / Choices or Options	not have to not need to be not required to	past, present, future	You **didn't have to** bring your notes. You **don't need to** study tonight. You **are not required to** bring your books.
Ability	can (not)	present, future	We **can** meet the professor at noon tomorrow.
	could (not)	past	I **could** understand the lecture, but I **could not** remember it.
	be (not) able to	past, present, future	She **wasn't able to** see very well from her seat.
	could have	past	I **could have** done well on that memory test.
	could not have	past	I **couldn't have** taken the test yesterday. I was in another state!
Probability	can't could (not) (not) have to must (not)	present	Hackers **can't** be interested in my data. He **could** be online now. She **has to** be at work right now. He **must not** be worried about data security.
	may (not) might (not) ought to should (not)	present, future	Your computer **may** be at risk of hacking. That software **might not** be good enough. That password **ought to** be strong enough. It **shouldn't** be difficult to find good software.
	could will (not)	future	The company **could** start using cloud computing next month. My sister **will** probably get a new computer soon.
	can't have could (not) have may (not) have might (not) have must (not) have	past	I **can't have** entered the wrong password! The expert **could not have** given you good advice. The company **may have** been careless with security. I **might have** written the wrong password down. Someone **must have** stolen all the passwords.

4. Noncount Nouns and Measurement Words to Make Noncount Nouns Countable

Category of noncount noun	Noun Examples	Measurement Words and Expressions
Abstract concepts	courage, luck, space, time	a bit of, a kind of *You had **a bit of** luck, didn't you?*
Activities and sports	dancing, exercise, swimming, tennis, yoga	a game of, a session of *They played **two games of** tennis.*
Diseases and health conditions	arthritis, cancer, depression, diabetes, obesity	a kind of, a type of *She has **a type of** diabetes called Type 2.*
Elements and gases	gold, hydrogen, oxygen, silver	a bar of, a container of, a piece of, a tank of *We have **tanks of** oxygen in the storage room.*
Foods	beef, broccoli, cheese, rice	a bottle of, a box of, a bunch of, a can of, a grain of, a head of, a loaf of, a package of, a piece of, a pinch of, a serving of, a slice of, a wedge of *I'll take **a serving of** rice and beef.*
Liquids	coffee, gasoline, oil, tea	a bottle of, a cup of, a gallon of, a glass of, a quart of *I would like **a cup of** tea.*
Natural phenomena	electricity, rain, sun, thunder	a bolt of, a drop of, a ray of *There hasn't been **a drop of** rain for three months.*
Particles	pepper, salt, sand, sugar	a grain of, a pinch of *My food needs **a pinch of** salt.*
Subjects and areas of work	construction, economics, genetics, geology, medicine, nursing	an area of, a branch of, a field of, a type of *There are a lot of specialty areas in **the field of** medicine.*
Miscellaneous	clothing, equipment, furniture, news	an article of, a piece of *I need **a piece of** furniture to go in that empty corner.*

5. Order of Adjectives Before Nouns

When you use two (or more) adjectives before a noun, use the order in the chart below.

Opinion	Size	Quality	Age	Shape	Color	Origin	Material	Nouns as Adjectives
beautiful comfortable delicious expensive interesting nice pretty rare reasonable shocking special ugly unique	big fat huge large long short small tall thin wide	cold free heavy hot safe	ancient antique new old young	oval rectangular round square triangular	black blue gold green orange purple red silver yellow white	American Canadian Chinese European Japanese Mexican Peruvian Thai	cotton glass gold leather metal paper plastic silk silver stone wooden woolen	computer evening government rose safety software summer training

Examples:

*That was a **delicious green Canadian** apple!* (opinion before color before origin)
*I saw the **shocking government** report on nutrition.* (opinion before noun as adjective)
*Wei got a **small oval glass** table.* (size before shape before material)

6. Verbs That Can Be Used Reflexively

allow oneself	challenge oneself	hurt oneself	remind oneself
amuse oneself	congratulate oneself	imagine oneself	see oneself
ask oneself	cut oneself	introduce oneself	take care of
be hard on oneself	dry oneself	keep oneself (busy)	talk to oneself
be oneself	enjoy oneself	kill oneself	teach oneself
be pleased with oneself	feel sorry for oneself	look after oneself	tell oneself
be proud of oneself	forgive oneself	look at oneself	treat oneself
behave oneself	get oneself	prepare oneself	
believe in oneself	give oneself	pride oneself on	
blame oneself	help oneself	push oneself	

7. Verbs Followed by Gerunds Only

admit	keep (= *continue*)
avoid	mind (= *object to*)
consider	miss
delay	postpone
defend	practice
deny	propose
discuss	quit
enjoy	recall (= *remember*)
finish	risk
imagine	suggest
involve	understand

8. Verbs Followed by Infinitives Only

afford	help	pretend
agree	hesitate	promise
arrange	hope	refuse
ask	hurry	request
attempt	intend	seem
choose	learn	struggle
consent	manage	tend (= *be likely*)
decide	need	threaten
demand	neglect	volunteer
deserve	offer	wait
expect	pay	want
fail	plan	wish
forget	prepare	would like

9. Verbs Followed by Gerunds or Infinitives

begin	like	regret*
continue	love	start
forget*	prefer	stop*
get	remember*	try*
hate		

*These verbs can be followed by a gerund or an infinitive, with a difference in meaning.

10. Expressions with Gerunds

Use a gerund after certain fixed verb expressions.

Verb expressions	
spend time / spend money	I **spent time helping** in the library.
waste time / waste money	Don't **waste time complaining**.
have trouble / have difficulty / have a difficult time	She **had trouble finishing** her degree.

Use a gerund after certain fixed noun + preposition expressions.

Noun + preposition expressions	
an excuse for	I have **an excuse for not doing** my homework.
in favor of	Who is **in favor of not admitting** him?
an interest in	He has **an interest in getting** a scholarship.
a reason for	He has **a reason for choosing** this school.

11. Verbs + Objects + Infinitives

advise	force	remind	ask*
allow	get	request	choose*
cause	hire	require	expect*
challenge	invite	teach	help*
convince	order	tell	need*
enable	permit	urge	pay*
encourage	persuade	warn	promise*
forbid			want*
			wish*

* These verbs can be followed by an object + infinitive or an infinitive only, with a difference in meaning.

Examples:
My boss **advised me to go** back to school.
They **urged the advertisers not to surprise** people.
My department **chose* Sally to create** the new ads.
My department **chose* to create** the new ads.

12. *Be* + Adjectives + Infinitives

be afraid	be delighted	be encouraged	be lucky	be sad
be amazed	be depressed	be excited	be necessary	be shocked
be angry	be determined	be fortunate	be pleased	be sorry
be anxious	be difficult	be fun	be proud	be surprised
be ashamed	be easy	be happy	be ready	be upset
be curious	be embarrassed	be likely	be relieved	be willing

13. Verbs + Prepositions

Verb + *about*	Verb + *by*	Verb + *of*	Verb + *to*
ask about	be affected by	be afraid of	admit to
care about	be raised by	approve of	belong to
complain about	**Verb + *for***	be aware of	confess to
be excited about	apologize for	consist of	listen to
find out about	apply for	dream of	look forward to
forget about	ask for	be guilty of	refer to
hear about	care for	hear of	talk to
know about	look for	know of	be used to
learn about	pay for	take care of	**Verb + *with***
read about	be responsible for	think of	agree with
see about	wait for	be warned of	argue with
talk about	**Verb + *from***	**Verb + *on***	bother with
think about	graduate from	concentrate on	deal with
worry about	**Verb + *in***	count on	start with
be worried about	believe in	decide on	work with
Verb + *against*	find in	depend on	
advise against	include in	insist on	
decide against	be interested in	keep on	
Verb + *at*	involve in	plan on	
look at	result in	rely on	
smile at	show in		
be successful at	succeed in		
	use in		

14. Adjectives + Prepositions

Adjective + **about**	Adjective + **by**	Adjective + **in**	Adjective + **to**
concerned about	amazed by	high in	accustomed to
excited about	bored by	interested in	due to
happy about	surprised by	low in	similar to
nervous about	Adjective + **for**	Adjective + **of**	Adjective + **with**
pleased about	bad for	accused of	bored with
sad about	good for	afraid of	content with
sorry about	ready for	ashamed of	familiar with
surprised about	responsible for	aware of	good with
upset about	Adjective + **from**	capable of	satisfied with
worried about	different from	careful of	wrong with
Adjective + **at**	safe from	full of	
amazed at	separate from	guilty of	
angry at		sick of	
bad at		tired of	
good at		warned of	
successful at			
surprised at			

15. Verbs and Fixed Expressions that Introduce Indirect Questions

Do you have any idea…?	I'd like to know…	I don't know…
Can you tell me…?	I wonder / I'm wondering…	I'm not sure…
Do you know…?	I want to understand…	I can't imagine…
Do you remember…?	Let's find out…	We don't understand…
Could you explain…?	Let's ask…	It doesn't say…
Would you show me…?	We need to know…	I can't believe…

16. Tense Shifting in Indirect Speech

Direct Speech	Indirect (Reported) Speech
simple present She said, "The boss **is** angry."	**simple past** She **said** (that) the boss **was** angry.
present progressive He said, "She **is enjoying** the work."	**past progressive** He **said** (that) she **was enjoying** the work.
simple past They said, "The store **closed** last year."	**past perfect** They **said** (that) the store **had closed** last year.
present perfect The manager said, "The group **has done** good work."	**past perfect** The manager **said** (that) the group **had done** good work.
will He said, "The department **will add** three new managers."	***would*** He **said** (that) the department **would add** three new managers.
be going to She said, "They **are going to hire** more people soon."	***be going to* (past form)** She **said** (that) they **were going to hire** more people soon.
can The teacher said, "The students **can work** harder."	***could*** The teacher **said** (that) the students **could work** harder.
may Their manager said, "Money **may not be** very important to them."	***might*** Their manager **said** (that) money **might not be** very important to them.

* Note: *should, might, ought to,* and *could* do not change forms.

17. Reporting Verbs

Questions	Statements				Commands and Requests	
ask inquire question	admit announce assert assure claim comment complain confess	convince exclaim explain find indicate inform mention note	notify observe promise remark remind reply report shout	show state suggest swear yell	advise ask command demand order	request say tell urge warn

8. Passive Forms

	Active	Passive
present progressive	People are speaking English at the meeting.	English is being spoken at the meeting.
simple present	People speak English at the meeting.	English is spoken at the meeting.
simple past	People spoke English at the meeting.	English was spoken at the meeting.
past progressive	People were speaking English at the meeting.	English was being spoken at the meeting.
present perfect	People have spoken English at the meeting.	English has been spoken at the meeting.
past perfect	People had been speaking English at the meeting.	English had been spoken at the meeting.
simple future	People will speak English at the meeting.	English will be spoken at the meeting.
future perfect	People will have spoken English at the meeting.	English will have been spoken at the meeting.
***be going to* (future)**	People are going to speak English at the meeting.	English is going to be spoken at the meeting.
Questions	Do people speak English at the meeting? Did people speak English at the meeting? Have people spoken English at the meeting?	Is English spoken at the meeting? Was English spoken at the meeting? Has English been spoken at the meeting?

19. Relative Clauses

	Identifying	Nonidentifying
Subject Relative Clauses	*Many people **who / that support the environment** recycle.*	*My sister, **who lives in Maine**, loves being outside.*
	*Electricity **that / which saves energy** is a good thing.*	*People power, **which is a way to create energy**, is popular.*
	*They are the scientists **whose research has won awards**.*	*Brad Pitt, **whose movies are well known**, gives a lot of money to environmental causes.*
Object Relative Clauses	*Detectives are people **(who / whom / that) I respect tremendously**.*	*The character Sherlock Holmes, **who / whom Arthur Conan Doyle created**, was a fictional detective.*
	*Evidence **(which / that) criminals leave at the crime scene** is called forensic evidence.*	*Evidence from criminals, **which we call forensic evidence**, can help police solve cases.*
	*The person **whose car the thieves stole** was a friend of mine.*	*Arthur Conan Doyle, **whose medical clinic not many patients attended**, had time to write his stories.*
Object Relative Clauses as Objects of Prepositions	*There's the police officer **(that / who / whom) I spoke to**.* (informal) *There's the police officer **to whom I spoke**.* (formal)	*There's Officer Smith, **who / whom I spoke to yesterday**.* (informal) *There's Officer Smith, **to whom I spoke yesterday**.* (formal)
	*Police found evidence from the crime scene under the chair **(that / which) I was sitting on**.* (informal) *Police found evidence from the crime scene under the chair **on which I was sitting**.* (formal)	*The door, **which I entered through**, had been broken during the robbery.* (informal) *The door, **through which I entered**, had been broken during the robbery.* (formal)

Relative Clauses *(continued)*

	Identifying	Nonidentifying
Relative Clauses with *Where* and *in Which*	*It's a city **where you can find Wi-Fi almost everywhere**.* *It's a city **in which you can find Wi-Fi almost everywhere**.*	*The city of Atlanta, **where my sister lives**, is very large.* *The city of Atlanta, **in which my sister lives**, is very large.*
Relative Clauses with *When* and *During Which*	*Night is a time **when many students study for exams**.* *Night is a time **during which many students study for exams**.*	*Joe prefers to study at night, **when his children are asleep**.* *Joe prefers to study at night, **during which his children are asleep**.*
Participle Phrases	*Students **concerned with the environment** should get involved in environmental groups on campus.*	*Millennials, **raised in the era of technology, cell phones, and the Internet**, understand technology very well.*
	*The expert **giving tomorrow's talk on Millennials** is very well known.*	*The movie Twilight, **starring Millennials**, is based on a book by Gen Xer Stephenie Meyer.*
Prepositional Phrases	*The computers **in our classroom** are fast.* *Young workers **low in self-esteem** are unusual.*	
Appositives		*Jan Smith, **the president of Myco**, will be speaking at noon today.* *Jan Smith (**the president of Myco**) will be speaking at noon today.* (formal writing)

20. Conditionals

Situation	Tense	*If* clause	Main clause	Example
Real Conditionals	present	simple present	simple present	If a website **is** popular, people **talk** about it.
	future	simple present	future	If you only **listen** to one station, you **will hear** only one opinion.
Unreal Conditionals	present	simple past or past progressive	*would, could, might* + base form of verb	If I **studied** every day, I **would pass** all my tests. If I **weren't dreaming** all day, I **would pass** all my tests.
	future	simple past	*would, could, might* + base form of verb	If our school **closed** next year, we **wouldn't have** a place to learn.
	past	past perfect	*would have, could have, might have* + past participle	If the city **had hired** more teachers, the schools **might have improved**.
Wishes	**Tense**	*that* **clause**		**Example**
	present	simple past, past progressive, could		I wish (that) schools **were improving**.
	future	*were going to, would, could*		I wish (that) the teachers **were going to** give us a party.
	past	past perfect		I **wish** (that) I **had studied** more.

21. Academic Word List (AWL) Words and Definitions

The meanings of the words are those used in this book. ([U1] = Unit 1)

Academic Word	Definition
academics (n) [U25]	the subjects that you study in high school or college
access (n) [U5] [U6]	the opportunity or ability to use something
access (v) [U8]	get information, especially when using a computer
accurate (adj) [U22]	correct and without any mistakes
adapt (v) [U2] [U26]	change something so that it is suitable for a different use or situation
adequately (adv) [U20]	good enough but not very good
adult (n) [U4] [U8] [U9]	someone (or something such as a plant or animal) grown to full size and strength
affect (v) [U5] [U10] [U14] [U15] [U17] [U19] [U20] [U24] [U27]	have an influence on someone or something
aid (n) [U12]	help or support, especially in the form of food, money, or medical supplies
aid (v) [U9]	help or support
alter (v) [U20]	change a characteristic, often slightly; cause something to happen
alternative (adj) [U21]	available as another choice
alternative (n) [U18]	something that is different, especially from what is usual; a choice
analyst (n) [U24]	someone who studies or examines something in detail, such as finances, computer systems, or the economy
analyze (v) [U22]	study something in a systematic and careful way
appreciation (n) [U17]	being grateful for something
approach (n) [U2] [U15]	a method or way of doing something
approximately (adv) [U19]	almost exact
area (n) [U19] [U26] [U28]	a particular part of a country, city, town, etc.
attitude (n) [U1] [U15]	the way you feel about something or someone, or a particular feeling or opinion
author (n) [U7] [U9] [U17]	a writer of a book, article, etc.; a person whose main job is writing books
automatically (adv) [U22]	done in a manner as a natural reaction or without thinking
available (adj) [U14] [U18]	ready to use or obtain
aware (adj) [U8] [U21]	knowing that something exists; having knowledge or experience of a particular thing
beneficial (adj) [U10] [U20]	tending to help; having a good effect
benefit (n) [U11] [U20]	a helpful service given to employees in addition to pay; a helpful or good effect

Academic Word	Definition
challenge (n) [U8]	something needing great mental or physical effort in order to be done successfully
challenge (v) [U7]	test someone's ability or determination
challenging (adj) [U23]	difficult in a way that tests your ability or determination
chemical (n) [U20] [U27]	any basic substance that is used in or produced by a reaction involving changes to atoms or molecules
cite (v) [U20]	mention something as an example or proof of something else
civil rights (n) [U3]	the rights of every person in a society, including equality under law
classic (adj) [U10]	having a traditional style that is always fashionable
colleague (n) [U23]	one member of a group of people who work together
communication (n) [U5]	the exchange of messages or information
complex (adj) [U8] [U17]	having many, but connected, parts making it difficult to understand
computer (n) [U5] [U6] [U8] [U9] [U22] [U23] [U28]	an electronic device that can store, organize, and change large amounts of information quickly
computing (n) [U6]	the use of computers to complete a task; the study or use of computers
concentrate (v) [U7] [U12]	direct your attention and thought to an activity or subject
conclude (v) [U24]	cause something to end; end
conclusion (n) [U24]	a decision made after a lot of consideration
consequently (adv) [U16] [U28]	as a result; therefore
consist of (v) [U12] [U20]	be made up or formed of various specific things
constant (adj) [U5]	not changing
constantly (adv) [U1]	nearly continuously or very frequently
consumer (n) [U13] [U26]	a person who buys goods or services for their own use
contact (v) [U4]	have communication with a person or with a group or organization
contribute (v) [U3] [U10]	help by providing money or support, especially when other people or conditions are also helping
controversial (adj) [U4]	causing or likely to cause disagreement
convert (v) [U21]	change the character, appearance, or operation of something
convince (v) [U13] [U15] [U24]	cause someone to believe something or to do something
corporation (n) [U3]	a large company
create (v) [U1] [U2] [U7] [U15] [U17] [U20] [U21] [U26] [U28]	cause something to exist, or to make something new or imaginative
creation (n) [U16] [U19]	something that is made
creative (adj) [U13] [U18]	producing or using original and unusual ideas
creatively (adv) [U18]	done in a new or imaginative way

Academic Word	Definition
creator (n) [U28]	a person who creates something
crucial (adj) [U7] [U10]	extremely important because many other things depend on it
cultural (adj) [U15] [U19] [U26]	relating to the way of life of a country or a group of people
culture (n) [U2] [U14] [U19] [U26]	the way of life of a particular people, especially shown in their ordinary behavior and habits, their attitudes toward each other, and their moral and religious beliefs
data (n) [U6]	information collected for use
debate (n) [U4] [U20]	a discussion or argument about a subject
demonstrate (v) [U1]	show how to do something; explain
depressed (adj) [U27]	unhappy and without hope
design (v) [U18] [U20]	make or draw plans for something
despite (prep) [U28]	used to say that something happened or is true, although something else makes this seem not probable
device (n) [U5] [U6] [U8]	a piece of equipment that is used for a particular purpose
distribution (n) [U20]	the division of something among several or many people, or the spreading of something over an area
dominant (adj) [U4]	more important, strong, or noticeable
dominate (v) [U19]	control a place or person, want to be in charge, or be the most important person or thing
dramatically (adv) [U10]	suddenly or noticeably
economic (adj) [U14] [U21] [U24]	connected to the economy of a country
eliminate (v) [U6]	remove or take away
energy (n) [U9] [U21]	the power to do work and activity
environment (n) [U4] [U10] [U13] [U17] [U20] [U21]	the conditions that you live or work in, and the way that they influence how you feel or how effectively you can work; the air, water, and land in or on which people, animals, and plants live
error (n) [U23]	a mistake, especially in a way that can be discovered as wrong
ethnic (adj) [U3]	relating to a particular race of people who share a system of accepted beliefs and morals
evidence (n) [U16] [U22]	something that helps to prove that something is or is not true
expert (n) [U6] [U7] [U9] [U18] [U19] [U22] [U23] [U25]	a person with a high level of knowledge or skill about a particular subject
external (adj) [U17]	relating to the outside part of something
facility (n) [U11]	a place where a particular activity happens
file (n) [U6]	a collection of information in a computer stored as one unit with one name
final (adj) [U7]	last

Academic Word	Definition
finally (adv) [U4] [U12] [U16] [U18] [U20] [U28]	at the end, or after some delay
financial (adj) [U11] [U12] [U16] [U27]	relating to money
flexible (adj) [U18]	able to change or be changed easily according to the situation
focus (v) [U11] [U17] [U21]	direct attention toward someone or something
found (v) [U3]	start an organization, especially by providing money
foundation (n) [U3]	an organization that provides financial support for activities and groups
furthermore (adv) [U6] [U15] [U28]	also and more importantly
generate (v) [U6] [U21]	produce
generation (n) [U23]	all the people within a society or family of about the same age
global (adj) [U2] [U3] [U19] [U20]	relating to the whole world
globalization (n) [U26]	the increase of business around the world, especially by big companies operating in many countries
globally (adv) [U26]	pertaining to the whole world
goal (n) [U3] [U4]	an aim or purpose, something you want to achieve
grade (n) [U17]	the measure of the quality of a student's schoolwork
grant (n) [U12]	money that a university, government, or organization gives to someone for a purpose, such as to do research or study
guarantee (v) [U8]	promise that a particular thing will happen
identical (adj) [U4]	exactly the same
identify (v) [U22]	recognize or be able to name someone or something; prove who or what someone or something is
identity (n) [U19]	who a person is, or the qualities of a person, thing, or group that make them different from others
image (n) [U2] [U7] [U22]	an idea, especially a mental picture, of what something or someone is
immigrant (n) [U26]	a person who has come into a foreign country in order to live there
impact (n) [U4] [U10]	the strong effect or influence that something has on a situation or person
implicit (adj) [U1]	suggested but not communicated directly
inappropriate (adj) [U2] [U25]	unsuitable, especially for the particular time, place, or situation
inconclusive (adj) [U22]	not leading to a definite result or decision; uncertain
individual (n) [U4] [U18]	a person, especially when considered separately and not as part of a group
individualism (n) [U15]	the quality or state of being different from other people

Academic Word	Definition
innovation (n) [U11]	something new or different
institute (n) [U9] [U11]	an organization where people do a particular kind of scientific, educational, or social work
internal (adj) [U17]	happening inside a person, group, organization, place, or country
investigate (v) [U1] [U4] [U22]	try to discover all the facts about something
investigation (n) [U22]	the search for facts
investigator (n) [U22]	a person who examines the particulars of an event in an attempt to learn the facts
isolated (adj) [U24]	separated from other things
issue (n) [U11] [U12] [U14] [U20] [U24]	a subject or problem that people are thinking and talking about
job (n) [U11] [U12] [U14] [U19] [U23] [U24] [U28]	the regular work that a person does to earn money
legislator (n) [U25]	a member of an elected group of people who has the power to make or change laws
link (n) [U9] [U24]	a connection; a word or image on a website that can take you to another document or website
link (v) [U20]	make a connection
locate (v) [U26]	put or establish something in a particular place
location (n) [U6]	a place or position
maintain (v) [U7]	make a situation or activity continue in the same way
maintenance (n) [U23]	the work that is done to keep something in good condition
major (adj) [U2] [U9] [U21]	more important, bigger, or more serious than others of the same type
media (n) [U24]	newspapers, magazines, television, and radio considered as a group
mental (adj) [U7]	relating to the mind, or involving the process of thinking
method (n) [U18] [U22]	a way of doing something
minority (n) [U3]	a part of a group that is less than half of the whole group, often much less
modify (v) [U20]	change something in order to improve it
motivate (v) [U17]	cause someone to behave in a certain way, or to make someone want to do something well; give a reason for doing something
motivation (n) [U17]	enthusiasm to do something
negative (adj) [U23]	not happy, hopeful, or approving
nondominant (adj) [U7]	not as important, strong, or noticeable
nonetheless (adv) [U6] [U25]	despite what has just been said or referred to
occupy (v) [U4]	fill or use

Academic Word	Definition
occur (v) [U8] [U22] [U23] [U24]	happen
option (n) [U12]	a choice
participant (n) [U18]	a person who becomes involved in an activity
percent (adv) [U11] [U14] [U21] [U27]	for or out of every 100
physical (adj) [U9]	relating to the body
plus (conj) [U12]	added to
policy (n) [U24] [U25]	a set of ideas or a plan of what to do in particular situations that has been agreed on by a government or group of people
portion (n) [U9]	the amount of food served to, or suitable for, a person
pose (v) [U6]	cause a problem or difficulty
positive (adj) [U13] [U15] [U17] [U23] [U24]	happy or hopeful
potential (adj) [U20]	possible but not yet achieved
predict (v) [U5] [U16]	say that an event will happen in the future
prediction (n) [U24]	events or actions that may happen in the future
principle (n) [U3]	a rule or belief which influences your behavior and is based on what you think is right
prior (adv) [U25]	existing or happening before something else
priority (n) [U7]	something that is considered more important than other matters
process (n) [U1] [U18]	a series of actions or events performed to make something or achieve a particular result, or a series of changes that happens naturally
professional (adj) [U18] [U21] [U27]	relating to the workplace; engaging in as a career; relating to a skilled type of work
project (n) [U7] [U16]	a piece of planned work or activity that is completed over a period of time and intended to achieve a particular aim
psychologist (n) [U1] [U17]	someone who studies the mind and emotions and their relationship to behavior
range (n) [U24]	the level to which something is limited, or the area within which something operates
react (v) [U1] [U13]	feel or act in a way because of something else
refined (adj) [U9]	made more pure by removing unwanted material
relaxed (adj) [U10]	comfortable and informal
relaxing (adj) [U10]	feeling happy and comfortable because nothing is worrying you
reliable (adj) [U6]	to be trusted or believe
relocate (v) [U14]	move to a new place
rely (v) [U24]	need or trust someone or something
require (v) [U18]	need something, or to make something necessary

Academic Word	Definition
research (n) [U1] [U2] [U4] [U5] [U10] [U14] [U15] [U16] [U17]	the detailed study of a subject or an object in order to discover information or achieve a new understanding of it
research (v) [U1]	study a subject in order to discover information
researcher (n) [U3] [U4] [U5] [U15] [U17]	a person who studies something to learn detailed information about it
reveal (v) [U1]	allow something to be seen that had been hidden or secret
role (n) [U4]	the duty or use that someone or something usually has or is expected to have
route (n) [U7]	the roads or paths you follow to get from one place to another place
schedule (n) [U16]	a list of planned activities or things to be done at or during a particular time
secure (adj) [U6]	safe
seek (v) [U27]	search for something
sequence (n) [U28]	a series of related events or things that have a particular order
series (n) [U2]	several things or events or the same type that come one after the other
similar (adj) [U2] [U3] [U4] [U24]	looking or being almost the same, although not exactly
similarity (n) [U4]	when two things or people are almost the same
similarly (adv) [U10]	in almost the same way
site (n) [U6] [U11] [U13] [U24]	a place where something is, was, or will be; a place on the Internet with one or more pages of information about a subject
source (n) [U21] [U24]	origin or beginning of something
specific (adj) [U20]	relating to one thing and not others; particular
specifically (adv) [U1]	for a particular reason or purpose
strategy (n) [U11] [U13] [U26]	a plan for achieving something or reaching a goal
stress (n) [U11]	a feeling of worry caused by a difficult situation
style (n) [U10] [U13]	a way of doing something that is typical to a person, group, place, or time
sum (n) [U6]	an amount of money
survey (n) [U6]	a set of questions to find out people's habits or beliefs about something
survive (v) [U15]	continue to live, especially after a dangerous situation
team (n) [U12] [U22] [U23]	a group of people who work together, either in a sport or in order to achieve something
technique (n) [U7] [U18] [U22]	a specific way of doing a skillful activity
technological (adj) [U8]	relating to or involving technology

Academic Word	Definition
technology (n) [U5] [U6] [U20] [U21] [U22] [U23] [U28]	the method for using scientific discoveries for practical purposes, especially in industry
tradition (n) [U15]	a custom or way of behaving that has continued for a long time in a group of people or a society
traditional (adj) [U13] [U18] [U22] [U25]	established for a long time, or part of a behavior and beliefs that have been established
traditionally (adv) [U15]	relating to or involving tradition
transfer (v) [U12]	move someone or something from one place to another
trend (n) [U9]	the direction of changes or developments
unbiased (adj) [U24]	not influenced by personal opinion
unique (adj) [U28]	different from everyone and everything
uniquely (adv) [U26]	in a manner that is unusual or special
variation (n) [U18]	a change in quality, amount, or level
varying (adj) [U10]	different
version (n) [U18]	a form of something that differs slightly from other forms of the same thing
virtual (adj) [U28]	created by a computer
visualization (n) [U7]	an image in your mind of someone or something
visualize (v) [U7]	create a picture in your mind of someone or something
voluntary (adj) [U11]	done or given because you want to and not because you have been forced to

22. Pronunciation Table International Phonetic Alphabet (IPA)

Vowels	
Key Words	**International Phonetic Alphabet**
cake, mail, pay	/eɪ/
pan, bat, hand	/æ/
tea, feet, key	/iː/
ten, well, red	/e/
ice, pie, night	/aɪ/
is, fish, will	/ɪ/
cone, road, know	/oʊ/
top, rock, stop	/ɑ/
blue, school, new, cube, few	/uː/
cup, us, love	/ʌ/
house, our, cow	/aʊ/
saw, talk, applause	/ɔː/
boy, coin, join	/ɔɪ/
put, book, woman	/ʊ/
alone, open, pencil, atom, ketchup	/ə/

Consonants

Key Words	International Phonetic Alphabet
bid, jo**b**	/b/
do, fee**d**	/d/
food, sa**f**e	/f/
go, do**g**	/g/
home, be**h**ind	/h/
kiss, ba**ck**	/k/
load, poo**l**	/l/
man, plu**m**	/m/
need, ope**n**	/n/
pen, ho**p**e	/p/
road, ca**r**d	/r/
see, re**c**ent	/s/
show, na**ti**on	/ʃ/
team, mee**t**	/t/
choose, wa**tch**	/tʃ/
think, bo**th**	/θ/
this, fa**th**er	/ð/
visit, sa**v**e	/v/
watch, a**w**ay	/w/
yes, on**i**on	/j/
zoo, the**s**e	/z/
bei**g**e, mea**s**ure	/ʒ/
jump, bri**dg**e	/dʒ/

Glossary of Grammar Terms

action verb a verb that describes an action.
*I **eat** breakfast every day.*
*They **ran** in the 5K race.*

active sentence a sentence that focuses on the doer and the action.
***Jorge played** basketball yesterday.*

adjective a word that describes or modifies a noun.
*That's a **beautiful** hat.*

adjective clause *see* **relative clause**

adverb a word that describes or modifies a verb, another adverb, or an adjective. Adverbs often end in -ly.
*Please walk **faster** but **carefully**.*

adverb clause a clause that shows how ideas are connected. Adverb clauses begin with subordinators such as *because, since, although, and even though.*
***Although it is not a holiday**, workers have the day off.*

adverb of degree an adverb that makes other adverbs or adjectives stronger or weaker.
*The test was **extremely** difficult. They are **really** busy today.*

adverb of frequency an adverb such as *always, often, sometimes, never,* and *usually* that describes how often something happens.
*She **always** arrives at work on time.*

adverb of manner an adverb that describes how an action happens.
*He has **suddenly** left the room.*

adverb of time an adverb that describes when something happens.
*She'll get up **later**.*

agent the noun or pronoun performing the action of the verb in a sentence.
***People** spoke English at the meeting.*

appositive a reduced form of a nonidentifying relative clause. Appositives are formed by removing the relative pronoun and the verb *be*, leaving only a noun phrase.
*Jan Smith, **an expert on Millennials**, will be speaking at noon today.*

article the words *a/an* and *the*. An article introduces or identifies a noun.
*I bought **a** new MP3 player. **The** price was reasonable.*

auxiliary verb (also called **helping verb**) a verb that is used before a main verb in a sentence. *Do, have, be,* and *will* can act as auxiliary verbs.
***Does** he want to go to the library later? **Have** you received the package? **Will** he arrive soon?*

base form of the verb the form of a verb without any endings (*-s* or *-ed*) or *to*.
come   go   take

clause a group of words that has a subject and a verb. There are two types of clauses: **main clauses** and **dependent clauses** (*see* **dependent clause**). A sentence can have more than one clause.

MAIN CLAUSE   DEPENDENT CLAUSE   MAIN CLAUSE

I woke up when I heard the noise. It was scary.

common noun a word for a person, place, or thing. A common noun is not capitalized.

mother   building   fruit

comparative the form of an adjective or adverb that shows how two people, places, or things are different.

*My daughter is **older than** my son.* (adjective)

*She does her work **more quickly** than he does.* (adverb)

conditional a sentence that describes a possible situation and the result of that situation. It can be a real or unreal condition / result about the present, past, or future.

If a website is popular, people talk about it. (present real conditional)

If I had studied harder, I would have passed that course. (past unreal conditional)

conjunction a word such as *and, but, so, or,* and *yet* that connects single words, phrases, or clauses.

*We finished all our work, **so** we left early.*

Some more conjunctions are after, as, because, if, and *when.*

consonant a sound represented in writing by these letters of the alphabet: ***b, c, d, f, g, h, j, k, l, m, n, p, q, r, s, t, v, w, x, y,*** and ***z.***

count noun a person, place, or thing you can count. Count nouns have a plural form.

*There are three **banks** on Oak Street.*

definite article *the* is the definite article. Use *the* with a person, place, or thing that is familiar to you and your listener. Use *the* when the noun is unique – there is only one (*the sun, the moon, the Internet*). Also use *the* before a singular noun used to represent a whole class or category.

The *movie we saw last week was very good.*

The *Earth is round.*

The *male robin is more colorful than **the** female.*

dependent clause a clause that cannot stand alone. A dependent clause is not a complete sentence, but it still has a subject and verb. Some kinds of dependent clauses are adverb clauses, relative clauses, and time clauses.

After we return from the trip, *I'm going to need to relax.*

determiner a word that comes before a noun to limit its meaning in some way. Some common determiners are *some, a little, a lot, a few, this, that, these, those, his, a, an, the, much,* and *many.*

These *computers have **a lot** of parts.*

*Please give me **my** book.*

direct object the person or thing that receives the action of the verb.

*The teacher gave the students **a test**.*

direct question a type of direct speech (see **direct speech**) that repeats a person's question.

The president asked, ***"Who were your best employees last month?"***

direct speech (also called **quoted speech**) repeats people's exact words. A direct speech statement consists of a reporting clause and the exact words of a person inside quotation marks.

The manager said, ***"Workers need to use creativity."***

factual conditional *see* **present real conditional**

formal a style of writing or speech used when you don't know the other person very well or where it's not appropriate to show familiarity, such as in business, a job interview, speaking to a stranger, or speaking to an older person who you respect.

Good evening. I'd like to speak with Ms. Smith. Is she available?

future a verb form that describes a time that hasn't come yet. It is expressed in English by *will, be going to,* and present tense.

*I'**ll meet** you tomorrow.*

*I'**m going to visit** my uncle and aunt next weekend.*

*My bus **leaves** at 10:00 tomorrow.*

*I'**m meeting** Joe on Friday.*

future real conditional describes a possible situation in the future and the likely result. The *if* clause uses the simple present. The main clause uses a future form of the verb.

***If** you only **listen** to one station, you **will hear** only one opinion.*

future unreal conditional describes an imaginary situation in the future. The *if* clause uses the simple past. The main clause uses the modals *would, could,* or *might*.

***If** teachers **prepared** students better for exams, more students **would pass**.*

gerund the *-ing* form of a verb that is used as a noun. It can be the subject or object of a sentence or the object of a preposition.

*We suggested **waiting** and **going** another day.*

*Salsa **dancing** is a lot of fun.*

*I look forward to **meeting** you.*

habitual past a verb form that describes repeated past actions, habits, and conditions using *used to* or *would*.

*Before we had the Internet, we **used to** go to the library a lot.*

*Before there was refrigeration, people **would** use ice to keep food cool.*

helping verb *see* **auxiliary verb**

***if* clause** the condition clause in a conditional. It describes the possible situation, which can be either real or unreal.

***If it rains tomorrow,** I'll stay home.*

imperative a type of clause that tells people to do something. It gives instructions, directions to a place, and advice. The verb is in the base form.

***Listen** to the conversation.*

***Don't open** your books.*

***Turn** right at the bank and then **go** straight.*

indefinite article *a/an* are the indefinite articles. Use *a/an* with a singular person, place, or thing when you and your listener are not familiar with it, or when the specific name of it is not important. Use *a* with consonant sounds. Use *an* with vowel sounds.

*She's going to see **a** doctor today.*

*I had **an** egg for breakfast.*

indefinite pronoun a pronoun used when the noun is unknown or not important. There is an indefinite pronoun for people, for places, and for things. Some examples are *somebody, anyone, nobody, somewhere, anywhere, nothing, everything*, etc. Use singular verb forms when the indefinite pronoun is the subject of the sentence.

***Everybody** is going to be there.   There is **nowhere** I'd rather work.*

indirect object the person or thing that receives the direct object.

*The teacher gave **the students** a test.*

indirect question (also called **reported question**) tells what other people have asked or asks a question using a statement. There are two kinds of indirect questions: *Yes/No* and information questions. Indirect questions follow the *subject-verb* word order of a statement.

*Mia **asked whether** we **would begin** Creative Problem Solving soon.*

*The president asked **who** my best employees **were** last month.*

indirect speech (also called **reported speech**) tells what someone says in another person's words. An indirect speech statement consists of a reporting verb (see **reporting verb**) such as *say* in the main clause, followed by a *that* clause. *That* is optional and is often omitted in speaking.

*He **said** (that) she **was enjoying** the work.*

infinitive *to* + the base form of a verb.

*I need **to get** home early tonight.*

infinitive of purpose *in order* + infinitive expresses a purpose. It answers the question *why*. If the meaning is clear, it is not necessary to use *in order*.

*People are fighting **(in order) to change** unfair laws.*

informal is a style of speaking to friends, family, and children.

Hey, there. Nice to see you again.

information question (also called **Wh- question**) begins with a *wh*-word (*who, what, when, where, which, why, how, how much*). To answer this type of question, you need to provide information rather than answer *yes* or *no*.

inseparable phrasal verb a phrasal verb that cannot be separated. The verb and its particle always stay together.

*My car **broke down** yesterday.*

intransitive verb a verb that does not need an object. It is often followed by an expression of time, place, or manner. It cannot be used in the passive.

*The flight **arrived** at 5.30 p.m.*

irregular adjective an adjective that does not change its form in the usual way. For example, you do not make the comparative form by adding *-er*.

good → *better*

irregular adverb an adverb that does not change its form in the usual way. For example, you do not make the comparative form by adding *-ly*.

badly → *worse*

irregular verb a verb that does not change its form in the usual way. For example, it does not form the simple past with *-d* or *-ed*. It has its own special form.

go → *went*   *ride* → *rode*   *hit* → *hit*

main clause (also called **independent clause**) a clause that can be used alone as a complete sentence. In a conditional, the main clause describes the result when the condition exists.

After I get back from my trip, **I'm going to relax**.

If I hear about a good story, **I move quickly to get there and report it**.

main verb a verb that functions alone in a clause and can have an auxiliary verb.

They **had** *a meeting last week.*

They have **had** *many meetings this month.*

measurement word a word or phrase that shows the amount of something. Measurement words can be singular or plural. They can be used to make noncount nouns countable.

I bought **a box** *of cereal, and Sonia bought* **five pounds** *of apples.*

modal a verb such as *can*, *could*, *have to*, *may*, *might*, *must*, *should*, *will*, and *would*. It modifies the main verb to show such things as ability, permission, possibility, advice, obligation, necessity, or lack of necessity.

It **might** *rain later today.*

You **should** *study harder if you want to pass this course.*

non-action verb *see* **stative verb**

noncount noun refers to ideas and things that you cannot count. Noncount nouns use a singular verb and do not have a plural form.

Do you download **music**?

noun a word for a person, place, or thing. There are common nouns and proper nouns. (*see* **common nouns, proper nouns**)

COMMON NOUN   PROPER NOUN

I stayed in a **hotel** *on my trip to New York.*   *I stayed in the* **Pennsylvania Hotel**.

object a noun or pronoun that usually follows the verb and receives the action.

I sent **the flowers**. *I sent* **them** *to* **you**.

object pronoun replaces a noun in the object position.

Sara loves exercise classes. She takes **them** *three times a week.*

participle phrase a reduced form of an identifying relative clause. Participle phrases are formed by removing the relative pronoun and the verb *be*. Participle phrases can be used when the verb in the relative clause is in the form verb + *-ing* (present participle) or the past participle form.

He is the person **using the Internet too much at work**.

particle   a small word like *down*, *in*, *off*, *on*, *out*, or *up*. These words (which can also be prepositions) are used with verbs to form **two-word verbs** or **phrasal verbs**. The meaning of a phrasal verb often has a different meaning from the meaning of the individual words in it.

passive sentence   a sentence that focuses on the action or on the person or thing receiving the action. The object is in the subject position.

*English **was spoken** at the meeting.*

past participle   a verb form that can be regular (base form + *-ed*) or irregular. It is used to form perfect tenses and the passive. It can also be an adjective.

*I've **studied** English for five years.*

*The **frightened** child cried.*

past progressive   a verb form that describes events or situations in progress at a time in the past. The emphasis is on the action.

*They **were watching** TV when I arrived.*

past unreal conditional   describes a situation that was not true in the past. Past unreal conditionals describe something that was possible but did not happen. The *if* clause uses the past perfect. The main clause uses the modals *would have*, *could have*, or *might have* and the past participle form of the verb.

***If** we **hadn't had** a hurricane, the schools **wouldn't have closed**.*

phrasal verb   (also called **two-word verb**) consists of a verb + a particle. There are two kinds of phrasal verbs: separable and inseparable. (*see* **particle, inseparable phrasal verbs, separable phrasal verbs**)

> VERB + PARTICLE

*They **came back** from vacation today.* (inseparable)

*Please **put** your cell phone **away**.* (separable)

phrase   a group of words about an idea that is not a complete sentence. It does not have a main verb.

across the street   ***in the morning***

plural noun   a noun that refers to more than one person, place, or thing.

students   ***women***   ***roads***

possessive adjective *see* **possessive determiner.**

possessive determiner   (also called **possessive adjective**) a determiner that shows possession (*my*, *your*, *his*, *her*, *its*, *our*, and *their*).

possessive pronoun   replaces a possessive determiner + singular or plural noun. The possessive pronoun agrees with the noun that it replaces.

*My exercise class is at night. **Hers** is on the weekend.* (hers = her exercise class)

preposition   a word such as *to*, *at*, *for*, *with*, *below*, *in*, *on*, *next to*, or *above* that goes before a noun or pronoun to show location, time, direction, or a close relationship between two people or things. A preposition may go before a gerund as well.

*I'm **in** the supermarket **next to** our favorite restaurant.*

*The idea **of** love has inspired many poets.*

*I'm interested **in** taking a psychology course.*

prepositional phrase a reduced form of an identifying relative clause. Prepositional phrases are formed by removing the relative pronoun and the verb *be,* leaving only a prepositional phrase.

*The computers **in our classroom** are fast.*

present perfect a verb form that describes past events or situations that are still important in the present and actions that happened once or repeatedly at an indefinite time before now.

*Lately scientists **have discovered** medicines in the Amazon.*

*I**'ve been** to the Amazon twice.*

present perfect progressive a verb form that describes something that started in the past, usually continues in the present, and may continue in the future.

*He **hasn't been working** since last May.*

present progressive a verb form that describes an action or situation that is in progress now or around the present time. It is also used to indicate a fixed arrangement in the future.

*What **are** you **doing** right now?*

*I**'m leaving** for Spain next week.*

present real conditional (also called **factual conditional**) describes a situation that is possible now and its result. Present real conditionals describe general truths, facts, and habits. The *if* clause and the main clause use the simple present.

***If** you **control** the media, you **control** public opinion.*

present unreal conditional describes an imaginary situation in the present. The *if* clause uses the simple past or past progressive. The main clause uses the modals *would, could,* or *might*.

***If** I **studied** every day, I **could pass** all my tests.*

pronoun a word that replaces a noun or noun phrase. Some examples are *I, we, him, hers, it*. (see **object pronoun, subject pronoun, relative pronoun, possessive pronoun, reciprocal pronoun, reflexive pronoun.**)

proper noun a noun that is the name of a particular person, place, or thing. It is capitalized.

Central Park** in **New York City

punctuation mark a symbol used in writing such as a period (.), a comma (,), a question mark (?), or an exclamation point (!).

quantifier a word or phrase that shows an amount of something. In addition to measurements words, some other quantifiers are *much, many, some, any, a lot, plenty, enough*, etc.

*We have **three bottles** of juice and **plenty of** snacks.*

quoted speech *see* **direct speech**

reciprocal pronoun a pronoun (*each other, one another*) that shows that two or more people give *and* receive the same action or have the same relationship.

*Mari and I have the same challenges. We help **each other**.* (I help Mari, and Mari helps me.)

reflexive pronoun a pronoun (*myself, yourself, himself, herself, ourselves, yourselves, themselves*) that shows that the object of the sentence is the same as the subject.

*I taught **myself** to speak Japanese.*

regular verb a verb that changes its form in the usual way.

live ⟶ live**s**

wash ⟶ wash**ed**

relative clause (also called **adjective clause**) defines, describes, identifies, or gives more information about a noun. It begins with a relative pronoun such as *who, that, which, whose,* or *whom.* Like all clauses, a relative clause has both a subject and a verb. It can describe the subject or the object of a sentence.

*People **who have sleep problems** can join the study.* (subject relative clause)

*There are many diseases **that viruses cause.*** (object relative clause)

relative pronoun a pronoun (*who, which, that, whose, whom*) that connects a noun phrase to a relative clause

*People **who** have sleep problems can join the study.*

*There are many diseases **that** viruses cause.*

reported question *see* **indirect question**

reported speech *see* **indirect speech**

reporting verb a verb used to introduce direct speech or indirect speech. *Say* is the most common reporting verb. Other such verbs include *admit, announce, complain, confess, exclaim, explain, mention, remark, reply, report, state,* and *swear,* and *tell.*

*The president **said**, "We will change our system of rewarding employees."*

*The president **stated** that they would change their system of rewarding employees.*

result clause *see* **main clause**

sentence a complete thought or idea that has a subject and a main verb. In writing, it begins with a capital letter and has a punctuation mark at the end (. ? !). In an imperative sentence, the subject (*you*) is not usually stated.

This sentence is a complete thought.

Open your books.

separable phrasal verb a phrasal verb that can be separated. This means that an object can go before or after the particle.

***Write down** your expenses.*

***Write** your expenses **down**.*

simple past a verb form that describes completed actions or events that happened at a definite time in the past.

*They **grew up** in Washington, D.C.*

*They **attended** Howard University and **graduated** in 2004.*

simple present a verb form that describes things that regularly happen such as habits and routines (usual and regular activities). It also describes facts and general truths.

*I **play** games online every night.* (routine)

*The average person **spends** 13 hours a week online.* (fact)

singular noun a noun that refers to only one person, place, or thing.
*He is my best **friend**.*

statement a sentence that gives information.
Today is Thursday.

stative verb (also called **non-action verb**) describes a state or situation, not an action. It is usually in the simple form.
*I **remember** your friend.*

subject the person, place, or thing that performs the action of a verb.
***People** use new words and expressions every day.*

subject pronoun replaces a noun in the subject position.
***Sara and I** are friends. **We** work at the same company.*

subordinator a conjunction that connects a dependent clause and an independent clause. Some common subordinators include *although*, *because*, *even though*, *in order to*, *since*, and *so that*.
***Although** many people like to shop, some people shop too much.*

superlative the form of an adjective or adverb that compares one person, place, or thing to others in a group.
*This storm was **the most dangerous** one of the season.* (adjective)
*That group worked **most effectively** after the disaster.* (adverb)

syllable a group of letters that has one vowel sound and that you say as a single unit.
There is one syllable in the word lunch *and two syllables in the word* breakfast. (Break *is one syllable and* fast *is another syllable.*)

tag question consists of a verb and pronoun added to the end of a statement. Tag questions confirm information or ask for agreement. The tag changes the statement into a question.
*They don't live in Chicago, **do they?***   *Geography is interesting, **isn't it?***

tense the form of a verb that shows past or present time.
*They **worked** yesterday.* (simple past)
*They **work** every day.* (simple present)

third-person singular refers to *he, she,* and *it* or a singular noun. In the simple present, the third-person singular form ends in *-s* or *-es*.
***It looks** warm and sunny today. **He washes** the laundry on Saturdays.*

time clause a phrase that shows the order of events and begins with a time word such as *before, after, when, while,* or *as soon as.*
***Before** there were freezers, people needed ice to make frozen desserts.*

time expression a phrase that functions as an adverb of time. It tells when something happens, happened, or will happen.
*I graduated **in 2010**. She's going to visit her aunt and uncle **next summer**.*

transitive verb a verb that has an object. The object completes the meaning of the verb.
*She **wears** perfume.*

two-word verb *see* **phrasal verb**

verb a word that describes an action or a state.

*Alex **wears** jeans and a T-shirt to school. Alex **is** a student.*

vowel a sound represented in writing by these letters of the alphabet: **a, e, i, o,** and **u**.

***Wh*- question** *see* **information question**

***Yes/No* question** begins with a form of *be* or an auxiliary verb. You can answer such a question with *yes* or *no*.

*"**Are** they going to the movies?" "**No**, they're not."*

*"**Can** you give me some help?" "**Yes**, I can."*

Index

Art Credits

Illustration

Shelton Leong: 62, 116, 164, 346; **Maria Rabinky:** 261; **Monika Roe:** 6, 90, 193, 308, 309: **Rob Schuster:** 139, 225, 322

Photography

2 ©Yuri Arcurs/Shutterstock; 11*(top to bottom)* ©Glow Images/Getty Images; ©Comstock/Thinkstock; ©Jose Luis Pelaez Inc/Blend Images/Getty Images; 16 *(top to bottom)* ©Gavin Hellier/Robert Harding World Imagery/Getty Images; ©Angus McComiskey/Alamy; 18 ©Joseph Wright of Derby/The Corcoran Gallery of Art/Corbis; 27 ©David Young-Wolff/PhotoEdit; 30 ©Dinodia Photos/ Hulton Archive/Getty Images; 31 ©Sean Gallup/Getty Images; 33 ©Luxxtek/ iStockphoto; 34 *(top to bottom)* ©Purestock/Getty Images; ©Caroline Schiff/ Blend Images/Getty Images; ©The Agency Collection/Getty Images; 37 ©Evan Agostini/Getty Images; 41 *(top to bottom)* ©AP Photo/Al Behrman; ©Beck Starr/FilmMagic/Getty Images; 46 ©Picture Partners/Alamy; 49 ©Ingram Publishing/Punchstock; 50 ©Laurence Monneret/Taxi/Getty Images; 54 ©Barbara Penoyar/Photodisc/Getty Images; 55 ©Juan Manuel Silva/age footstock; 57 ©Fuse/Getty Images; 65 ©Mark Evans/iStockphoto; 72 ©Rich Legg/Vetta/Getty Images; 76 ©Hakan Caglav/iStockphoto; 80 ©Andersen-Ross/Flame/Corbis; 93 ©Image Source/Blend Images; 95 ©Corbis Bridge/ Alamy; 102 ©Blickwinkel/Alamy; 106 ©Punchstock; 108 ©Samotrebizan/ Shutterstock; 109 *(top to bottom)* ©Ace Stock Limited/Alamy; ©Blend Images/Punchstock; 111 ©Blend Images/Punchstock; 120 *(left to right)* ©Yamix/Shutterstock; ©Vasilevich Aliaksandr/Shutterstock; 124 ©Robert Ginn/Index Stock/age footstock; 128 ©Mozcann/iStockphoto; 129 *(clockwise from top left)* ©Ratikova/Shutterstock; ©Carlos Gawronski/iStockphoto; ©Юра Белошкурский/iStockphoto; ©Jaimie Duplass/Shutterstock; ©Hemera/ Thinkstock; ©Monticello/Shutterstock; 131 ©Eising Food Photography/ StockFood; 136 ©AsiaPix/SuperStock; 143©Universal Images Group/Getty Images; 150 ©Mixa/Getty Images; 167 ©Kayte Deioma/PhotoEdit; 172 ©Alberto Pomares/iStockphoto; 190 ©Stockbroker xtra/age fototostock; 197 ©Fuse/Getty Images; 202 (top to bottom) ©MPI/Stringer/Archive Photos/ Getty Images; ©North Wind Picture Archives/Alamy; 205 ©Somos Images/ Alamy; 209 ©John Hauser/The Bridgeman Art Library/Getty Images; 216 ©Library of Congress; 219 ©Getty Images; 228 ©Jon Feingersh/Blend Images Getty Images; 234 ©Jack Hollingsworth/Photodisc/Getty Images; 236 ©Larry Williams/Photographer's Choice/Getty Images; 244 ©Corbis/Blend Images; 246 ©Rayes/Riser/Getty Images; 247 ©Corbis/Blend Images; 250 ©Design Pics/Punchstock; 254 ©Photos.com/Thinkstock; 259 ©Thomas Roetting/Look Getty Images; 264 ©Nathan Benn/Alamy; 268 ©Carl Swahn/iStockphoto; 272 ©iStockphoto/Thinkstock; 274 ©AP Photo/Paul Sakuma; 277 ©Joe Ciaramell. iStockphoto; 282 ©Echo/Cultura/Getty Images; 286 ©Julián Rovagnati/ iStockphoto; 289 ©Freddy Eliasson/Alamy; 291 © ZUMA Press/Newscom; 29(©Peter Coombs/Alamy; 299 ©Orjan F. Ellingvag/Dagbladet/Corbis; 300 ©AP Photo/Dan Lassiter; 311 ©Inti St Clair/Blend Images; 313 *(top to bottom)* ©Sarah Golonka/Hill Street Studios/Blend Images/Getty Images; ©Mimi Haddon/Digital Vision/Getty Images; ©Ryan McVay/Photodisc/Getty Images 315©Fuse/Getty Images; 327 ©Artur Marciniec/Alamy; 329 ©AP Photo/ Laurent Cipriani; 331 ©Fuse/PunchStock; 336 ©NOAA/Science Source/Photo Researchers /Getty Images; 340 © Reynold Mainse/Design Pics/ Perspectives Getty Images; 343 *(top right)* ©Huntstock_Images/iStockphoto; *(left to right)* ©Steven Kazlowski/Science Faction/Getty Images; ©Frans Lemmens/ Alamy; ©Elena Kalistratova/Vetta/Getty Images; 350 © Used by permission of RF Binder; 354 *(left to right)* ©TinaFields/iStockphoto; ©morningarage/ iStockphoto; 355 ©Peter Horree/Alamy; 358 ©iStockphoto/Thinkstock; 362 *(clockwise from top left)* ©Photolibrary/Getty Images; ©Mixa/Alamy; ©Melba Photo Agency/Alamy; ©Photossee/Shutterstock; ©Istockphoto/ Thinkstock; 366 ©Andrew Bret Wallis/Photographer's Choice RF/Getty Image 369 ©AP Photo/Gregory Bull; 372 *(left to right)* ©Richard Levine/Alamy; ©Arcaid Images/Alamy; 378 ©Justin Sullivan/Stringer/Getty Images; 381 ©YoshikazuTsuno/AFP/Getty Images; 385 *(top to bottom)* ©Image Source/ Alamy; ©Tom Williams/CQ-Roll Call Group/Getty Images